Peter Dobson, who is happily married, lives in a Cambridgeshire village and left school at fourteen to sweep up in a machine shop. He has served in the RAF, built racing cars, sold motorcycles, worked as a barman, run a successful picture framing business, and managed a large block of flats in London.

Apart from a lifelong love of bicycles, his interests include thoroughbred cars, classic motorbikes, railways, reading, jazz ancient and modern, and black and white photography.

Formative influences were Ma Rainey, Aldous Huxley, Fausto Coppi, Geoff Duke, Dizzy Gillespie, and riding a Claud Butler around the English countryside.

Previous publications include three books of railway photographs, many light-hearted articles and serious photographs in enthusiasts' magazines, and a light-headed book about his dogs, and their bad habits, acquaintances and friends.

The Corgi Book of Bicycles and Bicycling

PETER DOBSON

CORGI BOOKS

THE CORGI BOOK OF BICYCLES AND BICYCLING

A CORGI BOOK 0 552 99069 8

First publication in Great Britain

PRINTING HISTORY

Corgi edition published 1985

This book is set in 10/11pt Plantin

Corgi Books are published by
Transworld Publishers Ltd.,
Century House, 61-63 Uxbridge Road,
Ealing, London W5 5SA

Printed and bound in Great Britain by
Cox & Wyman Ltd, Reading

Contents

Acknowledgements and Bibliography

The author is greatly indebted for information, not only to the books mentioned below but to the *Freewheel Annual Equipment Guide* and to Richmond Cycles' Catalogue, and to numerous articles in *Cycling, Cycling World, Cyclists' Monthly, Bicycle Magazine* and *Bicycle Times*.

The author would also like to thank John Collins, the curator of Harlow Council's Mark Hall Cycle Museum, and his staff for the many happy hours spent in their company, and for their kindness in letting him ride and photograph some of the bicycles in the collection. Thanks also to Harry Bickerton, Tim Close of Solec Cycles, Harry Quinn, Ken Rogers, Condor Cycles, Jack Taylor Cycles and all the other pleasant and friendly people in the cycle trade who have been so helpful.

Alderson, F.   *Bicycling. A History*
Alderson, F.   *The Cyclists' Companion*
Ballantine, R.   *Richard's Bicycle Book*
Kolin, M. J. and de la Rosa, Denise M.   *The Custom Bicycle*
Kossack, J.   *Bicycle Frames*
Oakley, W.   *Winged Wheel*
Ritchie, A.   *King of the Road*
Thomas, N.   *City Rider*
Watson, R. and Gray, M.   *The Penguin Book of the Bicycle*
Whitt, R. W. and Wilson, D. G.   *Bicycling Science*
Wilcockson, J.   *Cycle Racing*
Wilkinson-Latham, R.   *Cycles in Colour*

Chapter 1

YOU ONLY GET WHAT YOU PAY FOR

At first glance the price of bicycles might seem exorbitant, but after a little thought one comes to realize that they are in fact good value for the money especially when considering the prices asked for other, much less durable, forms of personal transport.

The most basic motorbike, for example, will cost at least £500. True, it won't *look* very basic but – with the exception of one or two machines from Eastern Europe – all that a buyer will be getting for his money will be an ephemeral package of ersatz metal, 'styled' with built-in obsolescence very much in mind, that will be superseded as the latest model in a few months time by something gaudier with even less mechanical integrity. Because of over-production it will be worth very little in part-exchange as the motorcycle showrooms of the Western world are packed with similar, and un-saleable, machines. Due to the appalling price of spares (assuming spares can be obtained), it will be economically if not completely life expired – to use a genteel term – within five years, at the most.

Cars are somewhat more durable but a great deal more expensive and the dullest form of four-wheeled transport known to man will cost something in the region of £4,000. Anything at all sprightly will cost at least £6,000, and anything elegant and remotely interesting double that amount.

None of these vehicles, however much one pays, are going to last more than ten years – and very likely less – and during their brief lifetime will cost a terrifying amount of insurance, road tax, petrol, oil, spares, tyres and servicing.

Looked at in this light the bike is almost unbelievably good value. The most beautiful bicycle that one can buy would cost, at the most, £1,200 and would be constructed of Titanium and other precious metals, while at the other end of the scale an honest, everlasting, upright roadster may only cost a twelfth of that amount. £250 buys you a very nice sports bicycle indeed, and not one of them will cost you anything in fuel; unless you think of food as fuel and even the most indolent motorist has to eat. A bicycle costs very little for oil, tyres or spares, and not much for insurance, and maintenance is so simple and straightforward that you can do all, or most of it, yourself. Even a lightweight bike that is well looked after will last a lifetime, although the rider himself will benefit from the fresh air and healthy exercise. A heavy roadster bicycle will easily outlast the owner, and many already have.

In fact, it is quite obvious that nobody can afford to be without a bicycle so having sensibly decided that you must buy one, the next thing to decide is what sort of bike to buy, and equally important, where to buy it. And do you want a new bike, or a second-hand one, or a tandem or a tricycle, or what?

The categories of bicycles now available do tend to overlap a little, but divide conveniently into five broadly defined groups. These are the small wheeled 'shopping' bicycles and the folding bicycles; the roadsters, light and heavy; the commuting bicycle; the sports tourer; and the racing bicycle.

You will get a lot of useful guidance on what sort of bike to buy if you visit a specialist cycle shop. Discount houses are all very well for electric chip fryers, power drills, or a lawn mower, but there is a lot to buying a bike. Whilst there is no doubt that you can buy one more cheaply at such places the salesman may be more interested in commission than in bicycles, and you are very unlikely to get any sensible advice. If he is a good salesman, and you don't know a lot about the subject, you could well end up with something quite unsuitable for no better reason than the firm have bought too many of the type and need to shift a few.

Something else that you certainly won't get is help with any problem that may arise, for such sources are not interested in offering an after-sales service. They have no repairs or servicing facilities – one reason that they can afford to sell so cheaply – and after you have parted with your money you are on your own; although they would, if pressed, return a machine to the makers if it had a serious defect, or had broken in half.

Buying your bike cheaply at a discount house and then trotting round with any problems to your local cycle shop, expecting them to help you out, takes a bit of nerve, and I wouldn't recommend it unless you are endowed with exceptional charm. Naturally, the specialist cycle dealer strongly resents the discount houses cutting prices to the bone, taking a huge share of the business and offering little in return.

In fact, the local man will help you out, when he has calmed down and has the time. His own customers have priority and he would be a lot more welcoming had you been a customer in the first place. His attitude is reasonable and fair. There is very little profit in repairs and servicing, which is why the discount houses don't want to know, and they are ruining his trade. Bicycles after all are not expensive and when the comparatively small sum that you save by buying from 'cowboys' is weighed against the disadvantages it simply isn't worth the risk. Your local specialist is usually a keen cyclist and knows what he is talking about. He can genuinely save you money by giving knowledgeable advice that can be trusted. Not that he is a sort of cycling Albert Schweitzer who doesn't care about a profit, but he hopes to stay in business and the only way that aim can be achieved is by earning a good reputation. One dissatisfied customer with a grievance, imaginary or real, can do a local business a lot of harm.

There are of course specialists, and specialists. Your local cycle shop will be the ideal place to buy a bicycle in any of the first three categories. But unless it is quite remarkable, the choice of sports bicycles will be very limited, and the choice of racing bicycles will be even more restricted. They can, of course, order any make that you might want, but it is not a very satisfactory way of buying a bicycle.

It is far better to go to a sports and racing specialist in the first place for advice and help. A glance through the advertisements in the cycling magazines and newspapers will soon tell you where they can be found. You will probably find a couple of keen clubmen in cycling gear behind the counter. They ride the kind of bikes they sell so do not be put off by their easy expertise and your own comparative ignorance. Cyclists are very decent people, and if you go along in a spirit of enquiry and are prepared to listen, you will find them most forthcoming and informative, particularly if you have a genuine desire to buy.

This last advice also applies to buying a sporting tandem or

11

tricycle, although your local man could easily supply a shopping tricycle of the kind that are now becoming popular again.

One of the fundamental things when buying a bike is getting one that fits, and that, I promise you, is not as simple as it sounds. There are at least half a dozen theories on correct frame sizing currently being debated involving a variation of 3″ or more for the same rider, and some of these theories are very complicated indeed. Americans are writing books about the subject and it's all getting rather out of hand. We will go into it in detail in Chapter 2, but my own view is that deducting 10″ from your inside leg measurement is as good a guide as any and will not be far out; not more than 1½″ either way that is. Take advice from the experts. They will sit you on a bike and move the bars and saddle up and down, and back and forth. Listen to what they have to say, see what you prefer for looks and comfort, and make up your own mind. All the theories work out wonderfully well in practice, if one is to believe their respective advocates, so it probably isn't all that critical. Just bear in mind that the bigger frame will be slightly heavier and marginally less stiff. But you would have to be very sensitive to notice it.

Any cycle shop will encourage you to buy the best, and never mind whether you can afford it or not; though I doubt if they would try to sell you a titanium-framed racer for a thousand quid unless you looked as though you could. This attitude could be described as enlightened self interest, for their percentage on the larger sum, while still the same percentage, adds up to more money. Nevertheless it's good advice. Always buy the best you can afford. If you don't you will regret it later, and, being dissatisfied with what you bought, will probably go back and part exchange it for a better bike and that *will* cost you money.

When buying a bike always try to think ahead and foresee if what you intend to buy now will be as suitable as you imagine in a few months time. Say, for example, that you buy a small wheeler, or a roadster on which to ride to work, which isn't far away, and then find out that you like cycling: it has become more than just a money-saving way to avoid the hacking, coughing, fag-smoking, time-wasting, expensive wretchedness of public transport. You may like to try a short ride in the country. If you enjoy the country ride and want to go again, will the bike that you have chosen be adaptable enough for this new purpose, or for any other presently unimagined development, like moving to another job a greater distance from your home?

It is difficult, I know, to 'think on' in this way. But it is a good idea to realize the possibility of a change of circumstances, or a developing interest in bicycles and cycling, and to cater for it by buying, not just the best bike that you can afford, but also the most versatile. This, without doubt, is the 10-speed sports machine, with mudguards and a carrier. The only thing it won't do is fold up, unless you run it into something. I know it is quite possible to tour the world on a small wheeler just as it is possible to row across the Atlantic in a small boat, but the rider, if not the rower, would be a lot better off on a sports bicycle, in every way except initial outlay. The only drawback to the good quality sports machine is that it costs about £100 more than a small wheeler or a roadster. Buying a better machine will save you money in the long run, and you can always consider hire purchase.

SMALL WHEELED AND FOLDING BICYCLES

We will start a detailed examination of the categories of bicycles with a critical look at the two sorts of small wheeler available, which are those that fold and those that don't.

When Alex Moulton – now Sir Alex Moulton – introduced his revolutionary rubber sprung, small wheeled bicycle to a delighted public in the early sixties it revived interest in cycling. It had acquired a rather dreary image in a flashy car orientated society, and it quickly became trendy to buy, and actually to ride about on a small wheeler, although many of the mini cyclists wouldn't have been seen dead on a conventional machine.

This first Moulton design was very good indeed and was significant in as much as it was the first commercially successful alternative to the diamond frame in over sixty years, but it also created a fashion for small wheeled bicycles that were less well engineered.

Discomfort is a basic problem inevitable with small wheels for they do not ride easily over irregularities of road surface, they drop into potholes rather than roll smoothly over them, and, being much more rigid than a larger wheel of the traditional 26" or 27" diameter, they transmit road shocks to the rider.

The cheapest and simplest solution – and consequently the one most commonly adopted – is to increase the wheel size to 20" and use wide rims and big, fat, tyres to soak up bumps. Whilst this solves the problem it creates another, for such tyres have a terrific rolling resistance that also soaks up energy, which explains why 'shopping' type small wheelers are such labour-intensive things to ride.

The most elegant solution, although naturally the most expensive, is the front and rear suspension system used by the ingenious Sir Alex for his new and delightful 'separable' space frame bicycles, which are the only small wheeled bicycles designed – and practical – for general use that are as good as a conventional machine of comparable quality.

The fact is that there are few advantages, and several drawbacks, to owning a non-folding small wheeler and the myth that they are more stable than a conventional bicycle due to a low centre of gravity is total rubbish and needs knocking on the head. It's only true of a riderless small wheeler which is of little use to anybody. In fact, with an adult rider in the saddle, they are a lot less stable because of the unhappy relationship between the rider's weight, which is high up, and the low wheel centres. The effect is rather like putting a rider fifteen feet tall onto an ordinary bicycle.

To be fair, if all you need is just one utilitarian bike that the entire family can use for local shopping and short journeys, a small wheeler is the answer with its enormous range of seat and handlebar adjustment; but due to the geometric weakness of the 'open' type of frame used to achieve such versatility it has to be constructed of heavy, thick-walled tubing, and although there isn't much of it, the small wheeler weighs more than any other type of bicycle (apart from the stately roadster), and excessive weight is death to happy cycling. Pick up a small wheeled bicycle when you are next in a cycle shop and you will be surprised. Prices are in the region of £80 to £100.

Having said all that, quite a good case can be made for owning a small wheeler, so long as it folds up, and where the small wheels are not just a stylist's gimmick but do have a definite space saving advantage. There are two basic types of folding bicycle available. The first type simply folds in half for storage in a cupboard or whatever, and if you are very short of storage space, or live in a vandal-infested tower block and have to keep a bike indoors, or need to put the bicycle into the boot of a car, then this type of 'folder' is convenient but not ideal.

For cheapness of production, this type of bicycle is otherwise identical with the non-folding small wheelers in the maker's range and will have the same 20″ diameter wheels. Smaller wheels, for all their other disadvantages, would take up much less space in a car boot, or a cupboard, but would involve the manufacturer in producing an entirely new and separate model at probably unjustifiable expense. These machines are still quite large when folded up, but if this rather limited facility is adequate to meet your needs, and you do not want to spend a lot of money, then they do provide an acceptable compromise at reasonable cost.

Two good examples are the Raleigh Safari, and the Dawes Kingpin. Both have Sturmey-Archer 3-speed hub gears. The Raleigh has a large diameter curved tube frame, and is priced at £90. With a graceful straight tube frame, braced at the bottom bracket and the steering head, the Dawes is lighter. It costs almost £40 more than the Raleigh, but it is a better bicycle.

In the second category of folding, small wheeled, bicycle there are three examples currently available. They are the Bickerton, the new Moultons and the Brompton, though strictly speaking the Moultons are 'separaters' and not 'folders'. There are several other designs in the offing which may or may not make it to the market.

As with most good things the only serious drawback is their price, but whereas the comparatively cheap folding bikes already mentioned are very heavy – which means that they are not much fun to ride and even less to carry – both the Bickerton and the Moultons are little more than half their weight. The 3-speed Bickerton weighs only 22 lbs, exactly the same weight as the top of the range 'racers' from both Dawes and Raleigh, and at least 4lbs less than a great many expensive sports machines. Both the Moulton models weigh only 2lbs more than the Bickerton but, sad to say, the Brompton is the same weight as a Dawes Kingpin.

When it comes to folding up and general portability there is no contest. The first category of folders are really only shoppers which have been cut in half and a hinge inserted in the frame so that they fold back on themselves, and on some of the 'cheapies' it has been known for the hinge and consequently the wheels to be a little out of line.

The purpose-built Bickerton goes in for a controlled collapse, and with a bit of practice can be reduced to hand luggage, and reconstituted into a bicycle, in under a minute and a half, and when packed into its nice blue 'holdall' it occupies a space only

30″ x 20″ x 10″. Alternatively, you can hang the holdall on the handlebars and use it for the shopping.

This combination of light weight and compactness is what you pay the money for. At first glance a Bickerton looks rather odd, its aluminium box section mainframe containing the bottom bracket and keeping the small wheels apart – only 18″ from the ground – the light alloy handlebars sticking up like narrow antlers, and the saddle perched high up on an aluminium pole. There is no spurious styling about a Bickerton, just proper engineering, and the functional appearance soon grows on you. In polished alloy with a little chrome it is a delight to look at, folded or unfolded. Even the chain is nickel plated. There is a myth that it needs no messy lubrication which in fact it does, so perhaps a chainguard would be useful. The inventor Harry Bickerton agrees, but says that nobody has ever asked for one.

Riding a Bickerton is a strange experience, but strange or not, it is enjoyable and owners tend to rave about it. Stand beside a Bickerton and gently pull the bars towards you, at the same time pushing gently on the saddle and the whole bicycle will seem to twist. For that reason I didn't fancy scooting off and throwing a leg over the saddle, but there is no need to do that anyway. I shoved a size twelve shoe across the frame, sat down, and set off carefully. Besotted owners say that it feels less like a bike than an extension of themselves. To me it seemed like riding on a small, sweet natured animal that has its nose down following a scent. The antlers flex and move under your hands, the saddle sways about, the front end darts here and there but not alarmingly and the whole bicycle feels alive and unmechanical. I don't think that I'd care to stand up on the pedals but I didn't feel the need. I don't know that it felt '30% easier to pedal' as the adverts claim and I don't think that I'd care to rush down hills or tear round corners on one. It is not that sort of bicycle, but essentially a gentle, gentlemanly one. I only had a brief ride on a brand new bike on wet and muddy roads, but I was most relaxed and comfortable and found it easy to understand why owners become so fond of Bickertons and call them by pet names.

To sum up, if you need a folding bicycle the Bickerton is superb, and oddly beautiful. I don't need a Bickerton but would love to own one just to look at, if I could justify the outlay.

Prices, including VAT, are £169 for a single speed model, £179 for a 3-speed model and £199 for the 5-speeder. A bag to put them in costs £14.50.

In some ways even more attractive than the Bickerton, but at twice the price, are the new Moulton bicycles, although the AM2 Town version which has flat handlebars is by far the better looking, as the dropped bars of the AM7 Country model do look a bit ungainly.

Whereas Harry Bickerton has cleverly used a general lack of rigidity to overcome the problem of discomfort inherent in bicycles with small and very rigid wheels, so Alex Moulton has opted for the equally valid, but much more complex and expensive solution of front and rear suspension to keep road shocks from the rider via the stiff structure of his multi-tubular space frame.

The springing for the leading link front forks is ingeniously placed inside the steering head tube and the entire rear triangle pivots behind the bottom bracket and is cushioned by a rubber cone – the cone shape has a naturally progressive spring rate – mounted on the back of the seat tube. This type of rear suspension has been in use on motorcycles since the 1920s, using springs instead of rubber – and similar systems were used by at least three makers of 'spring frame' bicycles in the 1880s.

Reynolds 531 tubing is used throughout the Moulton frame which can be separated at a central 'king pin' so that the two halves will fit neatly into bags – Moultons call them 'Carry Sacks' – that together occupy a space 42" x 21" x 14", small enough to slip in behind the seats of British Rail's high speed trains where normal bicycles are banned on weekdays.

Both Town and Country models have 17" x ¼" wheels but the AM2 Town version has a Fichel-Sachs automatic 2-speed back pedal-operated gear and the AM7 Country has a 7-speed Sun Tour Superbe derailleur. The AM2 costs £399 and the AM7 costs £489. Front and rear carriers in Reynolds 531 and the Carry Sacks are optional extras that push the price of the 'Country' model well over £550. I had hoped that they might eventually become somewhat less expensive, as happened with the earlier Moulton bicycle when the novelty wore off, but Moultons say that the likelihood is that they will soon become even more expensive.

Finally we come to the Brompton, which is a true 'folder' although at a quick glance it does look very like a 'shopping' bike and weighs a similar amount. Weight is the Brompton's only disadvantage for it folds up very neatly to occupy a space 22″ x 20″ x 10″, which is smaller than even the Bickerton achieves.

The back wheel folds underneath the frame so that the carrier becomes a stable platform for the folded bicycle to rest upon. The front wheel folds backwards from a hinge close behind the steering head so that it sits companionably beside the rear wheel, and the handlebar stem folds down and sideways so that the handlebars are inverted and parallel to the front wheel. You can sit very comfortably on a folded Brompton while waiting for a train. It is altogether a well thought out, nice looking bicycle. It's a great pity that it isn't 5 or 6lbs lighter but there is 'owt for nowt' in engineering and in this case weight is the penalty that must be paid for such a compact folded package. With a 3-speed Sturmey Archer hub as standard, the Brompton costs £197 including VAT, much the same price as a 5-speed Bickerton. A bag is £12.50 extra.

THE LIGHT ROADSTER

A short step up from the small wheeler, or the 'shopper', is the light roadster, and there is really not much of interest to say about them. They have been around for years, getting lighter and brighter perhaps, but still the basic bicycle. Most big manufacturers still offer a model for both sexes. They all have the modern equivalent of the mattress saddle, an upright bend of handlebar, three or five speed Sturmey Archer hub gears. The more you pay, the more equipment, such as carriers and saddle bags, you get. The average model weighs about 35lbs and costs about £90.

Remember the homily on versatility and think very deeply before you buy one. They are upright, honest and reliable, and deadly dull. If you are completely sure you only want to ride to work, and are not intending to enjoy the ride, then the roadster is OK. Provided that you work no more than ten minutes ride away. The broad saddle that looks so comfortable is actually fiendishly uncomfortable for anything other than a quick buzz to the shops. If you want a bike you can neglect the roadster is for you. It may grunt and squeak and scream for oil, but if you can put up with that, so can the bike. Roadsters are hard work, the large section tyres and weight will see to that. If you want, at least, to enjoy your ride to work, another £30 to £40 will buy you a lighter, more responsive commuting bike, which would give you a short range touring capability and riding that would be less of a chore. Think on.

THE HEAVY ROADSTER

This brings us to the heavy roadster, which is hard to find these says, as its role of sturdy workhorse has been taken over by the flashy, lighter roadster and the flibberty-gibbet commuter bike. The heavy roadster models that survive have become very grand indeed and are direct descendants of the dignified and stately bicycles made for the nobility and gentry of Edwardian times. Beautifully finished and fully appointed as they are, it is hard to imagine which market they are aimed at. They are very suitable for vicars, certainly, if only vicars could afford them, for they are expensive at prices approaching twice that of a lightweight roadster. And such nobility and gentry that are left tend to roar about in foreign motorcars.

Probably for this reason only Pashley, who specialise in heavy duty commercial carrier machines, and Raleigh who specialise in every sort except commercial types, still catalogue such charmingly old fashioned bicycles. Both offer a ladies' model: unusually, the head angle of the Pashley version is shallower than its seat angle. Sadly, neither ladies' model has cords to keep skirts out of the spokes. Of the two, the Raleigh Superbe is the more fully equipped, and both are currently on sale at £120 to £140. Which is the better buy? Well, the Raleigh dealer will tell you Raleigh and the Pashley dealer will tell you the reverse. One dealer who sells both told me he preferred the Pashley. Both are quite delightful.

Expensive as they are the heavy roadsters represent good value for money, and if you want a machine to take a pride in that will provide comfortable, safe and sedate progress for short distances, requires a minimum of maintenance and yet will last a lifetime, then buy a roadster. With their fully enclosed transmission, hub gears and hub dynamos, carriers, large section rims and tyres, domed mudguards, ample saddles, rod operated brakes and swept back, sit-up-and-beg handlebars there is a comforting feeling of continuity in just having one around. The sober, tasteful colours give an accurate impression of solid dependability, and solid they most definitely are. They may have lost the sturdy workhorse image but a roadster rider will need to be a sturdy workhorse if he intends to ride up hills, as the current breed weighs 40lbs or more. Nevertheless, they are very attractive, even to the writer, who hates hard work, and whose own vulgar preference is for a 10-speed sports machine.

THE COMMUTING BICYCLE

The commuting bike is a comparatively recent arrival on the cycling scene. A hybrid, or first cross out of the light roadster and the sports machine. All the big manufacturers – Raleigh, Peugeot, Saracen, Elswick, Falcon, Puch etc. – offer a choice of gentlemens' and ladies' models and, almost without exception, all refer to these models as tourers, or light tourers. One of them actually catalogues a 'gents tourer' – presumably intended for students of the turbulent history and florid architecture of the public lavatory. I find the 'touring' tag misleading and much prefer the term 'commuter', as it more accurately describes their function. *Bicycle* magazine quite frequently includes a Buyers' Guide in which they categorize these bicycles as 'uprights', defining their use for commuting or light touring, and a study of these guides – *Cyclist* also publish one from time to time – can be a great help in making a decision.

To simplify the choice as much as possible, remember that in this life you only get what you pay for. But it is possible to pay too much for what you get. At worst – which means the cheapest – the 'commuter' bicycle is just an uprated light roadster. At best – and most expensive – it means a down graded sports machine that can easily be upgraded once again. In terms of versatility, the latter class are obviously a better buy. You would hardly wish to convert a 'commuter' back into a roadster.

In its purest form, if one can say that kind of thing about a hybrid, the 'commuter' bike has a 5-speed derailleur gear, alloy cotterless chainset, high tensile steel frame, mattress type saddle, flat handlebars, mudguards and a carrier. Some makers offer a rather dinky little chainguard on their ladies models. All commuters have 27" x 1¼" rims. The Dawes Ambassador, currently retailing at £164.95 is a good example of a middle-of-the-range machine. The Falcon Super Tourist, which has a

Reynolds 531 frame, and which is generally regarded as absolutely super value, costs about £170. The parameters of prices for commuter bikes are from £120 to around £210. The Raleigh Merlin, and the 'mixte' framed Misty are priced at around £135, the Peugeot Sapphire at around £145, normal framed and 'mixte' framed versions of the Raleigh Richmond are priced in the region of £155, and the diamond framed, and open framed Coventry Eagle Elites cost £165. If you can afford an extra £40 the Saracen Town Tourist is probably the best value.

Naturally the less you pay, the more they weigh, and weights vary from 34lbs for the cheaper models to around 28lbs for the more expensive. There is little difference between the better class commuter bike and the lower scale of sports machine, if you change the handlebars for drops which are more practical, fit a double chainwheel – doubling the choice of gears – and throw away the mattress saddle substituting a narrow saddle in its place. Changing the saddle is a good idea anyway, particularly if you intend to do 'light touring' – whatever that may be. My own experience is that a mattress saddle will soon give you a sore behind; they never wear in and become comfortable, no matter how you persevere, as the width creates friction just where you need it least. A new, narrow, leather, or plastic, saddle will probably be uncomfortable at first but after 500 miles or so it will break in to your shape, and you soon won't know that you are sitting on it. We will go into details about saddles, the various types and makes available and their respective merits, in Chapter 7, but on second thoughts don't throw the old mattress saddle away. Put it back on the bike should you wish to sell it, and keep your own personalized saddle for the next bike that you buy.

A brief word to ladies about ladies' bicycles. If you are interested in cycling and intend to buy a 'commuter/tourer' or a sports machine, then from most angles, except perhaps modesty, you would be better off with a man's bicycle. Modesty hardly comes into it anyway, as most girls wear shorts or trousers – so much more practical for serious riding than skirts. Men's bicycles have stronger, lighter, more responsive frames than the open, or the 'Mixte' twin cross tube type frames used in ladies' models. Men's bicycles are also available in a greater range of sizes, colours, and models. But if you are only interested in a bike as local transport to the shops, and don't habitually wear jeans or trousers, then a ladies' model will be more convenient.

Before launching into the fascinating subject of sports bicycles, a word of caution. There are a lot of so-called sports bikes about selling at around £80 to £100 and, although at a brief glance they look the part, they definitely aren't. Even the better ones from reputable manufacturers are bogus, for it simply is not possible to build a decent sports bike for the same price as a rugged basic roadster. Some of the less well made are little more than rubbish. The low price is achieved by slapdash assembly and poor quality components and materials. Do not be tempted into thinking that you could buy one, and by working on it, sort it out into a sound machine. In many cases you could certainly improve on the assembly but there is nothing to be done with poor quality wheels and gears, or brakes; or with a heavy lifeless frame. If things are really tough and you cannot afford a better new machine then buy a good second-hand bike instead. If you buy a cheapy you will regret it later and you will find it very hard to sell.

SPORTS AND RACING BICYCLES

Just as the better class of commuter bicycle merge imperceptibly into the lower orders of sports tourers, so the more expensive touring bicycle merges into the racing bicycle, making it difficult to decide where tourers stop and road racing bicycles begin. In fact, many machines are used for both purposes, have similar frames made up for the most part from the very same materials, and use the same, or very similar, components. For these reasons, and to avoid going over the same ground twice, we will examine the sports tourer and the road racing bicycle together, being careful to avoid confusion between the design and components intended purely for touring, and the design and components of thoroughbred racers.

Almost every bicycle maker, big or small, offers a number of sports and racing machines. Most of the small firms make nothing else, and taken together this abundance of models gives a buyer a seemingly infinite variety of choice from medium weight tourers to exotic ultra-lightweights. Or, to make matters even more complicated, many of these makers will just supply a frame, from which you can build up your own idea of what the perfect bicycle should be, from a bewildering choice of components. Alternatively, you can have a custom frame made specially for you that will take into account the measurements of your arms and torso, as well as the vital statistics of your inside leg. The frame maker will have very definite ideas on the angles, lugwork, and fittings that he thinks you ought to have. You have to be strong minded and knowledgeable to get what you want from a frame maker. Frame makers always know best. The trouble is that they mostly do know best and you would be foolish to ignore such good advice.

The price parameters of sports and racing bicycles are from around £180 to £1,000. Before we go any further on the subject, I think I ought to mention that you can buy a very nice machine indeed for £200 to £250. If you were to spend £1,000 it would not necessarily mean that you could ride much further and much faster. With the better kind of bicycles the differences between the good and the superb are fairly subtle and their performance is ultimately down to you – which can be a most depressing thought.

Pride of possession is all very well, but I once knew a wealthy art collector who had turned his house into a type of cage to stop dishonest persons getting at his paintings. If you are going to worry about owning a beautiful, expensive, bicycle it might be best to buy a cheaper one. Cycling should be relaxing and enjoyable.

The sports bicycle with the 10 or more speed derailleur gear is the most versatile of all bicycles. There are very few kinds of riding for which it isn't almost perfect, and it is easily the most effortless and comfortable whatever the distances involved. Versatile as it is, it will help you to buy the bicycle ideally suited to your needs if you can be sure just what those needs are, or, and this is more difficult, can accurately predict just what they are likely to be.

For the sake of simplicity and sanity we will leave the complexities of buying a ready-made frame, or a custom-made frame, to the next chapter. If you are intending to build up your own bike in this way it is necessary to know a little about frame design and construction, and quite a lot about the choice of components available, and we will go into all that at the same time.

For the moment, let us examine the range of excellent ready-made bicycles that are available in Britain. The top names are Raleigh, Peugeot, Puch, Falcon, Dawes, Carlton, Claud Butler, Holdsworth, Saracen, Clements, and Coventry Eagle. It would be tedious and confusing to try to list all the advantages, and disadvantages, of several hundred bicycles, but an analysis of the makers' catalogues shows that in a given price bracket you will get a similar quality bicycle from all of them, often with the same components. To reduce the subject to more manageable proportions we will have a detailed look at four popular sports tourers. The Raleigh Royal, the Claud Butler Majestic, the Dawes Galaxy, and the Coventry Eagle Touristique, priced at £225, £245, £250, and £252 respectively.

The Dawes has a Reynolds 531 frame, and all the others have 531 frames and forks. The Raleigh, the Claud Butler, and the Dawes have 10-speeds with rear mechanisms made by SunTour, and the Coventry Eagle has 12-speeds with a rear mechanism by Shimano. The makers of the front changers are not mentioned but they will certainly be Japanese. The Raleigh probably has the best rear gear mechanism, and the worst front changer. None of the four bicycles have very special wheels. The Raleigh and the Dawes have 27" x 1¼" Weinmann rims. The Coventry Eagle has similar rims from Rigida, and the Claud Butler has the same sized, but slightly better rims from Super Champion. All have inexpensive hubs. Small flange, quick release Maillard Atoms on the Raleigh, and Claud Butler. Large flange, quick release Normandy hubs on the other two. All have similarly priced alloy chainsets from Japan, and all have the same centre pull brakes from Weinmann. So much for exhortations to Buy British, although, of course, there are no British components to be had.

The makes of saddles are not mentioned, but the Raleigh and the Claud Butler have nameless things in mock suede plastic which are best done away with. All the bicycles will, almost certainly, be fitted with exactly the same ESGE mudguards, all have carriers, and all weigh around 28lbs.

Dawes and Claud Butler make 'Mixte' frame models. Raleigh offer an open framed ladies model, and the Coventry Eagle is for men only. All are extremely good value, and the only way to choose between them is on a preference for a colour, or the maker's name.

The same price and quality equation applies further up the scale with production racers, but any manufacturer is only as good as his workforce. If one of the workers is having an off day, and his off day should coincide with lapses in inspection, you can buy ɔr workmanship from almost anybody, however good their ɛputation. Closely inspect any new bicycle that you intend to buy. Never mind who made it, if you don't like what you see, say so before you part with your money, and make sure that the defects are put right.

Apart from such occasional falls from grace, you will get an excellent bicycle from all the makers in the list above. The old saying that 'you pays your money and you takes your choice' is hackneyed but applicable. If a particular bicycle in your price range is fitted with an especially good and expensive chainset or derailleur it will make up for that extravagance elsewhere with cheaper brakes or pedals. If you want a bicycle with components of superb quality throughout you may have to build your own, and it will cost you. £400 isn't at all out of the way for turning a frame and forks into a bicycle, and that doesn't include the cost of the frame and forks.

Even if you can afford an expensive racing bike there is absolutely no point in doing so if you are only intending to use it for touring, or impressing the girls at the Young Communist League meetings or the tennis club. And that is not said to save you money, but rather to spare you disappointment and discomfort. The girls at the tennis club won't be impressed anyway, and apart from that sad social reflection, it is doubtful whether the bike would have any provision, or room, for the fitting of mudguards, which will make riding in the rain a messy business. It will also have a hard and unyielding ride and quick, nervous, steering and handling due to being designed for speed rather than for comfort. All the components will be much lighter than their touring counterparts and will consequently demand more attention, and the gear ratios will probably be too close together.

AERODYNAMIC BICYCLES

Several manufacturers offer 'low profile' or aerodynamic frames made of oval section tubing, ostensibly to cut down on wind resistance and reduce the effort involved in cycling to a minimum. Wind resistance is a severe handicap to cyclists, and aerodynamics are very important, as the astonishing performance of the streamliners at the British Human Powered Vehicle Championships prove. But their beautiful shells encompass both recumbent bike and recumbent rider and wouldn't be very suitable for touring in the Peak District. The rider of a conventional bicycle sticks up in the air like a sore thumb and is responsible for a good two-thirds of the wind resistance that takes up 90% of his energy at 25mph, and streamlining the bike instead of the rider in such a marginal manner is not going to help very much. Nevertheless, any reduction in drag should be welcomed, always providing that it doesn't create any problems that negate the advantages.

Oval tubing is marginally less resistant to lateral forces and consequently more liable to 'whip' than normal round section tubing. But Reynolds have introduced their own aerodynamic 531 Speedstream double butted oval tubing, so it cannot be too serious a problem. Reynolds offer an oval, changing to round section, seat tube to accept a standard metric seat pillar; and all the Reynolds oval tubing is drawn to that shape, rather than flattened.

Frame lugs cannot be used in the construction of aerodynamic frames due to the shape of the tubing, and framesets have to be bronze, or silver, soldered. On ballance it seems very unlikely that an aerodynamic frame is in any way better than a lightweight frame made of traditional round tubing, except in the eye of a biased beholder who prefers the appearance.

The aerodynamic Cinelli Laser is probably the most beautiful bicycle ever made, and probably the most expensive. The Kronos front brake is tucked in behind the front forks whilst the rear brake is cowled over and hidden behind the bottom bracket. The handlebars and brake levers are aerodynamic and the control cables are routed inside the frame. Even the spokes and rims are constructed to lessen wind resistance – a lovely bike if you can afford it.

CUSTOM BICYCLES

Several of Britain's better bike shops, Beta Bikes of West Hampstead in North West London, and Harry Hall Cycles of Manchester, to name but two (see List of Useful Addresses), offer their own complete bicycles, in addition to custom-made frames and the products of most of the top manufacturers. The Harry Hall Super Tourists model has a top quality hand-made frame of Reynolds 531 double butted tubing (double butted tubes are thicker at both ends where the extra strength is most needed), with very nice lug work. Fully equipped with good quality components, it costs almost £400.

Beta Bikes offer their Revell range of touring and racing bicycles in ascending degrees of price and splendour. The Revell Ritmo, Giro, Elite, Rapide, Romany and Custom are all nicely made and finished, and are equipped with components of quality consistent with their respective cost. Prices range from £200 to almost £700.

I don't think one could say that the products of these specialist shops are greatly superior to those of the better known makers mentioned above, but if you want something a little different in an increasingly uniform world then these bicycles represent excellent value for money.

TRICYCLES

W .R. Pashley Limited (the makers of what used to be termed 'tradesmens bicycles'), TGA Cycles, Broadway Bikes, and Ken Rogers all offer homely 'shopping' trikes (see Addresses). Because of their load-carrying capacity, stability and ease of parking, these sober and respectable three wheelers are becoming increasingly popular with mothers needing to transport young children, and with older people.

With the exception of the two Trident models – basic and De-luxe, from Broadway Bikes – all these tricycles have 20″ wheels. Broadway go in for 26″ wheels which makes them more suitable for touring but slightly trickier to ride at first.

Pashley offer a single speed, 3-speed hub, or 5-speed derailleur alternatives. The basic Broadway Trident has a 3-speed Shimano hub and the De Luxe version, a 5- or 10-speed derailleur. Ken Rogers has standardised on a 5-speed Positron derailleur, and TGA Cycles will fit any suitable gear to order.

Prices range from £200 for the basic Unisex 'trike' from Ken Rogers, which at 19 kilos is easily the lightest, up to £325 for the attractive TGA Tri-Treka with two child seats in moulded fibreglass above a luggage locker.

All are very adequately braked, with callipers on all three wheels of Broadway's Tridents, and a mixture of callipers and drum brakes on the others. Pashley and TGA fit brakes on front wheels only.

Due to problems with storage space, most dealers are reluctant to carry stocks of tricycles, so cycle shops selling TGA and Pashley products are fairly few and far between, and Ken Rogers and Broadway Bikes only sell direct.

Whilst the 'shopping' type of tricycle is a stable enough mode of transport if ridden sensibly and gently, do not imagine that a sports tourer or racing tricycle will be similarly docile. A lightweight 'trike' can be a very difficult machine to get the 'hang of'. And hang is the right word, for it will lift an inside wheel, and may even tip right over, until a rider can get used to shifting his weight and 'hang' into the corner to counteract centrifugal force. And he must also learn to steer with the handlebars instead of relying on leaning over, as with a conventional two wheeler.

Once you have mastered the eccentricities of the handling, a tricycle is enjoyable and remarkably quick, and a lot more relaxing to ride than a two wheeler on wet or icy roads. Ken Rogers of Middlesex and T & J Cycles of Burton-on-Trent (see Addresses) both offer simple tricycle conversion kits that bolt onto a normal bicycle, a recent development that allows a rider to have the best of both worlds; a bike if he prefers it for the summer and a trike for the winter when the roads are bad. These conversion kits come without rims or tyres for about £50, or complete with wheels for an extra £20.

The components of a tricycle are much the same as for a bicycle but tricycles are more expensive because of the extra frame tubes, the axle and the extra wheel. I doubt whether you would get much change out of £400 for the cheapest hand-built lightweight trike (very nice to ride in town as there is no need to put your foot, or feet down, at the traffic lights). See Useful Addresses for a list of specialist tricycle makers. The weekly paper *Cycling* carries a great many advertisements, whilst the monthly paper *Cycling World* rather goes in for tricycles and gives them a lot of coverage, including an occasional feature called 'Trike Talk'.

TANDEMS

Tandems are wonderfully efficient machines and it is sad that they seem to be so rare these days. In fact, there are only three production models available in this country and they are made by W. R. Pashley Limited, Cycle Peugeot and Gitane, all three makers offering 'double gents' or 'ladyback' alternatives. Pashley make the least expensive tandems, two D Types and an E Type, names which make them sound like sports cars. This is a bit misleading as the D Types weigh 66lbs each, and the E Types 55lbs, daunting weights which must make them uphill work. One D Type has a 3-speed hub, the other a 5-speed derailleur, and both are reasonably priced at £322. The lighter E Type has a 10-speed derailleur gear but is a great deal more expensive, but good value, at £471.50.

The more sporting Peugeot models have 10-speed derailleurs and, weighing only 46lbs and costing around £450, are both lighter and less expensive than the E Type Pashley. The Gitanes, at around £400 have a slightly shorter wheelbase than the others and have 15-speed derailleurs.

For a really superb lightweight tandem, weighing something in the region of 35 to 40lbs you will have to go to one of several firms that specialize, and expect to pay between £600 and £1,000 – rather more than the cost of two solo bicycles of comparable quality. For a husband and wife who are keen to go cycling together a tandem is the ideal solution, much faster and much less effort than separate bicycles. With three quarters of the weight and half the wind resistance they absolutely sail along, and do away with the hazard of riding side by side in order to converse. Whoever isn't steering can look around and enjoy the scenery. With two strong lads on board, a lightweight tandem is terrifically fast.

Tandem components are very similar to those of the sports touring, or racing bicycle, but tyres, rims, hubs and brakes have to be more robust to stand up to the greater stresses put upon them. Brakes are particularly important due to the greatly increased weights and speeds involved. A mixture of cantilever and disc or drum brakes give the best results. You will find the names of all the leading tandem specialists in our list of useful addresses, and also the addresses to write to for *Freewheel Tandem*, a supplement to the very useful and informative *Freewheel Annual Equipment Guide*, and for the beautifully produced mail order catalogue from Richmond Cycles which includes their range of tandems and components.

CHILDREN'S BICYCLES

Everything that we have previously said about buying the best you can afford is particularly applicable to children's bicycles. Don't put little Wayne or Marlene off cycling for life by buying them some cheap rubbish to be going on with, just in case they don't enjoy it. If you buy them something cheap and nasty they certainly won't enjoy it, and you won't save any money, even in the short run, because children are even harder on bikes than they are on parents. If it isn't a good bike it won't survive long enough for you to sell it when they get fed up, or it gets 'grown out of' and they need a bigger bike.

Some children seem to be quite fearless, and to have fantastic reaction times. To watch a four year old ace three wheel drifting his kiddie trike through downhill bends is both exciting and enjoyable, provided it is someone else's child doing the drifting, of course. Even if it is your own child and the sight frightens you to death, remember that competent handling of a vehicle is character forming and a great confidence builder, and increase your public liability cover.

Children are ready for their first two wheeler when they are four or five. Don't buy them something on horrid solid tyres, especially if your child is the sort that likes fast cornering, as these tyres have poor road holding qualities, apart from being uncomfortable to ride.

Do not make a great production about teaching them to ride. If you are a relaxed and cheerful tutor, the chances are that you will have a relaxed and happy pupil who will learn more quickly. Cycling, after all, is supposed to be fun, especially at that age. A park is a good place for tuition – on the grass, not on the paths. If they fall off they won't hurt themselves. Let them paddle the bike along, picking up their feet from time to time. They will soon get the hang of balancing and steering. Remember: enjoy, enjoy. Call encouraging remarks. Do not shout threats and insults.

A good quality bicycle in the four-to-seven year old range, with stabilisers, proper steel ball bearings rather than the plastic ones which soon wear out, a chainguard, and no dangerous, sharp, edges, will cost between £50 and £60.

After that a well made bicycle with 16″ wheels will be suitable for several years, provided that you buy one that has a 3-speed gear, or has a chainwheel large enough to give a sensible, single, gear ratio. The Dawes Junior Kingpin priced around £100 is a good example of this type of bicycle. Small framed BMX bikes are also suitable, although they tend to be expensive.

Make sure that the bicycle you buy is the right size for your child. Too big a bike that he, or she, is intended to 'grow into' and not 'out of', thus saving money, is very dangerous as it will increase the tendency to wobble. Most schools invite the police, and road safety officers, to give cycling proficiency lessons and riding tests. Make sure that your child attends the classes, and passes the test. Survival is just as important as 'O' levels.

After the age of twelve, or thereabouts, 20″ wheels are in order, which gives you a wide choice of adult 'shopping' bicycles, BMX bikes, or sports machines. For non-enthusiastic child cyclists the 'shopper' is the best value as it is virtually impossible to outgrow its enormous range of handlebar and seat adjustment. Rugged BMX 'burners' for this age group are even more expensive than the smaller models, and drop handlebar sports machines are priced midway between the two. The Raleigh Micron, with a 5-speed derailleur gear and a 16½″ frame, costs around £100, and Marlborough make similar bicycles with 20″, and 24″, wheels.

BMX BICYCLES

BMX bicycles are marvellous fun, and if your child shows interest, and there is anywhere reasonably close at hand where he can do some off-road riding, then it would be a good idea to buy him one. I am genuinely sorry that I am too old and large to ride one properly.

BMX stands for Bicycle Moto Cross so in a sense they are bogus as they are pedal cycles aping motorbikes. Most of the kids in our village, and probably every other village, have them, and I'm sure they never wear their front tyres out as they are always 'pulling wheelies' and riding on the rear wheel. BMX bikes aren't cheap, but anything that encourages children to take an interest in a healthy and confidence building outdoor activity must be a good idea, and as a bonus most of the action takes place in parks, on waste ground, or on specially constructed tracks, away from the menace of fast moving traffic.

BMX bicycles have small wheels, big studded tyres, sit-up-and-beg handlebars, light but strong frames, and indeed light and

31

strong everything else. All are carefully designed, and padded, to be as safe as possible.

Prices range from £120 to £150 for a machine quite good enough to provide a child with endless pleasure, up to £400 for very superior models intended for the higher forms of competition. You can also buy crash helmets and colourful protective clothing, which, by the way, are obligatory for all official competition.

I would suggest that you consult your child before going out to buy what you consider to be a suitable machine, as he, or she, is probably an expert. To sum up, it may cost you a fair amount of money, but it's worth remembering that BMX riders are not the sort to hang around streets getting into trouble, and complaining that there is nothing else to do.

ATBs, or 'MOUNTAIN' BICYCLES

All terrain bicycles, like BMX bikes, are a concept imported from America and are intended for the more severe type of off-road riding, not just gently pottering along smooth bridle paths, or dry 'green lanes'. The American, and Japanese, offerings have rugged names. Muddy Fox 'Adventurer', Cougar 'Mountain Lion', Specialized 'Stump Jumper' and Kuwahara 'Puma' are typical, and give some idea of their intended purpose. This new sport is 'taking off' and European manufacturers, F. W. Evans, Saracen, Madison, Dawes, Bob Jackson, and Peugeot, to mention just a few that are now in the business of making ATBs.

As a generalisation most 'Mountain' bikes will have 26″ x 2.125″ knobbly tyres, a 6-speed freewheel, and a triple chainwheel, giving 18-speeds, a handlebar gear changer, flat, or upswept handlebars, a padded saddle, cantilever brakes, and motorcycle type brake levers.

A well set up ATB is an attractive bicycle, but there is a snag and that is cost, particularly as an ATB is not ideal for any other purpose. Prices range from £200 to over £500, due, in part, to limited production. As the sport becomes more popular, and Raleigh enter the field, prices may come down a little. At the moment the best buys are probably the three 'Ridgeback' models made by Madison, priced between £230 and £350.

If you are thinking of buying an ATB remember that the bottom bracket will be much higher than it would be on a normal bicycle and you will need a smaller frame than usual if you wish to have safe access to the ground.

SECONDHAND BICYCLES

Finally we come to buying secondhand, and the same rules apply to all categories of bicycles and can be summed up neatly in the latin *caveat emptor* which is a legal term for 'watch it' or let the buyer beware. Even the nicest people will quite happily sell you a load of trouble rather than cope with it themselves. Decency and morality peter out at the edge of the second-hand market, but if you are careful it is better to buy a really good bike second-hand than settle for second-best new.

A good source of second-hand bikes, other than the cycling newspapers already mentioned, is the *Exchange & Mart*. The only drawback about it is that anything of interest to you is usually for sale 400 miles away. The local paper is better in this respect but won't have much to offer. You should not pay more than three quarters of the list price, and that is absolutely top whack, no matter how recent or in how good a condition the bike may be. Don't pay more than half list price for anything in only moderately good order, and if it isn't in moderately good order don't buy it anyway.

My own feeling about buying a second-hand bike is, if the wheels are in line, it looks as though it has been looked after, there are no signs of recent repairs to the frame, and it rides nicely and everything works smoothly, then it is probably OK. Don't worry too much about worn tyres or cables that need renewing, provided their condition is reflected in the price.

Don't be shy about trying to knock the price down. Everybody asks more than they expect to get and if you don't bargain for the lowest price the seller will be astonished.

Chapter 2

BUILDING YOUR OWN BICYCLE.
PART 1

THE FRAME AND FORKS

Whilst the primary concern of this chapter, and the next, is advice on buying a frame and building up your own sports or racing bicycle, it should contain much of interest even though you may already have decided to buy such a bicycle ready made. A quick glance through the text before you spend your money may not change your mind, or choice, but it will help you to ask the right questions in the cycle shop, and to understand something of bicycle construction and design.

We will begin at the beginning with the frame, as it is the heart of a good bicycle. A bicycle is only as good as its frame, and a frame is only as good as the thought, the materials and the craftsmanship that go into it. Don't be a cheapskate when buying a frame, either off the peg or when having one made to your specification, buy the best that you can possibly afford. Basically, the more you pay, the less a frame will weigh. But deciding what is best is where things get a little complicated. I suppose it could be defined as that which is best fitted for its purpose. For example, there would be no point in spending a fortune on a frame made of ultra light-weight tubing if you need a bike for touring with a heavy load. Equally, there would be no point in buying a frame designed for touring and then trying to race on it, no matter how good the materials. Actually, it is doubtful whether a good shop or a frame maker would sell you the wrong set up if you briefed them accurately about your needs, but it is nice to know the whys and wherefores of materials and frame design.

FRAME TUBING

Taking material first, there are five main suppliers of lightweight tube sets. They are Ishiwata and Tange – both Japanese – Atelier de la Rive, of France, A.L. Colombo of Italy and, lastly and easily the most popular, at least in Britain, Reynolds.

Saracen use Ishiwata, Koga use Tange and Peugeot use the Super Vitus tubing from Atelier de la Rive. All the Italian custom frame makers use Colombus from Colombo and everybody uses Reynolds 531 and 753 tube sets. Puch, Peugeot, Raleigh, Dawes, Holdsworth, Claud Butler, Condor, Hetchins, and certainly all the British specialist frame makers use them, as do most of the American custom frame makers.

There is very little difference between the weights of the various makers' tube sets supplied for similar types of frame, 11 tubes to a set. For example, for a touring frame, a Colombus tube set will weigh 2375 grms, a Reynolds set 2445 grms, and a Tange tube set 2400 grms. Nevertheless, Reynolds tubing is generally regarded as the very best – which would explain its popularity – with Colombus a close second – although Vitus 979 Duralinox is claimed to be a third lighter than Reynolds 753.

Any of these tube sets will make you a lively and resilient frame, something that can't be done with cheap and heavy thick walled tubing. Drop a good bike made of decent tubing on its wheels from a few inches up and it will bounce, whereas a cheap bike will have a dead and lifeless feel to it.

Titanium is a material that has been in limited use for a number of years but has never really caught on due to its shattering price. At the London Cycle Show of 1956, Phillips showed a titanium frame weighing about 2½lbs, which was roughly half the weight of a contemporary frame made of Reynolds 531 lightweight tubing. But the Phillips frame was never marketed. The Speedwell Gearcase Company of Birmingham produced 10,000 frames with titanium tubing in 1973, and these sold for around £130 – quite a lot of money for a frame in 1973 – and although they were light, weighing only 3½lbs, they were not very stiff and had a dead and unresponsive feel. Various people have built aluminium frames over the years, starting as early as 1896, but the cost and the disadvantages have always outweighed the advantages, and for the purposes of this chapter we need only consider the highly satisfactory, easily obtainable and sensibly priced steel alloy frame tubing already listed.

If you are buying a good, off-the-peg English frame and forks they will almost certainly be constructed of a suitable lightweight tubing from the Reynolds range. But make sure that they are, and that the entire frame, and the forks as well, are made from Reynolds, or at least from lightweight tubing. Some frame makers use Reynolds tubing for the main frame triangle and Columbus forks and stays, and there is nothing wrong with such a combination.

Reynolds offer several grades of lightweight butted and double butted tubing. Butted simply means that the tubing is internally thicker at one end where the strength is most needed. Double butted means that it is thicker at both ends. Plain gauge tubing is the same thickness all the way along and although correspondingly heavier it is cheaper to produce.

The lightest and most expensive of this tubing is known as Reynolds 753. It comes in two grades – 753 Track for pursuit racing and time trials, and 753 Race for road racing, cycle cross and sprints. Then comes the famous 531 in the usual bicycle equation of ascending weight, descending price. First is the 531 SL Speedstream – lightweight oval section for racing, then follow 531 Professional and 531 Competition also for racing, and 531 Special Tourist which is self-explanatory. Finally, there are two new additions to the range, designated Reynolds 501 Cromalloy and Reynolds 501 BMX for the less expensive touring and commuting bicycles and BMX bicycles respectively.

753 tubing has more torsional rigidity than titanium. But it is extremely thin walled and very difficult to work with. For that reason you should only buy a 753 frame from an absolutely top flight frame maker. Brazing temperatures are critical and there is no room for error in frame alignment.

LUGS AND BOTTOM BRACKET SHELLS

Having dealt a little with the subject of lightweight tubing – this chapter is only concerned with what you need to know about a bicycle, not all there is to know – let us have a look at the methods used for joining these tubes into the classic diamond frame. Put very simply, this is done with a bottom bracket shell and with, or without, lugs at the corners.

Both lugs and bottom bracket shells are available in cast or pressed mild steel and are 'bought out' by frame makers and cycle manufacturers from a number of sources. The suppliers of bottom bracket shells seem mainly to be French or Italian with such names as Dardenne, Gargatte and Dubois (nervex) or Cinelli. The big names in lug making are once again Dubois and Cinelli and also Prugnat, Fisher, Agrati and Bocama.

Pressed steel bottom brackets that have been stamped out and welded together are the lighter, the cast shell the stronger. Some frame makers prefer one type and some the other and so it seems quite probable that there is little to choose between them.

This is not the case with lugged, or lugless frame construction. As a general rule, and without getting deeply into technicalities and metallurgy, the great majority of top class lightweight frames are built with lugs. Most lugless frames are found on inexpensive or heavy duty bicycles that are made from thick and heavy cheaper tubing welded together.

BRAZING AND WELDING

There is a lot of loose talk about welded frames. Welding is a process that involves heating up two pieces of metal, or in this case tubing, to a molten state so that the metals run and merge together and, when cooled, form a joint. Although people speak of welded lightweight frames, such frames are, in fact, brazed or soldered. Thin walled tubing will not withstand the heat involved in welding without distortion and fatal loss of strength.

Brazing is a process in which the tubes that are to be joined together are preheated with a brazing torch, but not melted, and molten brass, or copper alloy, is flowed into the gaps between the tubes, and built up around them so that the brass or alloy, and not the metal of the tubing, forms the joint. Superficially this looks much like a weld.

In both the lugged and lugless frame the tubes are mitred to butt closely up together. In a lugless frame this mitring is critical, especially if the frame is to be soldered, as silver solder doesn't flow as easily as brass. Silver soldering is used for very thin walled lightweight tubing as the temperatures involved are lower, which means less weakening of the metal at the joint – just where it takes the highest stress loads and needs its strength most. Silver solder is very difficult to handle and there is no margin for error in the alignment of a frame, as ultra-lightweight tubing cannot be 'cold set' – which means bent into line after the soldering is done. For this reason some frame makers prefer not to use such tubing as Reynolds 753.

Lugless frames are not as resistant as lugged frames to downward thrusts upon the pedals, which means they tend to 'whip', and this is especially true of 'aerodynamic' frames of oval section tubing which, because of its shape, has less lateral strength anyway. Unless of course, the broader side is set against the direction of travel, which would rob it of any advantage it might have. And this comparative weakness is compounded by the lugless construction dictated by the difficulties of joining oval tubes.

Paradoxically, such a streamlined frame ostensibly built for speed might be very soft and comfortable for lightweight touring.

Provided that the tubes are mitred carefully, the lugged frame is much stronger. During the brazing process the molten brass flows into the lugs, as well as filling and joining the small gaps between the tubes, and makes a robust joint over a much greater area than in a lugless frame, thus distributing the stress loads instead of concentrating them in the small area where the tubes are joined.

MORE ABOUT LUGS

Lug is a rather ugly word for something that can be very beautiful. Most frame makers use stamped out steel lugs – cast lugs are heavier and tend to become brittle – and most of them file and cut away these lugs to their own distinctive style. Mercian of Derby offer a wide range of attractive hand-cut lugs of their own design but Hetchins Cycles must be the ultimate in this field with a long history of fancy lugwork with rather far-fetched names like 'Experto Credo', 'Nulli Secundus', 'Mountain King' and 'Gothic' down to the current 'Keyhole Superbe'. I find them all a bit too Gothic for my simple taste but this is only comment and not criticism, for in theory, the long tails of the decorated lugs do have a function in that they distribute the stress loadings over even greater areas. The Americans love Hetchins bicycles with their whorls and whimsical embellishments, and their functional curly seat and chain stays. They buy them to hang them up on walls as works of art, which indeed they are.

In spite of the elaborate filing and shaping of a Hetchins lug, plenty of metal is left where it is most needed. In fact such windows in a lug – hole would be too crude a word – do have a definite advantage in as much as the builder can see that the brass has flowed around the joint.

An American school of frame making favours thinning and lightening the lugs, and cutting weight-saving holes in bottom brackets. Neither of these practices have found favour here, the English craftsman's view being that the lug and bottom bracket are used to impart strength and rigidity to a frame and that there is little point in weakening either of them.

When ordering a frame, you may be asked to specify your choice of lugwork from a set of samples. Although I doubt if a decent frame builder would offer such a thing, do not choose lugs that are chopped off at the ends rather than tapered off. The sudden change in frame strength at the end of such a lug would mean a high stress concentration at this point and could cause a tube to break. Other than that, it doesn't really matter, except as a personal preference for plain or ornate lugs.

TUBE ALIGNMENT

After the tubes have been prepared and mitred, and the lugs, if lugs are to be used, have been cleaned up – most lugs come from the makers in a rough, unfinished state – or filed to exotic shapes, the actual construction of the frame can either be carried out in one of two ways, or in a mixture of both. One method is to assemble the tubes into the lugs against a board marked with the angles and positions of the tubes, and to join them with locating screws in holes drilled through the lugs and tubes, and then to braze or solder up the frame relying on the locating screws to hold the frame in its alignment.

The other method is to clamp the tubes in jigs and hold them firmly in configuration while the joining up is done. Obviously this latter method must be used for a lugless frame and in fact it does produce a more accurate alignment that will require less forcing into shape by cold setting. Cold setting sets up stress patterns in a frame that can eventually cause fractures and it is not permissible for frames made of ultra thin walled lightweight tubing. These have to be constructed with absolute accuracy in the first place.

Frames are easily checked visually for correct alignment. Sight along it from front to back and then from back to front. If anything is out of line don't touch it with a barge pole; it will be a misery to ride.

The standard of the brazing, soldering, or lugwork, can give a useful indication of the quality of a frame makers work, although a lot of rotten workmanship can be disguised by clever finishing. If what you can see looks slapdash, you can imagine the quality of what you cannot see. Your best bet for getting a good frame is to go to a top frame maker or to buy a frame with a good reputation.

FORK CROWNS, DROPOUTS AND CLEARANCES

When discussing your new frame with the builder – which is, incidentally, a lot more fun than ordering a suit – you will be asked to specify your choice of fork crowns and fork ends, or dropouts. The fork crowns come in three patterns, fully sloping, semi sloping and flat. All have something going for them. The fully sloping fork crown is the strongest and the heaviest and the flat fork crown the lightest. All of them are far stronger than the fork blades so it is really only a matter of what you think will look the best, although it's possible that a fully sloping crown will transmit more road shocks to the rider.

When choosing dropouts remember to specify the type with mudguard eyes, if you are intending to have mudguards, as some types have mudguard eyes and others don't. If you are building up a bike for serious touring then vertical rear dropouts with both mudguards and carrier eyes are probably the best, and if you are intending to fit mudguards make sure the frame maker knows this and leaves room for them. You should also tell your frame maker the size of the wheels that you intend to use, as a frame with close clearances intended to take the continental 700C will not have room for 27" diameters.

FRAME SIZING

Off-the-peg frame sizes have traditionally been decided by measuring the length of the buyer's inside leg and deducting about 10″, but nothing is simple anymore. Some 'experts' are now saying that we all ride bikes that are too big for us – which I don't think is true – and advocating a deduction of 11″ from a rider's inside leg dimension. Everybody seems to be in agreement about saddle height, so from a performance point of view I don't think seat tube length can be all that critical, and don't intend to get my skin tights into a twist about it.

Cino Cinelli, the famous Italian frame maker, has a method of frame sizing that is different but interesting. He takes the distance from the head of a client's femur to the floor, less 32 to 34cm depending on length of arm and torso, as a guide to seat tube length. In my case this distance is 100.33cm (39½″), so subtracting 32cm from that figure, as I have long arms and torso, leaves 68.33cm or a frame size of 26.90″. Just to cross check – if you can put up with all these intimacies – my inside leg measurement is 35″ which less 10″ gives a frame size of 25″, the size of the frame I ride and which suits me well enough.

All Italian vehicles are built for people with short legs and exceedingly long arms ('Standard Italian Ape' as this design philosophy is called in the car business). The results of sizing by the Cinelli system would suggest that we are all riding frames that are in fact too small. As a point of interest there was a fashion for small frames before the last World War when 'Standard English Apes' like me rode around with yards of seat pin sticking rudely out. There is a theory – that I don't quite follow – that 24″ is the limit for a good bike frame. Aesthetically, this may be true, but most tall people have long legs. A frame to suit a long body and short legs would be even less aesthetic.

To sum up I would say that subtracting 10″ from your inside leg length will give you a comfortable size for a touring frame. For time trials where keeping your head down to lessen wind resistance is more important than your comfort, and a high saddle, low handlebar position is acceptable, then you may find the 11″ deduction theory is more suitable.

DECISIONS, DECISIONS

There is a great deal more to buying a frame than agonizing over size. The greatest advantage of having a frame built instead of buying one off-the-peg is that the frame will fit you perfectly, instead of you having to adapt your own frame to fit the frame as best you can. The analogy with being measured for a suit is apposite, for careful noting of most of your vital statistics – including the emotive measuring of inside leg – will be necessary before work commences, so that top tube length, seat and chain stay length, bottom bracket height and wheelbase, as well as seat tube length, can be determined. Don't be surprised if your frame maker doesn't ask you to come back for a fitting. You can hardly try on a heap of loosely connected tubes and he can't take a tuck in, or cut pieces out of, a brazed up and finished frame. It has to be a case of right first time.

In order to determine the kind of frame you need, the frame maker, or the chap you buy your off-the-peg frame from – I wouldn't describe him as a salesman – will want to know if you intend to use your frame for touring, for road racing – by which I mean massed start racing – for time trialling, or even for a mixture of all three, in which case you will end up with a compromise not very suitable for anything.

Whilst it is quite true that the most important factor in a bike's performance is the rider's own power output and stamina, the old saying about horses for courses is also true enough and the bloke in an equal state of fitness, but on a bike intended for the purpose, will beat you every time. It all depends how keen you are. If you just want to take the mudguards off your touring bike and have a bash round in the club '25', just for the fun of it, that's fine. If you have any ambition to do well in racing you will need specialized machinery.

For road racing and touring you need a bike to be as light as is consistent with reliability and to steer and handle well. A time trial bike, or a track bike, must be a pretty uncompromising device; short, stiff, light, and to hell with stability and comfort. It is in the time trial bike that most scope exists for the aerodynamic frame. In a road race, the riders are mostly riding in a bunch, and wind resistance is a less important factor. It is in high speed riding in close company that the good handling and steering count. In a time trial the rider is on his own with nothing and nobody to shelter him, and even the smallest reduction in drag is very welcome.

FRAME ANGLES

The intended purpose of a frame will, to a great extent, dictate the head tube angle, and the degree of fork offset (the terms 'fork rake' or 'trail' mean the same thing) which is the distance, measured horizontally, between the centre of the front wheel and an imaginary line drawn downwards through the centre of the head tube to the ground. This line will pass behind the centre of the wheel, due to the forward curvature of the front forks. The less the curvature, the less the offset, rake, or trail. Straight forks would have absolutely none, as the imaginary line would run down through the centre of the fork blades.

Both the head angle and the fork offset are critical, in as much as they determine the characteristics of a bicycle in terms of steering, handling and comfort.

The angle of the seat tube is dictated by the need to achieve a 45% front, 55% rear weight distribution. A short-thighed rider needs a steep seat angle to place him nearer to the handlebars, and a tall rider with long thighs needs a shallow angle to place him further to the rear.

Shallow head angles and generous fork offsets make for stable steering, and soften the ride characteristics of a bicycle as road shocks tend to be absorbed rather than transmitted to the rider. They also extend the wheelbase, which is another factor that contributes to stability and comfort, and makes shallow angles a desirable design feature for touring bicycles.

As a rough guide, the ideal touring frame for the average sized rider would be one with both head and seat angles set at 72°, (or 72° parallel) a fork offset of 2½″, or slightly more, and a 42″ or even 43″ wheelbase. This type of frame will steer and handle well, and at the same time be very comfortable over poor road surfaces, increasingly important as our roads deteriorate through lack of maintenance.

For lighter steering, or a longer top tube to suit a taller rider, a combination of 73° for the head tube, and 72°, or less, for the seat tube would still be fine for comfort and stability. But there are no hard and fast rules to be observed, the most important thing

43

is your own preferences. In the late 1940s, and early 1950s, 74°/72°, and 73°/71°, were popular frame angles for touring, and for racing bicycles, and before the war the classic English time-trial bike had frame angles far shallower than used today for touring. 68° parallel was not uncommon, with a 3″ fork offset and a 46″ wheelbase – extreme in every way according to the current trends – but the truth is that frame design, like so much else, is influenced by fashion.

For time trials, and fast road work, the current trend is towards steeper angles – 74° parallel, or 75°/74° for instance – allied with 39″ or 40″ wheelbases, and these trends are creeping into designs intended for round-the-houses massed start races, now called 'Criteriums', and long distance road races. The aim is partly to achieve a 'stiffer' frame, in the sense that being shorter it will be more resistant to 'whip' or deformation caused by powerful thrusts exerted on the pedals, and will therefore absorb less energy and transmit more power to the rear wheel. The aim is also to place the rider more directly above the pedals, a good position for high power output for short periods.

These steep 'stiff' frames are excellent for climbing hills, but not so good for descending hills at speed. The steepness makes the steering light and over-sensitive, and the rider may feel rather insecure from being placed so far forward over the front wheel. Sitting directly above the pedals is not such a good position for transmitting moderate power outputs for long periods. Furthermore this kind of frame transmits road shocks to the rider far more than the longer, shallower, frame, and a harsh and jarring ride can be extremely tiring.

In fact the steep angles themselves do not contribute to the 'stiffness' of a frame, but only to the shortness of it. A long wheelbase frame with steep angles would be no stiffer than a shallower design. What makes for stiffness in a frame is a short rear triangle made possible by steeper angles. It is the chain and seat stays that are inclined to whip, and making them stronger, and as short as possible, is where the most advantage can be gained. Although, of course, a shorter top tube giving a more compact main triangle will also help.

Whether the modern frames with steeper angles are in fact faster than their earlier counterparts, it is difficult to say. During the last forty years so many advances have been made in weight saving materials, component efficiency and tyre design that no

44

comparisons of race times can be valid. It would be very interesting to have a robot of rider shape and size, programmed to ride bicycles of various designs and frame angles on rollers in a wind tunnel.

It is quite possible that the results would show little difference in performance between the shallow angles and long wheelbases of the 1930s and the products of the modern schools of thought.

Certainly the modern frame feels livelier, and for that reason probably feels faster. But with its steep angles, small fork offsets and shorter wheelbase, the modern bicycle has a hard, less comfortable ride, and less directional stability.

The ideal all-round frame would absorb road shocks but not power, be comfortable to ride, but wouldn't 'whip', would be excellent for climbing hills and just as good for coming down again. It would also be good for sprints, yet carry lots of touring gear. Naturally enough, such perfection is not attainable, at least not yet, with a conventional diamond frame. As is the case with almost everything you must decide on your priorities and settle for a compromise.

The 'Sun Manx TT' bicycle of the late 1940s was an interesting attempt to avoid compromise and to have the best of both worlds by combining a short wheelbase for frame stiffness with a shallow head angle and terrific fork trail for stability, both virtues very necessary for road racing on the Isle of Man where the TT course includes an ascent and descent from and to sea level over the shoulder of Snaefell mountain, which, while only just a mountain at 2034' is still a severe test of stamina, nerve and skill. In this design, the seat tube came down at a very shallow angle to meet the down tube six inches or so above the bottom bracket, which was braced with twin small diameter tubes from the seat tube. This allowed the backwheel to be tucked well in to give short chain stays and wheelbase.

The Hetchins 'curly' seat and chain stays, or 'Vibrant triangle' as the makers call it, is also very effective for creating a stiff rear triangle, although the actual intention was to give a comfortable ride when unyielding wooden wheels were fashionable wear for racing, and the road surfaces were worse than they are today. The Bates curly 'Duoarc' front forks were another successful design for minimizing road shocks.

Bottom bracket height is another factor worth considering, for as wheelbases have shrunk so bottom brackets have got higher.

This is all very well for racing cyclists as it enables them to keep the power on through a corner without the pedals digging in, but it has no advantages for tourists, for whom the facility to pedal through a corner doesn't matter in the least.

The higher the bottom bracket, the higher the top tube, and the saddle, from the ground, and this makes for long and unsightly head tubes, especially on larger frames. Racing has an enormous, and disproportionate, influence on bicycle design, and the current trend is for unnecessarily high bottom brackets on touring bicycles. 11" is not at all uncommon, when 10¼" would be more practical in every way.

Before we leave the subject of hand built frames, your frame maker will ask you to specify a headset, through which the front forks will be attached to the head tube of your frame, and these vary in price from about £8 for a set from Tange to just over £30 for the most expensive one from Campagnolo.

For pottering about and for gentle riding you would find the Tange adequate. For frames intended for racing and hard riding the Campagnolo Super Record, and the less expensive Record priced at £20 will be hard to beat and are almost standard equipment for many racing bicycles, but the light alloy Shimano Dura-Ace 600 EX is a great deal cheaper and will give good service.

For racing or for touring the Stronglight Super Pro set, which costs a little under £20, will prove very durable and smooth with its tapered roller bearings, but, in the short term, the choice isn't really critical. Ask the frame maker's advice and buy the best you can afford.

Now let me give you some idea of current prices. A good ready-made touring or racing frame and forks in Reynolds 531 butted tubing with nice but simple lugwork will cost you about £135 and a similar, but made-to-measure frame, about £190. Should you want Reynolds Special Lightweight tubing you will have to find another £30 at least. Beyond this standard it is difficult to say, as so much depends on details and refinements, but for a frameset in Reynolds 753 ultra lightweight tubing with moderately ornate lugwork you would certainly be looking at an outlay of between £250 to £300.

Chapter 3

BUILDING YOUR OWN BICYCLE.
PART 2

COMPONENTS

Before going on to take a general look at the enormous choice of lightweight cycle components available in this country, I should mention that the cheapest way of building up a bicycle is to decide on the components that you want and ask your frame maker to supply them all. That way he may be persuaded to pass some of his trade discount on to you.

If you are building up a racing bicycle and have no strong preferences for one make of derailleur, another maker's pedal, and yet another maker's hubs, then the easy way is to buy a racing 'grupo'. Campagnolo, SunTour, Shimano and several other manufacturers make 'grupos' which consist of brakes, pedals, derailleurs, control levers, chainset, headset, seatpost, freewheel and hubs. Some even offer handlebars and chain.

However, buying a 'grupo' won't be the cheapest way to build a bicycle. If you settle for a group of components from Campagnolo, whose beautifully hand finished products have a terrific reputation for reliability, it will be the best, but probably the most expensive, way. In passing, it is interesting to note how few ready-made bicycles are made up from components from just one manufacturer.

Both Shimano, with their Dura-Ace equipment, and SunTour offer excellent value for money, and in some cases their components are actually lighter and as good as those from Campagnolo – in fact, in some cases they are very similar – but there is a 'but'. The Japanese philosophy for 'market penetration' is innovation and frequent change, with a new model quickly superseding the last new model. This practice makes spares hard to get, and this has certainly been the case with Shimano. Also, the Japanese tend towards low first cost and high priced spares – if you can get them.

PRICES

As the cost of bicycles and bicycle components vary from shop to shop, the prices mentioned in this Chapter – and throughout the book – are intended only as a guide. At the time of writing (Summer 1984) I would say that they are about average. As prices have recently been fairly static, hopefully they won't be too inaccurate at the time of publication. All prices quoted include 15% VAT.

WHEELS

We will make a start on wheels, as they are next in order of importance for comfort and performance. In the context of the sports touring and racing bicycle there are only two wheel sizes – diameter, that is – and they are 27″ and 700 C. The difference is small but significant. 26″ wheels and smaller belong only on 'cooking' bicycles, except when used on recumbents and other unconventional machines outside our present scope.

Wheels fall into three basic categories. Firstly, light wheels for touring with a lot of luggage; secondly, even lighter wheels for fast riding, such as training, and light touring; and lastly – lightest of all – wheels purely for racing. You can buy your wheels already made, or buy the rims and hub and spokes separately, and have them built.

At the risk of being extremely boring, buy the best that you can afford. Cheap wheels are a pain and you will always be replacing spokes. But, once again, don't pay too much in the belief that because a rim, a hub, or a complete wheel, is twice the price of others it will be twice as good. £60 seems about the right price to pay for a good pair of ready-made touring wheels. There seems to be very little difference in the price of buying comparable bits and having a pair of wheels made up. The same sort of prices are charged for wheels suitable for training and for light touring, and for really lightweight racing wheels you can pay between £60 to £200 depending on your choice of rims and hub.

Taking wheel rims first. For our purposes, there are five basic types. Firstly, the widely used 27" x 1¼" size 'Endrick' rims that take only a 27" x 1¼" high pressure tyre; secondly the 27" x 1¼" rims that take both the standard size high pressure or HP tyres and the new narrow section HP tyres, which are 27" x 1⅛" or 27" x 1", and thirdly, 700C rims which are the standard continental size, 700mm in diameter and approximately a centimetre smaller than our standard 27". They are available in various widths from 32mm down to 20mm. Then there are the recently introduced 'Mixte' type of rim that will accept both 700C HP tyres and tubular tyres known as 'tubs' which are the same diameter as 700C, and finally there are the very light 'sprint' type of racing rim which will take only 'tubs'.

Most of the rims designed for use with narrow section HP tyres have a concave tyre well, or retaining ridges on the top inner edges of the well that lock into the tyre walls, making it easier to centre the tyres correctly on the rims, and less liable to being blown off the rims by the very high tyre pressures involved which can be 100lbs per square inch or more.

For touring you need nothing lighter than a 27" x 1¼" rim or a comparable 700C drilled for thirty-six spokes, or forty spokes for the rear wheel if you intend to carry heavy loads. If you intend to do a lot of Continental touring then the 700C are much the better buy as 27" tyres are all but unobtainable in Europe and a 700C tyre will NOT fit the British size of rim. Also spokes for 27" wheels are difficult if not impossible to get.

Weinmann and Rigida both offer excellent and reasonably priced rims in both the above-mentioned categories. The Rigida 27" x 1¼" rims are under £13 a pair.

For training and fast roadwork you will need either 27" or 700C rims that take the narrow section HP tyres, or the 'Mixte' type of rim that will accept both HP tyres or 'tubs'. The famous French firms Mavic and Super Champion both offer 27" x 1¼" and 700C rims that will take both ordinary HP and narrow section HP tyres at prices around £15 a pair with 36-hole drillings, and for a couple of pounds more, Super Champion offer a 40-hole rim for the rear wheel. They also offer 'Mixte' rims at around £17.50 a pair.

Very light racing or 'Sprint' rims that accept only 'tubs' are made by Ascenti, Super Champion and Mavic and all are available with 28-, 32- or 36-hole drillings. The Super Champion Arc-en-ciel are priced at £19 a pair, the Ascenti Stradas at £22 a pair, while the Mavic GP4s are £27. Or for £100 you can have a pair of the distinctive, grey finished, Mavic SSCs. If you like aerodynamic bicycle components the Japanese Araya company make a beautiful light alloy rim, heart-shaped in section and drilled for 28 or 32 spokes, at only £45 a pair.

TYRES

There are two types of tyres. The 'wired on' type – HP tyres are in this category – that rely on wire inside the edges of the tyre to hold it on the rim, and tubular tyres that are glued or cemented to the rim.

Only the lightest and naturally the most expensive tubular tyres are worth using – and then only for racing – as the much cheaper narrow section HP tyres now have a similar if not superior performance to the heavier grade of 'tub' although the 'tub' can be pumped up to a higher pressure without being inflated off, or 'blown off' the rim. You do not need 'tubs' for touring. Most of them are nowhere near as durable as HP tyres and puncture far more easily. Being more difficult to repair, it is necessary to carry a spare which can be a nuisance, especially if you ride to work, for it would be foolish to park your bicycle and leave a spare 'tub' on it.

Good 27″ x 1¼″ or 700C tyres are all that are necessary for touring and general purpose riding and narrow section 27″ or 700C HP tyres for all other uses except racing, but do remember that 27″ and 700C tyres are not interchangeable. The materials, construction and tread patterns of both HP and tubular tyres are a compromise between too much grip which will slow you down and too little grip which will give you trouble in the wet.

Experiments are said to have shown that below twenty miles per hour there is very little difference in the grip factor of tread patterns and in fact an almost smooth and virtually treadless tyre is as good as a tyre with a marked and presumably scientifically designed tread, but on a wet road it seems to me that a well defined and designed tread pattern could make a considerable contribution to your safety.

There is also a theory that comparatively heavy tyre construction and tread pattern make little difference to the frequency of punctures but it is my experience that a marked tread pattern does give one some protection although this type of tyre does make cycling somewhat harder work. The simple rule is that the lighter, narrower and harder the tyre the more punctures you will have.

A simple, light and cheap device known as a 'tyre saver' will afford some measure of protection against punctures. Made of alloy, wire and plastic tubing it can be fitted to the brakes or mudguards so that it lightly skims the tyre, clearing thorns, flints and other small sharp objects off the surface of the cover before they have a chance to penetrate. Punctures can be such a problem in some areas that riders use 'tubs' instead of inner tubes inside their HP tyres.

Probably the best solution to the puncture problem is to fit a Wolber 'Invulnerable', a narrow section HP tyre, or a 'tub', with a stainless steel mesh interposed between the cotton casing and the tread. Wolber, the makers, claim that the 'Invulnerable' is 30% less likely to be punctured than a normal tyre or 'tub', and although that doesn't sound quite like invulnerability, it is, nevertheless, the most puncture proof tyre that is currently available. Prices are around £10 for either type.

The cost of the average HP touring tyre, with tube, is in the region of £7 and narrow section HP tyres, with tubes, cost very little more. Michelin, Nutrak, Wolber, Hutchinson, Specialized and Clement all offer excellent HP tyres in both wide and narrow section, and in both 27″ and 700C.

From the heavier grades of tubular tyres such as the Wolber Junior to such ultra lightweight racing 'tubs' as the Clement Seta Extra, the prices vary from around £9 up to £25. Clement, Wolber and Hutchinson all offer a wide range.

Your choice of tyres should to a large extent be dictated by your needs, and of course the rims that you have chosen. The best thing is to buy both rims and tyres from a shop that is run by keen and knowledgeable cyclists. Ask their advice and be guided by their experience and expertise.

HUBS

Wheels, no matter for what purpose, must all have hubs. Hubs for lightweight bicycles are made of light alloy, unless specific mention is made of an alternative material, and fall into two categories. There are large flange hubs, once very popular with racing men but becoming less so, and small flange hubs which are becoming increasingly popular with racing men.

Large flanges allow the use of shorter spokes and give a slightly stiffer wheel, while small flanges need longer spokes that give a slightly softer ride. In actual fact the difference in performance between the two is marginal and you can safely make your choice on a preference for the appearance of one type, or the other.

Most of these hubs are available only with quick release axles but some makers offer the old fashioned nut and solid spindle as an alternative. The quick release hub with its hollow axle and pull-out 'skewer' is certainly the best for quick removal of a wheel to mend a puncture, or for removing both wheels for easy transportation by car, and for storage in a confined space. The only drawback is that the wheels are more easily stolen and in that respect the spanner and nut arrangement is the best.

If you are buying your wheels in bits and having them made up, don't forget to match the number of spoke holes in the hub flange to the spoke holes in your rims. If you are intending to ride a fixed sprocket rather than a 10-speed gear, get a hub that is threaded on both sides for the fitting of two sprockets for a change of gearing.

As to prices, Phil Wood & Co. make the most expensive hub. It has a small flange in alloy and a very large diameter stainless steel drum that houses the maintenance free bearings. These hubs are available with quick release axles or Allen key axle nuts and are really very splendid, but they do cost over £90. Next in order of expense are Maxicar who offer a beautifully made pair of large flanged, highly polished alloy hubs – also with a quick release or solid spindle option – for just under £60. For only £3.50 more you can have their interesting Hilo hub with a small flange on one side and a large flange on the other, which Maxicar claim increases the strength of a 'dished' rear wheel.

Although it must be very nice to be able to afford the most expensive there really is no need to spend a fortune. Campagnolo Record hubs in both large and small flanged versions are available for £52 and £48 respectively, and excellent and less expensive hubs are made by Shimano, Ofmega, Maillard, SunTour, Miche, Normandy and, surprisingly, by Campagnolo. The latter's large and small flanged Tipo hubs are priced at £30 and £25 and must represent good value. A pair of Miche Competition small flange hubs, anodised in black or silver are also good value for less than £20.

Shimano and Maillard both offer unusual rear hubs. The Shimano Freehub, priced at £40 has an integral freewheel block and requires the use of Shimano Uniglide chain, and the Maillard 700 series hubs has helicoidal grooves in place of the conventional thread. These grooves allow for easy removal and rapid replacement of the freewheel block.

SPOKES

If you are having a wheel built, you will of course need spokes, and these are suprisingly expensive. The best chromed double butted spokes (double butted means that they are thicker at the ends than in the middle) work out around £10 per hundred, while the stainless steel variety are £20 or more. It is also possible to buy aerodynamic spokes to match aerodynamic rims and these are less expensive at £17 for 75. Discuss the choice of spokes with your wheel builder.

GEAR RATIOS, CHAINSETS, FREEWHEELS AND GEAR CHANGE MECHANISMS

Before we go any further let me clarify the term 'gear ratio'. Strictly speaking we don't express gear ratios as ratios but as the effective diameter, in inches, of the driven wheel. This is a hangover from the days of the 'Ordinary' bicycle, or Penny Farthing, when the diameter of the directly driven front wheel determined the 'gearing' – the bigger the wheel the higher the gearing, the smaller the wheel the lower the gearing.

To calculate a gear ratio, divide the number of teeth on the chainwheel by the number of teeth on the rear sprocket, and multiply the answer by the size of the back wheel. For example, a 32 tooth chainwheel and an 18 tooth sprocket on a 27″ rear wheel will give a 48″ gear, the equivalent of riding a Penny Farthing with a front wheel 48″ in diameter.

As few of us have ridden a Penny Farthing, this may not mean much to you, so a more up to date example may have more relevance. For instance, a 44 tooth chainwheel driving an 18 tooth sprocket on a 27″ rear wheel will give a 66″ gear, typical gearing for a roadster bicycle with a single speed freewheel, or an equally typical middle gear for a similar machine with a 3-speed hub.

It is, of course, the physical size of sprockets and chainrings that determines the gearing. The teeth are only there to mesh into the chain and hold it in place to provide the drive. A quick glance through the buyer's guides that I mentioned earlier will show that the most popular combinations are a 42T/52T double chainwheel (the T stands for teeth) driving a 5- or 6-speed block with sprockets ranging from 14T up to 28T. Obviously these are a compromise for general use, giving a 100″ top gear and a 40.5″ bottom gear. For special purposes, such as touring with a heavy load in hilly country the Cyclists' Touring Club suggests 28T/46T chainwheels driving a 5-speed block with 15, 17, 19, 21 and 23 tooth sprockets. Such a combination gives a useful spread of reasonably spaced gears from an 82″ top gear down to a bottom gear of 32.9″.

You will find some more comments and advice on choosing gear ratios a few pages further on, in the section dealing with freewheels, but gearing is very much a matter of personal preference and only through experience will you find out what suits you best.

Incidentally, there is no need to go around with a sectionally serrated brow working out gear ratios with a calculator. Gear ratio charts are freely available.

CHAINSETS

Chainsets are quite a complicated subject so we will begin with basics. A chainset is made up of a bottom bracket spindle, and the cups and bearings that support the spindle in the bottom bracket housing of the frame. A pair of cranks, a chainring or chainrings, and their fixings complete the set.

The right hand crank – in all the better chainsets – has five arms radiating from it to which the chainring or chainrings are attached by countersunk Allen headed bolts. The five arms are called the 'spider' and the complete crank, 'spider' and chainring are called a chainwheel.

The Campagnolo chainwheel is universally admired and as a consequence has been widely copied by other manufacturers. These copies are referred to as 'Campag.' pattern and their chainrings are interchangeable with those from Campagnolo.

The best chainsets are forged. This, put very simply, means that the right hand crank and 'spider' are made in one piece and are therefore very strong. Only a few of the cheaper chainsets have a 'swaged' crank and 'spider'. This means that the two items are made separately and then pressed together, an arrangement which is less strong.

All the chainsets mentioned in this brief survey are of the 'cotterless' variety. This means that the tapered square holes in the 'big ends' of the cranks fit over the square tapers of the bottom bracket spindle and are held tightly in place by bolts instead of old fashioned cotterpins.

Big names in chainsets are Campagnolo, SunTour, SR (SR stands for Sakae Ringyo) Stronglight, Shimano Dura-Ace, TA, Nervar and Edco. All but the last three mentioned offer a choice of crank lengths between 165-180mm. By and large, shorter cranks suit short legs and longer cranks suit long legs. 170mm is the most popular length. If you have long legs and chose the longest cranks make sure that the pedals won't foul the front mudguard or tyre.

The cheapest chainsets do not have detachable rings, and cheap double chainsets may have only one ring that can be detached. This not only limits your choice of ratios but when the non-detachable ring is worn out – they usually last around 10,000 miles – then the whole chainwheel is useless and will have to be replaced.

Campagnolo make the best chainsets for racing but at a price. The Campag Super Record – which does have a super record – costs around £150 and the Nuóvo Record only £35 less. SunTour, SR, Stronglight and Ofmega all offer Campag pattern chainsets at considerably lower prices. However, the Super Record set does include a titanium bottom bracket spindle and is the lightest on the market. Campagnolo and Campag pattern chainrings are readily obtainable but because they are primarily intended to be used for racing or fast roadwork, 42T is the minimum size available, not much good if you need a set of very low gear ratios for touring with a heavy load.

Probably the best value for a touring chainset is the Stronglight

49D, or the Stronglight 99 priced at £45 and around £35 respectively, with double chainrings. Triple chainrings cost between £5 and £10 more, and Stronglight offer a wide choice of alternative chainrings that range from 26T up to 60T.

If you think it possible that you may sometimes wish to vary a set of ratios for some specific purpose by fitting a larger or a smaller chainring, do check up as best you can on the range, availability and the interchangeability of alternative chainrings before you definitely decide on a particular make of chainset. Both Shimano and SR have a poor record of availability. Most Shimano sets only accept Shimano rings and SR only accept Campag pattern – which means no choice of smaller chainrings – or their own make of rings.

On the credit side, Shimano do make one of the most beautiful chainsets it is possible to buy. Their Dura-Ace AX, an aerodynamic design that comes complete with matching pedals, is absolutely stunning although it does cost around £100. Equally beautiful is the aerodynamic Edco Competition which is similarly priced, but without pedals. Less expensive aerodynamic sets are available from Stronglight and SR.

The best way to make up your mind on which chainset you should buy is to decide how much you wish to spend. The price factor and the use to which you intend to put your bicycle will cut down on the choice and consequently the confusion. Have a good look at the chainsets on offer and discuss the details with a knowledgeable cycle dealer.

BOTTOM BRACKET SETS

If you have bought a chainset without a bottom bracket set – some of the 'cheap offer' chainsets one sees are cheap for this very reason – or wish to replace or update an existing set, there are some very attractive units on the market. But remember that some sets have spindles long enough to accommodate only double chainrings. If you use, or intend to use triple chainrings make sure that the spindle in the set that you choose is long enough.

Top names in bottom bracket sets are Campagnolo, SunTour, Stronglight, Galli and Phil Wood & Co. The Campagnolo Super Record set has a titanium spindle, or axle, dural cups and special bearings but costs well over £80. The Nuovo record has a steel spindle and cups and is somewhat heavier but at only £35 it is much cheaper. The set offered by Phil Wood & Co. almost matches Campagnolo's Super Record for expense but it is claimed to be a maintenance-free unit with sealed bearings and it also has special aluminium mounting rings that are adjustable from both sides to give an ideal chain line. A sealed bearing unit from SunTour costs only £28.50.

Priced at around £27, the Stronglight 651 bottom bracket set has a steel spindle in double or triple chainring lengths. The Stronglight 650 set is very similar but costs almost twice the price, as the spindle, which is offered only in the double chainring length, is of Titanium.

The Galli unit is an unusual design using taper roller bearings that spread the pedalling stresses over a greater area giving a longer bearing life. As in the Phil Wood unit, the cups can be adjusted from both sides for perfect chain alignment. The price is just over £20.

FREEWHEEL BLOCKS

Discounting the single speed freewheel used on old fashioned roadsters (and not relevant to this survey), there are only two basic types of freewheel blocks. They are the 5- and 6-speed blocks of standard width that will accept both the $\frac{3}{32}''$ chain and the recently developed narrow section, flush sided $\frac{3}{32}''$ chain; and the compact 6- and 7-speed blocks that are the same width as the 5- and 6-speed standard blocks, achieved by narrowing the distances that separate each sprocket. Because of this diminished spacing, these blocks only accept the narrow $\frac{3}{32}''$ chain.

As a rule, 5- and 6-speed blocks are used in conjunction with a double chainwheel, giving 10- or 12-speeds, or gears. Touring in hill country with a heavy load is a good reason for using a 5-speed block with a triple chainwheel. For a situation where one could be riding uphill for a whole morning – as is quite possible when touring in the Alps – a selection of ratios around and below 40 inches can be very useful, enabling a rider to sit down and twiddle steadily.

For example, a triple chainwheel with 44, 36 and 26 tooth rings driving a block with 16, 18, 20, 23 and 27 tooth sprockets will give a top gear of 74 inches and a bottom gear of 26 inches, with a useful range of medium, low and very low gears in between. You do not need big gears for descending the Alps whilst trying to stop a heavy load, or for lugging the load along the flat.

It is, of course, possible to have 18- and 21-speed gears by using 6- or 7-speed blocks with a triple chainwheel but there is little point in such arrangements as they give too many close gear ratios to be of use to tourists, and racing men don't need that wide a spread of gears, or the extra weight and complication.

The famous names in freewheels are Campagnolo, Maillard, SunTour, Normandy and Regina. First, we will look at standard width blocks.

Campagnolo make the ultimate 6-speed racing block in hardened alloy with two sprocket combinations with 13 to 21 teeth, or 14 to 26 teeth. These blocks cost around £100 and worn sprockets are replaceable.

Maillard also offer hardened alloy 5- and 6-speed blocks to special order and 13 to 28 tooth sprocket combinations can be specified at prices between £65 and £70. Maillard also make much less expensive 5- and 6-speed blocks in silver finished steel at prices between £17 and £19.

Regina make a reasonably priced range of bronze plated 'Oro' blocks. There is a 5-speed version in a variety of stock sizes from 13 teeth up to 21 teeth, and a 6-speed version in three combinations within the same range of sprocket sizes. Prices range from £10 to £12.50.

Normandy make an even cheaper range of standard width steel blocks with 14 to 34 tooth variations from £6.25 up to £8.25 according to the sizes of the sprockets. Larger sprockets are the more expensive, naturally.

The SunTour 888 range of inexpensive freewheel blocks are available in nine 5-speed variations from 14 to 34 teeth, prices from £7 to £8 and in a similar number of 6-speed variations at prices between £8 and £9. SunTour also make a range of more expensive 6-speed blocks at prices in the region of £13.

Now we will have a look at the narrow 6- and 7-speed 'compact' blocks from SunTour and Maillard.

SunTour's offerings are the Ultra 6 and the Ultra 7 ranges. The Ultra 6 has a standard width 5-speed freewheel body and the Ultra 7 has a standard width 6-speed freewheel body, but with less space between the sprockets which necessitates the use of narrow chains. There are five stock versions of the Ultra 6 with sprocket combinations between 13 and 32 teeth, and prices vary according to the ratios selected, from £14 up to £17. The Ultra 7 is also offered in five combinations, all starting with a 12 tooth top gear sprocket. A 32 tooth sprocket is the largest size available, and prices are from £15 up to £18.50. Ultra 6 and 7 freewheels to your own specification are available to order, within the same range of sprockets, costing around £20.

Maillard make both 6- and 7-speed compact blocks, the 6-speed in four stock combinations between 13 and 30 teeth, and the 7-speed in four stock combinations between 12 and 21 teeth. Prices are £17 and £18.50 respectively. Maillard also offer custom freewheel blocks with sprocket variations between 12 and 30 teeth for just a few pounds more.

Do remember when you are ordering a block that gear change mechanisms work more smoothly with moderate jumps of two to three teeth between ratios. The same thing applies of course to front changers and if you restrict the difference between the chainrings to ten or twelve teeth they too will work much more smoothly. Choosing sizes of sprockets and chainwheels requires quite a bit of thought. If you have wide gaps between the size of both you get a duplication of gears, whilst a small difference in size of chainrings, combined with large differences in sprocket sizes means that in order to progress properly through the gears you will have to change on both front and rear changers every time, or put up with huge leaps from gear to gear. The very thing that a multi-speed gear should make unnecessary.

GEAR CHANGE MECHANISMS

To simplify things a little, let us first dispose of the subject of hub gears which – for the majority of riders – have no relevance to touring or to racing bicycles. This is not to denigrate this type of gear which is excellent in many ways. The hub keeps the oil in and the dirt out, they have long lives and need very little maintenance. The chain runs in a straight line between the chainwheel and the sprocket (which increases chain life), and it can be easily removed for cleaning. For town riding you can stop in a high gear at a traffic light and change down while you are waiting, which is a great convenience. With a derailleur all gear changes must be made while pedalling. If you stop in a high gear you must start off again in the same gear and struggle to change down.

The drawbacks of the hub gear are heavy weight and lack of ratios. I cannot think of one cycle manufacturer who offers a sports tourer or a racing bicycle with a hub gear, and the objections to them raised above are probably the reason.

However, there are keen tourists who dislike a multiplicity of gears and who find a 3-speed hub ideal, while others prefer to use a 5-speed hub in conjunction with a derailleur mechanism to arrive at 10 or 15 gears, or even more. For the latter, the Cyclo Gear Company of Birmingham make both 2- and 3-speed freewheel blocks that can be quickly fitted to a Sturmey-Archer hub, and although the sprockets accept only a $\frac{1}{8}''$ chain it is possible to run that over chainrings intended for the smaller – $\frac{3}{32}''$ -size of chain.

DERAILLEURS

Now let us have a look at the derailleur gear. The only real critisism that one can make of them is that they are rather hard on chains, the chain constantly being 'derailled' from one sprocket, or one chainwheel, to another. In fact, with the chain on the inside chainring and the smallest (outside) sprocket, or on the outside chainring and the largest (inside) rear sprocket, it runs so badly out of line that it effectively robs a rider of two gear ratios. But, in spite of this drawback, derailleur gears do work extremely well.

REAR DERAILLEURS, OR CHANGERS

The spring loaded jockey arm of a rear derailleur swops the chain from sprocket to sprocket to give different gear ratios, and also keeps the chain taut. Racing changers have shorter jockey arms than touring changers because they do not have to operate over wide variations in sprocket sizes, and consequently are not required to take up excessive chain slack. Because of the short jockey arm, a racing changer gives slightly more positive gear changes.

If you intend to go in for wide ratio gears for touring, then be careful to pick a rear derailleur with enough capacity to cope with your choice of ratios. To calculate required capacity, add the difference between the number of teeth on the top and bottom gear sprockets to the difference between your chainwheel sizes. For example, a 14T top gear sprocket and a 28T bottom gear sprocket have a 14T difference, and that figure added to a 13T variation in chainwheel size gives a difference of 27 teeth which many racing changers cannot cope with.

Therefore, before you buy a rear derailleur do make sure that it has a suitable capacity, and also that it will work satisfactorily with the largest sprocket on your freewheel block. If you have no need for wide gear ratios it is best to buy a racing changer. They tend to be lighter than the touring mechanisms, and also slightly cheaper.

There is an almost bewildering choice of rear gear changers with the products of Campagnolo, Huret, SunTour, Shimano, Simplex, Zeus, Mavic, Ofmega Rino and Galli all clamouring for attention. To complicate things even further, each manufacturer offers several gears. To simplify the subject, we will examine only the products of the first five companies, not because there is anything wrong with the products of the last five, but because the first five are by far the most popular and the most readily available. We will look at racing changers first.

Campagnolo offer three models. The Super Record at £48.50, the Nuovo Record at £34.50 and an attractive 'cheapy', the 980, for around £15. The first two have bushed bearings so that when, eventually, they do get sloppy they can be rebuilt to be as good as new. The Super Record is made of titanium and duralamin and will cope with 5-, 6- and 7-speed freewheel blocks with a maximum 28T bottom sprocket. The Nuovo Record is very similar but, constructed entirely in duralamin, it is somewhat heavier – 201gms against 187gms for the Super. The 980 is very little heavier and is unbelievably good value.

Huret offer two racing rear changers, the Jubilee and the Super Success, both priced at around £30. The forged light alloy Jubilee is the lighter of the two mechanisms, weighing only 148gms, which makes it the lightest on the market, a suprising 23 gms lighter than the titanium and light alloy Success with its 'drilled for lightness' roller cage. Both changers have a 12 to 24 tooth rear sprocket range.

SunTour make three competition changers at competitive prices, the Superbe Pro at almost £23, the Cyclone Mark II at £20 and the VX for around £10. The Superbe Pro in anodised forged light alloy – do not expect to find titanium in low priced changers – weighs 168gms and has a 12 to 23 tooth sprocket capacity. The cheaper Cyclone model is made of similar materials but weighs a few gms more with a 13 to 26 tooth sprocket range. Both will cope with a 15T variation in chainring sizes. The cheapest model – the VX – is naturally the heaviest and can be used with a 28T bottom gear sprocket on the block.

Shimano offer their Dura-Ace AX aerodynamic changer for £32.50 and a cheaper unit, the 600 EX for around £16.50. Both are a little heavier than average and Shimano recommend that the aerodynamic AX should only be used with their own Uniglide chain and special Freehub. The 600EX can cope with a 28 tooth difference, but the AX can only manage 24.

The Simplex 6600 is the gear most widely used by the French road racing teams. It is heavier than the comparable Shimano gears, and at almost £40 is a great deal more expensive. However, it is Simplex policy to offer cheaper versions of their top quality components and their 610 rear changer is very similar to the 6600 but costs a quarter of the price.

Now we come to rear gear changers intended for the tourist. The only Campagnolo unit in this category is the Rally derailleur, derived from the Nuovo Record, but with a longer roller cage it costs a little less (£31) and weighs very little more. It differs from its sporting ancestor in that it will cope with 13 to 31 teeth on the rear sprocket.

The most expensive rear gear changer available – and the one that allows the greatest differences between both freewheel sprocket sizes and chainring sizes – is the titanium and light alloy Huret Duopar, priced at just over £50. Due to the expensive materials used in this unique twin parallelogram design it weighs only 254gms, surprisingly little for a sturdy touring unit with such an incredible capacity. The Duopar works smoothly with a 12 to 36 tooth freewheel and a 17T difference between chainrings.

The Huret Eco is a similar mechanism made in steel which pushes the weight up to 330gms and the price down to just under £22.

SunTour make a GT (Grand Touring) version of their racing Cyclone Mark Two which costs just over £20 and which will cope with a 13T to 34T block and a 15T chainring difference. They also offer a GT version of their inexpensive VX unit.

Simplex make only one rear changer for the tourist, a greater capacity version of their racing unit. It weighs a little more and costs just under £40.

The usual equation of price and purpose will further simplify your choice.

FRONT DERAILLEURS, OR CHANGERS

Front changers are much simpler than rear changers and are consequently lighter – approximately half the weight – and cheaper.

As front changers are all much of a muchness in performance – with the exception of one or two that are particularly suitable for use with triple chainrings – it seems logical to use both front and rear changers from the same maker, but there is no reason why you shouldn't mix makes if you wish.

The Campagnolo Nuovo Record and Nuovo Gransport changers are both handsome and hand-polished – as are all Campagnolo components – and cost around £18.50 and £12.50 respectively. The Huret Success is the heaviest of all front changers – 130gms – and is ideal for use with triple chainrings. It costs around £13.50.

Shimano offer their Superbe Pro and Cyclone changers for £16.50 and £12, while the aerodynamic Shimano Dura-Ace AX costs nearly £17.60. Their 600EX version is both lighter and cheaper, which is unusual, at £6.50.

At £17 the Simplex 523 front changer is the most expensive in the range and is ideal for use with triple chainrings. The Simplex 103 is an economy version of the 523 and costs less than half the price, and the Simplex racing changer, the 102, costs only £6.50.

GEAR CHANGE LEVERS

For gear change levers the same names crop up yet again. In fact, SunTour, Simplex, Campagnolo, Dura-Ace and Huret all make complete sets of front and rear changers and levers and if you are getting tired of decisions then you could settle for a suitable full set from any one of them and have done with it, although SunTour undoubtedly offer the best value for money.

Gear change levers for rear derailleurs are designed to be mounted in one of three positions, on the down tube, on the handlebar stem, or in the ends of the handlebars. This also applies to control levers for both front and rear derailleurs which are sold in pairs set side by side, with the exception of the handlebar end type which come as single units.

The down tube position is the most common and is ideal for racing when a lot of time is spent riding on the 'drops' with the levers close at hand. For touring when one spends more time with the hands resting on the 'tops' rather than the 'drops', the down tube position is rather less convenient and the handlebar stem mounting might be better. Handlebar end controls are really only suitable for racing and for hard riding.

SunTour offer levers for all three positions and their prices vary from £5.50 to £14.50, the handlebar end controls being the most expensive. Campagnolo offer down tube and handlebar end controls at reasonable prices from £8.50 for a pair of levers for the down tube, to £5.50 each for handlebar end fitting levers. A single lever for the down tube costs around £5.

Huret offer similar options; their twin levers for the down tube cost £12.50 for the Jubilee-Success-Duopar version, and a pair of handlebar end levers in light alloy cost nearly £14. Oddly, the right hand lever costs slightly more than a left hand lever. Aerodynamic Dura-Ace AX and 600EX for the down tube seem rather expensive at £16 and £6.50

The choice of gear control position is very much a matter of personal preference. The down tube controls, while slightly inconvenient for touring, do have the shortest and most direct cables and work extremely well. They are also the least expensive.

None of the controls mentioned above give a positive change. The gears have to be 'felt in' by moving the lever until it has the desired effect. It is very easy at first to select a gear above or below the one that you actually want, but you will soon get used to the feel of the control and the amount of movement necessary and will have no further trouble. It is not possible to buy a lever that gives a positive change without also buying a complete rear derailleur. Both Huret and Shimano offer such systems for around £20.

CHAINS

Chains are a messy but necessary part of a bicycle's transmission. They are available in three sizes: $\frac{1}{8}$", $\frac{3}{32}$" and narrow section $\frac{3}{32}$". (For further details refer to the section headed Chains in the chapter covering bicycle maintenance.)

$\frac{1}{8}''$ chain is used only on bicycles fitted with a single speed freewheel, or on those fitted with hub gears. Accordingly, $\frac{1}{8}''$ chains are not included in the following brief survey.

All bicycles fitted with single 'fixed wheel' sprockets or with derailleur gears need $\frac{3}{32}''$ chain. Those fitted with narrow section 6- or 7-speed freewheel blocks need narrow section, flush sided, $\frac{3}{32}''$ chain.

The big names in chains are Promex, Sedis, SunTour, Shimano, Regina and D.I.D. Lanner.

Promex make both standard and narrow $\frac{3}{32}''$ chain with silver plated links designed for easy gear changing, at prices in the region of £5 and £5.50 respectively.

The Sedisport narrow chain with bevelled inner edges on its outer links, for improved gear changing, comes in black, silver or gold finishes at prices ranging from £4.50 up to £5.75 and is recommended for use with SunTour Ultra and Maillard compact freewheel blocks.

Confusingly, the SunTour Ultra-Glide and the Shimano Uniglide chains sound very similar and both have bevelled links, but the SunTour is a narrow section chain for use with standard or narrow freewheels, while the Uniglide is a standard width chain for use with standard freewheels only. The silver coloured Ultra-Glide is priced at £6.50 and the Uniglide is £1 cheaper.

Regina offer both chain sizes in a gold finish. Their Record Oro narrow chain has side plates drilled for lightness, which can hardly save much weight but makes it twice the price of the standard width Regina Oro which costs around £5.

Finally, D.I.D. offer a standard $\frac{3}{32}''$ chain with specially shaped outer plates which they claim improves gear change performance. It can be used only with standard width freewheels and costs £5.10.

The recently developed Super Link priced at £3.75 is the only spring link that can be used with a derailleur gear and greatly facilitates chain removal.

All prices quoted refer to 116 links, long enough to cope with the widest gear ratios.

PEDALS

There are two types of pedals suitable for lightweight bicycles.

Cage pedals, with or without 'quill' ends, and platform pedals. The platform pedal is probably the best for touring as they offer better weight distribution for a rider's foot, and consequently don't cause aches and cramps as the narrow edges of cage pedals are inclined to do on long distance rides, or on quite short distance rides if the rider is not wearing proper cycling shoes.

Good makes are Campagnolo, SunTour, Shimano Dura-Ace, SR, Miche, Ofmega, Lyotard, Olympic, Galli, and Maillard. Lightest of the lot is the Campagnolo Super Record, while the Maillard 700 steel cage pedal is the heaviest, and quite expensive at almost £30. The cheapest pedal on the market is the French made Lyotard chrome steel platform which is good value, priced at £7, but very narrow. Remember, if you have broad feet you need broad pedals.

The dearest pedal on the market? Well, Campagnolo of course. Their beautiful Super Record costs almost £100, but they do offer a super range of seven different models, all cage type, of which the Gran Sport is the least expensive at a modest £22.50. The SunTour Superbe, for both road and track, are very elegant for around £45, and the best economy cage pedal is probably the Miche for £10.50.

Naturally, it is now possible to buy aerodynamic pedals. Ofmega, the Italian accessory firm, make a very attractive and unusual platform, called the Sintesi, which utilises high density nylon, and has integral toe clips. The price is in the region of £20. SR make very striking streamlined pedals that come complete with toe clips for only £19, and the same manufacturer's alloy platform pedal, without toe clips, costs £12.25.

I doubt if, in the short term, there is much to choose between the performance of any of the pedals mentioned, so, other than considerations of comfort and longevity, the choice is down to visual preference, and price.

BRAKES

Lastly, there are the brakes; there are the same names in the 'grupo' trio, plus some new ones. CLB, Dia Compe, Galli, Mafac, Modolo, Weinmann and Zues. There seems to be a bigger choice of brakes than of any other component. Mercifully, there are only two kinds of brakes that are of any interest to us here, and those are disc brakes and calliper brakes. The calliper brakes sub divide

66

into two species which are side pull and centre pull. The cantilever brake is a variation on the centre pull theme but pivots from bosses brazed to either side of the front forks, or to the seat stays.

Disc brakes for pedal cycles are a recent innovation that tend to be both heavy and expensive and are rather too much brake for a lightweight bike. They work very well in wet weather when too much brake power can do more harm than good. Some need to be built into a special hub, but like the much less expensive drum brakes they are ideal for tandems, tricycles and tandem tricycles, and touring bicycles if you intend to carry monstrous loads. Prices run up to £100.

A quick look at the list of calliper type brakes reveals that there are more than twice the number of side pull brakes on offer than there are the centre pull type; a clear case of racing influencing the market, for both types work equally well in terms of stopping power. Without writing a thesis on the subject, side pull brakes are slightly lighter and quicker acting, although greater force is needed at the lever, and this makes them very popular with sporting riders. Centre pull brakes have a more precise, progressive action, and high pressure on the levers can be converted into high pressure on the wheelrim which makes them popular with tourists who need to control heavy loads down long descents rather than just banging the brakes on before scratching through a corner.

Campagnolo lead the field again for excellence, if not expense, with their Super Record and Record side pull brakes priced at £97 and £92 respectively. The SunTour Superbe Pro design is very similar, except that SunTour made the mistake of not copying the Campagnolo quick release arrangement and their own is not as good. Nevertheless, it is good value at only half the price. The Dura-Ace AX and Modolo Kronos are both aerodynamic brakes, the Kronos, at £156.75, are intended to be tucked away behind the forks to cut down on wind resistance, while the Dura-Ace, a centre pull design, are meant for more traditional siting in the air stream and have the slightly less up-market price of only £90. Although aerodynamic components are very beautiful, and always cost a lot of money, it is worth remembering that they may not make the slightest difference to performance.

On a more pragmatic level, Galli make a very light and popular side pull brakes for slightly less than £30 but Weinmann offer the most comprehensive and least expensive range. Their 605 side pull model costs £33. The 500 model – also side pull – is available in black, red or gold, as well as in the more usual polished alloy finish and costs just under £19. Their centre pull design, the Weinmann C.P. Vainqueur 999 also costs around £20 and their cheapest model, the side pull 730 Silver costs little more than £13. Inexpensive as they are, the Weinmann brakes are very good and widely used on production sports and racing bicycles. Dawes, Raleigh, Claud Butler, Revell, Falcon, Puch, Holdsworth and Koga all fit Weinmann products.

All the brake makers offer some form of quick release facility fitted variously onto the calipers, brake levers, the front brake cable hanger at the headset, or on the seat pin cable stop.

In terms of braking performance there doesn't seem to be a lot to choose between them for to a great extent the efficiency of a brake depends upon proper adjustment and the type of brake shoes fitted.

Nor is there a lot – other than price – to choose between the levers of the brakes listed above. All of them are attractive and all have hoods of moulded plastic or rubber to make them comfortable. Some are drilled for lightness, and some are not. This, incidentally, is the only difference between the Campagnolo Super Record and the Record. The Super Record is drilled, so you pay £5 more for rather less metal.

That really completes the 'build your own bicycle' briefing. Seat pins, saddles, handlebar stems and handlebars come under the heading of riding position and comfort, and we will deal with them later on.

As we have seen, there are a great many beautifully engineered and very desirable components available from a variety of makers. A 'grupo' might be the simplest way of equipping a bicycle; the trouble is though, that you miss out on so many nice things.

Before we leave the subject, mechanical efficiency is currently a great selling point and quite extravagant advertising claims are made that 'Whatsits Hubs' or 'Thingies six speed freewheel', or whatever, will improve your times, put you out in front, or lighten a tourist's load. In fact they will do nothing of the kind. Most of the gear advertised like this is excellent enough but any slight gain in efficiency the makers may have achieved won't be enough to improve your times. The only way to do that is to get fitter, or to cut down on your frontal area.

Chapter 4

ACCESSORIES & GOODIES

Over the past twenty years, the cycle accessory business has become a growth industry and much thought and ingenuity has gone into producing all kinds of useful and attractive bits and pieces intended to make cycling easier, safer or simply more convenient. A brief survey of a sample of such items follows, if only to inform a newcomer that such nice things exist.

However, before we become involved with carriers, prop stands, rear view mirrors and the like, we had better take a look at cycle lights, as they are basic to safety and survival if you intend to ride at night.

BATTERY LIGHTING

In Chapter 6 we will examine the importance of siting lighting prominently on your bicycle, so we will restrict this survey to the types of lights that are available – except to mention that brackets can be bought for mounting lights on headsets, handlebars, or on front carriers, all places where front lights should be.

Lights fall into three categories; chargeable, or non-rechargeable battery lights, and those powered from a dynamo; neither type is much good for seeing where you are going. To have really effective lighting on a bicycle would involve so much extra expense and weight that it simply is not practical at present, although a Quartz Halogen bulb, or headlamp, will help a little. The best that we can hope for at the moment is to have lights that can be clearly seen by other road users.

Both types of battery lights are pretty dim, especially when compared with the lights of motor vehicles, but are adequate for town riding. Straightforward battery front and rear lights are cheap enough. The very popular sets from Ever Ready and the Wonder lights from Wonder (UK) Portable Power Ltd, sell at around £8 while sets from Raleigh and from Pifco are similarly priced, and old fashioned lamps from Octopus are even cheaper.

Rechargeable batteries are quite a different story, for chargers, like principles, are expensive. The Bonanza outfit from Ron Kitching costs over £30 and produces a usable light for a continuous three hours. The Ever Ready charger, complete with batteries, is priced in the region of £18 plus the cost of front and rear lamps, and will give a good light for a continuous four hours.

Rechargeable batteries give no more light than ordinary batteries, take 12 hours on average to recharge fully, and are no use at all for touring in the Andes, or any other area where mains electricity is hard to come by.

To sum up, non-rechargeable battery lighting is cheap initially and very simple, but replacing batteries is expensive because they don't last very long. Rechargeable battery lighting seems to me to fall between two stools, as it is a lot more expensive than dynamo lighting and nowhere near as bright. The only things that batteries do have going for them are lack of friction and, in some cases, slightly lighter weight.

DYNAMO LIGHTING

Dynamo lighting is undoubtedly better from a lighting point of view but dynamos do have their problems. The hub dynamo is probably the most efficient but they are heavy and unfashionable and therefore unattractive to riders of lightweight machines; however, a lightweight version might sell very well. Driving a dynamo from a tyre wall will obviously cause friction, which will in time cause tyre wear, and also makes the rider have to work just that bit harder to overcome the drag. In wet weather, this type of drive will tend to slip, which means dimmer lights just when good lights are needed most. Another endearing feature of the dynamo is its tendency for blowing bulbs. The faster you go the brighter get the lights, until they suddenly go out and you end up hurtling downhill in total darkness, but this can be overcome by putting a voltage stabiliser in the circuit.

Not only might these lights go out at speed, they will certainly go out when you stop, a state of affairs which, while legally permissible, can be inconvenient. The best way to overcome this problem is to buy a Sanyo Electronic Dynamo, which currently costs £16.50, and which has batteries included in its circuit. When the power from the dynamo falls below a certain level the batteries cut in.

Otherwise, the best buy is probably the Jayem Cibie, with the Sanyo Dynopower the next best buy. Unusually the Cibie is the least expensive, costing £9.50 against nearly £15 for the Sanyo, which is supplied with front light only.

The Sanyo has the advantage of being driven by the tyre tread instead of the tyre wall and fits neatly under the bottom bracket. Although the tread affords a better drive, even the Dynapower will lose adhesion under some conditions but a wet weather lash-up with an elastic band to increase the roller pressure will cure that problem.

Other well known makes of dynamo, all tyre wall drive, include Union, Bluemells, Miller, Soubitez and Sturmey Archer. Prices range from £7 to £16 with Sturmey Archer the most expensive, but the lightest of the lot.

Whether they are powered by dynamo or battery most cycle lamps slip easily onto mounting brackets, and will just as easily slip off again, either into someones pocket or to bounce destructively beside you down the road. For both these reasons it does seem sensible to bolt your front and rear lamps to the lamp brackets.

Flashing amber lights worn on the back of a belt, or clipped on the back of clothing are essential wear for safe night riding. Being mistaken for a council dustcart might not be very flattering but it is better for the image than being flattened. Two such lights are the Belt Beacon and the Pulseguard and both retail at around £10.

Just to make sure that motorists can see you there are reflective 'Sam Browne' belts, and sashes, arm and leg bands, reflective mudflaps and reflective trouser clips, and even reflectors to fit onto spokes and pedals. If you should be run down when wearing all that lot I think you can only assume that someone is out to get you!

71

CYCLE BAGS

Unless you are a 'toothbrush and spanner' man, some means of carrying things on a bicycle will be of interest, and even the most unencumbered cycle purist with his spare 'tub' and tool roll strapped underneath the saddle must occasionally need to pick up something from the shops on his way home. For this purpose, the 'musette' or lightweight nylon bag worn on the back, is the simplest and cheapest answer, if you don't mind being used as half a sandwich board by the shop that sold it, as musettes are always used for advertising. At one time every keen cyclist wore one but now they are no longer fashionable.

The next stage up is the simple saddle bag which has not evolved a lot, but great advances have been made in pannier and luggage carrying equipment. The long distance tourist's bicycle can now carry loads that would dismay a camel without handling like a camel, as used to be the case when all the weight was piled up behind the rider, although this arrangement did diminish front tyre wear as the front tyre hardly touched the ground.

The trend is now for a more sensible distribution of such enormous loads with the weight shared between front and rear panniers, and much lower down. But if you really do need to carry so much stuff, it is best not to load the front panniers too heavily as that will make the steering very sluggish.

It is quite possible to carry enough gear for a weekend in a good sized saddlebag (provided that you don't dress for dinner), but if one bag isn't quite sufficient, a handlebar or front bag will increase capacity and balance things up very nicely. In fact, many riders are now using a handlebar bag in preference to a saddle bag. They do give a measure of protection from bad weather and if fitted with a transparent envelope on top are very useful for carrying an open map, or route card. Centre pull brakes are prevalent on touring bikes these days and both front and rear bags of any size need supporting frames to keep them clear of brake cables that run parallel with steering head tubes or seat stays, and also to stop them swaying about.

It is pleasant to report that British cycle bags and British pannier and carrier gear is the best available in Britain, and therefore probably in Europe, although the Americans make some really great outdoor life equipment, that country having more great outdoors than most.

Karrimor, Carradice, Pakit, and Andrew Hague are some of the top names in cycle bags of every sort, and they all quote the carrying capacities of their goods in litres. We will look first at some of Karrimor's products as they are probably the most popular, and certainly provide the widest choice.

Karrimor make their panniers and bags in three materials: a heavy duty nylon, that looks like cotton duck, called KS-100e which is offered in orange/blue, or red; a lightweight nylon called Silvaguard in the traditional Karrimor green; and a standard nylon packcloth in red, or navy. KS-100e is the most expensive, Silvaguard is slightly cheaper, and the standard nylon is used for the Karrimor Koronet economy range of luggage bags.

A 10-litre Bardale handlebar bag in KS-100e costs £21.75, in Silvaguard the same bag costs £19.50, and in nylon packcloth a similar bag costs only £8.50. The Karrimor Iberian pannier set with a carrying capacity of 45 litres costs £39.50 in KS-100e. The same set, but in Silvaguard, costs £36.25, and is not offered in the cheaper nylon. The Standard 38 litre panniers cost just under £30 in Silvaguard, just under £20 in packcloth, and isn't offered in KS-100e. Karrimor also make a cylindrical 10-litre bag called a Stuffsac for £8, in Silvaguard, and 25- and 20-litre saddlebags in the same material cost £22.50 and £19.50 respectively.

Karrimor also make an up-market Kabriolet range of panniers and bags in orange and blue KS-100e. The 35-litre rear panniers cost almost £40. A 20-litre pannier set to fit front or rear carriers costs £33.50. Karrimor also offer an attractive bag, complete with shoulder strap, that can be attached to front or rear carriers, or used as a handlebar or saddlebag. The price is £16.95.

I won't rummage through every pannier and bag made by the other manufacturers I mentioned, but will have a quick look at some prices to provide a yardstick for comparison.

Carradice bags are made from closely woven and hard wearing nylon, red or blue. Their 36-litre Overlander panniers cost £30.75. Their 14-litre saddlebag costs £15, and their 7-litre handlebar bag with shoulder strap and map case, costs nearly £18.

Pakit offer 20-litre aerodynamic Trimline panniers in their distinctive blue material, and suitable for front or rear, for £38.50, and a 5-litre streamlined Seatpak for £18. Un-aerodynamic 45-litre Expedition panniers with rigid aluminium back plates cost a whacking £59, and their 9-litre handlebar bag costs £31.

Andrew Hague make their bags in heavy duty waterproof

Cordura, in an extensive range of colours. 50-litre rear panniers are £39.59, a large saddlebag is £22.50. 18-litre front panniers are £25.25, and a handlebar bag complete with frame costs £22.50.

Octopus, Raleigh, and others offer full ranges of well made bags that will give good service, and at prices well below those of the rather grander products discussed above. The best way to decide is to shop around and see what suits you best in terms of price, quality, purpose and availability.

For more specialized purposes, Bicase make a pair of rigid panniers in white extruded polypropylene. They are ideal for carrying cameras, or fragile items, and are very reasonably priced at £16 a pair. Freedom Bike-packing of Exeter make a pair of briefcase panniers for the cycling commuter. Designed to carry files and documents they can be zipped together for convenience, which disguises the attachments; very smart and practical at £36.50.

CARRIERS

In the field of luggage carrying hardware, Jim Blackburn products are the very best. All the Blackburn carriers and pannier frames are made in aircraft grade aluminium, heliac welded at the joints. The fittings are all made of stainless steel, and they are very practical and handsome, but at a price.

The point of carriers on bicycles is simply to carry things and when they are fulfilling their function you won't see very much of them as they will be buried under heavy bags. With no disrespect to Mr Blackburn, whose products are very good indeed and in terms of materials and workmanship well worth the prices asked for them, I doubt if they are three times as durable as those from some other manufacturers.

For instance, a serviceable black plastic coated front carrier from Karrimor, with a very useful lamp bracket welded to it, costs £8, and a rear carrier from Karrimor costs £9.40. The equivalent items from Jim Blackburn are nicer looking but both cost £21.50. Aluminium front and rear carriers from Andrew Hague cost around £12, and carriers from Raleigh approximately half that amount.

If you intend to fit front panniers to spread the load it is well worth considering Jim Blackburn's Low Rider pannier frames, which can be used with or without a carrier. Carrying the weight at the centre of the front wheel, instead of high above it, greatly improves the steering and handling of a laden bicycle. Low Rider frames cost £24.95. Similar frames from Andrew Hague cost just over £10.50.

Leda, Showa, Pletscher, and Nagaoka all make moderately priced carriers, and Karrimor, Carradice and Leda all offer handlebar bag and saddlebag supports at prices in the region of £4.

TRAILERS

If you hate the thought of festooning your bicycle with panniers, and carriers and all kinds of stuffsacs and bags, then you could buy a trailer to carry your stuff. I have no experience of towing a trailer, at least not with a bicycle, but I imagine you would need to be exceedingly careful when descending hills. Pedley Equipment of Saffron Walden in Essex make a neat moulded box on two wheels for just £90 which no doubt they would be delighted to demonstrate to you. They also offer a trailer chassis kit for just under £40.

Bike Hod Limited of Croydon in Surrey sell a brightly coloured bag on two small unsprung wheels called a Bike Hod which looks just like a towable shopping trolley, and that is just what it is. It costs £50, and in one of their adverts is shown carrying what looks like a double bass – a rather too valuable item to pull through the streets on a trolley more suited for heavy and less vulnerable loads.

BIKE CARRIERS

Just as it is sometimes convenient or necessary to carry luggage on a bicycle, it can be equally convenient or necessary to carry a bike, or bicycles, as luggage on a car. Despite the anti-car nonsense that one reads in one or two of the cycling magazines, many cyclists are also motorists (it would be interesting to know what the figures are). I know several enthusiastic racing cyclists who own fast sporting motorcars, and many racing men who take their bikes to events on top of cars. One gentleman in a recent letter to a magazine claimed that his car was the 'ultimate cycle accessory'.

Some way of carrying bicycles by car is also useful for the touring cyclist as it makes it possible to have days out exploring areas many miles from home. For example, it is quite practical for a north London based rider to take a bike by car and be in Wiltshire, Oxfordshire, Berks, Bucks, Beds, or Warwickshire, Northants, Leicestershire, Lincolnshire, Cambridgeshire, Norfolk, Suffolk, distant parts of Essex, Kent and Sussex and furthest Hampshire, all in approximately two hours. Some determined driving on the motorways will bring Gloucestershire, Worcestershire and Derbyshire well within range. North West or West Country riders are even better placed, and with three or four riders sharing expenses, the cost of a delightful days riding in otherwise inaccessible country would be quite reasonable. I am not suggesting that one would want to do it every weekend, but it does make for a pleasant change of scene.

There are three methods of carrying bikes on cars, four ways if you include shoving one into the back of an estate car. More than one bike in such a car can be rather destructive, unless they are insulated from one another very carefully, and they do take up an awful lot of room, so you are really better off with them outside the car. One method is to hang bikes onto the back of a car, another is with bikes either way up on a roof rack and lastly with bikes strapped down, wheels uppermost, resting on polymer pads on the car roof.

My own preference is for hanging them on the back of the car from an AM Cycle Carrier, which looks rather like a walking frame with padded arms to take two bicycles, and can be quickly fitted to any type or make of car. Being on the back instead of on the roof means that one can drive quite quickly without risking damage to the bicycles, but this may not help fuel consumption as the laden rack probably creates massive interference drag. It costs £25.50 and is not a huge and awkward thing to store.

The first of the top-of-the-car alternatives is the LP Cycle Rack which has universal fittings that can be adjusted to fit into the guttering of any make of car. The Model 2G, which costs £46, will carry two bicycles upside down, with wheels in place, with quick release clamps holding the saddles and the handlebars. Model 1 holds only one bicycle in the same manner but is designed to fit onto other makes of roof racks. It costs £18.50.

Models 2, 3 and 4 each carry the number of bicycles suggested by the model numbers, but right-side-up with the front wheels removed and carried alongside the rear wheel of each bicycle. Model 2 costs £44, Model 3 costs £58 and Model 4 £71.50. It seems an expensive way to carry bicycles, and one which must create a lot of wind resistance and wind roar, but the bikes are securely held well out of harm's way should anything run into the back of the car, and the racks take up less storage space than the AM Cycle carrier.

The second of the rooftop methods is the Zulu, which uses nylon straps with gutter hooks to secure two bicycles upside down onto roof protecting pads. This has the same advantages and disadvantages as the roof rack system, except that it is easier to store when not in use. Around £25 it is the least expensive way of carrying two bicycles.

Whilst on the subject of transporting bicycles, taking bicycles by train can be a good way of having a day out, except that in this country train travel is hideously expensive.

Furthermore, bikes are not allowed on British Rail's Inter City high speed trains on weekdays, with the exception of one or two inconveniently timed trains per day, and then subject to reservation. The cost of this concession is half fare for your bicycle up to a maximum of £3 for a single ticket and £6 for a return, plus 70p for reservation, which means that accompanied bicycles can travel from London to Edinburgh and back for just £6.70 which is not unreasonable. On all other BR trains bikes travel free of charge at any time, and are allowed free travel on 125s at weekends.

CHILD SEATS

Before leaving the subject of ways and means to carry things, I do feel that children are one thing that should not be carried on a bicycle. Children have soft skulls that are easily damaged in the slightest accident, and even just dropping a stationary bicycle could injure a child quite severely. When strapped into a kiddie seat they have a long way to fall and are pretty defenceless. Carrying a child on a bicycle is dangerous enough in the country, where on a dry day the roads can be unexpectedly slippery from mud or from cows' nasty, or at 'loony time' in the morning and evening when the workers from the local industrial estate are

77

belting through the lanes in motorcars, late to clock on, or desperate to get home for whatever purpose. Carrying a child on a bike in a big busy town is absolute madness, and it doesn't matter how careful you are, cyclists are very vulnerable to the idiocy of others. On wet roads made treacherous by metal studs, rubber, and diesel oil you could deposit your Marlene or Marcus under the wheels of a bus, and even in dry weather it is only too easy, as all of us know, to get knocked off a bicycle by one of the 'I never saw you' brigade zooming out of a side turning or opening a car door right in your path. For the solo rider this is infuriating, or painful, if not worse. For a child helplessly lashed to a bouncing bicycle it could easily prove to be fatal.

If you simply must carry a child like a sack of potatoes, don't make a lash-up from a small saddle and footrests and hang the lot on the cross bar. It is good fun for kids to hang onto the handlebars but they can't be strapped on and there is no way of stopping them toppling off, and grabbing them suddenly when they do start to go isn't good for control or stability. If you have to carry a child, for heaven's sake buy a tricycle, or a kit to convert your bike into a tricycle. There are two of these at present on the market, both priced around £75, complete with wheels. If you are based in or near London, contact Ken Rogers at 71, Berkeley Avenue, Cranford, Middlesex. If you do not live in the south, try T. J. Cycles Ltd., 114, Blackpool Street, Burton-upon-Trent, Staffordshire. A tricycle will minimize the danger to a large extent, as tricycles are not prone to falling over, although of course they can be turned over, or run into by idiots.

Make sure that any child seat that you buy has a high back, which will give the child's head some measure of protection in the event of a spill, a safety harness, and some method of keeping the child's feet away from the spokes. There are several makes on the market that have all these features for around £20.

CRASH HELMETS

In spite of that homily on the folly of carrying children on bicycles, I am not a safety neurotic, but there are a lot of them about these days. Crash helmets are not the answer for safer cycling, just as they have proved not to be the answer for safer motorcycling. Crash helmets, especially the horribly ugly and sinister 'full face' variety lull young motorcyclists into a false sense of invulnerability, have caused a great many accidents due to riders getting drowsy from breathing in used up air, don't help much anyway in any accident that happens at more than 30 mph, and usually fall off in a really bad shunt – I have seen that happen several times during the TT races. If they do stay on, the weight will quite often break the rider's neck, and they have to be heavy to be any use. It is very probable that the invulnerability factor alone has killed more young motorcyclists than crash helmet compulsion has saved.

Not that the invulnerability factor applies to a cyclist. Motorcyclists tend to wear thick heavy clothing and boots, and you feel rather differently about biting the dust when just wearing shorts and a shirt. What could so easily apply to cyclists is crash helmet compulsion, if enough of us are silly enough to wear the things. They might perhaps be a good thing for children carried on the back of bicycles, but they would only be of marginal benefit, and a good quality helmet for a child costs nearly £30.

The best way for a cyclist to avoid a calamity is to use his wits and to ride defensively, and to lobby his MP for better facilities for cyclists. There is a House of Commons cycling club, so some MPs are sympathetic to our cause, and the Government is known to be disturbed by the increase in injuries to cyclists which is costing them £10,000,000 a year in London alone. Whilst it is possible that a crash helmet would save you from serious head injury in the event of an accident, it is by no means certain that it will. What is certain is that you will look quite ridiculous, and a helmet won't do much for your face, or your spine, or your lungs or your kidneys, which are all important. Unless you are prepared to ride about in full body armour looking like an amalgamation of a Samurai and the Tin Man from 'The Wizard of Oz', I'd forget about crash helmets. Unless you do have a problem with a fragile skull, in which case a padded leather strip track racing helmet is not unaesthetic and might be a good idea.

MIRRORS

Rear view mirrors should also be looked into. The current trend towards aerodynamics must be giving the mirror makers cause for reflection, for wherever you mount a bicycle mirror, it has to be reasonably large and prominently placed to be any use at all. Whilst I always use both inside and outside mirrors on motorcars, and handlebar mirrors on motorcycles, I don't find a mirror necessary when I ride a bicycle. In a car, or on a motorbike when wearing a crash helmet, you cannot hear vehicles coming up from behind as you can on a bicycle and a mirror is necessary to provide information that you must have before overtaking anything. You don't overtake much when riding a bike, unless cycling through a slow moving or stationary traffic jam, but spend most of the time in the opposite situation, and there is nothing a cyclist can do about traffic approaching fast from behind, other than keep out of its way. The only time that you really need to know about the speed and the nature of the heavy metal bearing down on you is when turning right, and in those circumstances I find a glance over the shoulder is more reliable than a glance in a wobbling mirror.

However, if you find that you are happier with a mirror, then the mirror to have is the Mirrycle, which isn't just a clever name, but a cleverly designed product especially for bicycles with dropped handlebars, for it fits very neatly on to the top of a brake lever, with the brake cable passing through the centre of the hollow mounting bolt. The Mirrycle is extremely effective, as bike mirrors go, for as the brake lever is on the extreme outside edge of the bicycle the mirror is ideally sited. Made from tough Lexan, which sounds like some sort of cowboy, the Mirrycle is 3″ in diameter and costs nearly £7.

The Mirrycle, and the Japanese Cati handlebar end fitting mirror that will fit into all types of bars, are much more effective than the mirrors made for upright or flat pattern bars as the long stems that are necessary make them unsightly and vulnerable, and they tend to shake and vibrate too much to be a great deal of use.

BELLS AND HOOTERS

There are many quite frivolous accessories for sale that have no place at all on a lightweight bicycle, or on any other kind of bicycle unless you are fond of bric-a-brac. Cycle bells and hooters are just two examples. Anything from a polite cough to a terrified yell, according to the circumstances, cost and weigh nothing and work just as well – and a wide open mouth must surely help to slow you down when braking hard. Hooters look and sound foul, with overtones of aggression, and are likely to get you into all sorts of trouble with pedestrians, car drivers and dogs.

BOTTLES

Twin bottles for carrying thirst quenching and high energy drinks have long been banished from pride of place in front of the handlebars – where they got in the way of the wind, or the handlebar bag – and sent down to a place on the down tube where many bicycles now have brazed-on bottle cage fittings waiting to receive a single bottle. Apart from giving a sporting image to a bike and its rider, bottles are a sensible accessory, especially on hot days. Jim Blackburn makes the aluminium Rolls Royce of bottle cages in dignified silver or black, with a leak proof bottle to fit, at a suitably up-market price of £7.50. Rhode Gear USA (available from Freewheel in company with Jim Blackburn equipment) do a very attractive range of cages and bottles, including Thermo bottles for keeping hot drinks hot and cold drinks cold, and their brightly coloured Mariplast bottles at just over £1.35 each are worth having just for their looks. Rhode Gear even make an aerodynamic bottle and cage. If you don't have brazed on fittings (and many frame makers do disapprove of them on the grounds that they weaken a frame), there is no need to feel deprived, or thirsty, as many manufacturers make clip-on cages. Bike shops have a lotta bottles, which are not expensive, look rather smashing, and are very useful things to have.

PUMPS

Bicycle pumps are not only useful, they are essential, and there is not much point in carrying a puncture outfit if you don't also carry a pump. Borrowing a pump from a passing cyclist can't be relied on, as cyclists, like policemen, are thin on the ground when you most need one. Selecting a pump is not quite the simple matter it used to be as the very high tyre pressures now prevalent – 100 lbs psi (pounds per square inch) is nothing out of the ordinary – are really too much for the traditional short pump to cope with. A long, thin pump is much better in this respect, and there is a spin-off bonus in that brazed-on pump fittings are no longer needed as a long pump is long enough to snuggle up to the seat tube with its specially shaped base in the vee above the bottom bracket and its concave handle top tight against the underside of the top tube. Take into account the size of your bike frame when buying such a pump, as some pumps are longer than others, and there is no way a pump meant for a 25in frame will fit into anything smaller.

These frame-fitting pumps push directly and sideways onto a Presta valve, an arrangement that I find rather awkward, and less efficient than the good old-fashioned pump connector. A little saliva in the push-on area makes them much easier to remove from the valve. Most shopping bicycles and roadsters now have car type Schrader valves so that their tyres can be inflated at a garage. It would be nice if high pressure, and tubular tyres had Schrader valves, as hand pumping anything more than 75lbs psi is very hard work, but the narrow section touring and racing rims would be seriously weakened by the large hole that is necessary.

However, it is possible to buy – for 50p – a Presta/Schrader valve adapter that will enable you to use a car pump or a garage air line. But do be careful and keep a close watch on the tyre pressure as it is very easy to over inflate and blow a tyre clean off the rim.

The best of the frame fitting pumps are the plastic bodied Bluemels and Trufflo GTX that retail at around £3 each. The aluminium bodied Trufflo SL sells for about £4.50. The best of the lot and the most expensive at £13.50 is the Zefal Preset but this does have a pressure gauge that can be pre-set, making it impossible to over-inflate.

As pumping high pressures with a portable pump is such very hard work, a stirrup-type pump for home use is an excellent thing to have by you, leaving the portable pump for emergency. In fact, if you intend to use 'tubs' which need 115 lbs psi pressure, then an upright workshop pump with a tee-piece handle that you can get your back into, and steadying brackets to stand on, is a definite must, as I doubt if you'll make it without one. Prices vary from £9 to £24.50 according to grandeur.

Bicycle tyre pressure gauges are becoming another necessity. Most high pressure tyres have recommended pressures embossed on the tyre walls, and such very high pressures are difficult to guess at correctly. Be careful when buying a gauge as even tyre pressures are more complicated than they used to be, and can be expressed as Kilograms per square centimetre, as well as atmospheres, or bars, and pounds per square inch. The French Zefal Pressographe is quite good and gives psi in addition to atmospheres. It is very accurate, has a reset button, and costs about £4.

Chapter 5

LOCKS, VILLAINS AND INSURANCE

Riding a beautiful, expensive and well set up bicycle is one of life's greatest pleasures, but, such is the high level of bicycle theft that having to leave that bicycle unattended in a public place, even for a very short time, is a worry that does gnaw away at the pleasure.

In 1981 109,843 bicycles were stolen in England and Wales alone. The figures for 1982 were considerably higher at 124,992. At the time of writing, the figures for 1983 are not available but it seems realistic rather than pessimistic to expect them to be even worse. The Home Office have no statistics for bicycles recovered – I would be surprised if there were very many – but they do give a figure of approximately 13% for what they call a 'clear up rate'. This does not mean that 13% of stolen bicycles are re-united with their owners, but only that the police have found out who stole them.

In fact, it is now possible, if you are in with the wrong lot and know the right people, to actually order the make, size and type of stolen bicycle that you want. 'Just give us the details, squire. We'll see you alright. Know wot I mean'.

I don't think that I could bring myself to commute on a really nice bicycle, or even just one I was fond of, unless I had a safe place to put it whilst beavering the day away. Not that riding a tatty and boring old lump to work, and leaving it in the street, is any guarantee that it will still be there when you need it again. The only thing that can be said for having a dreary old bicycle stolen is that it hurts rather less than having a nice new one stolen, but is just as inconvenient.

It is not sufficient to lock up a bicycle with a cheap padlock and chain and walk away and leave it. Cheap chains are easily cut. I think that gangs of bicycle thieves must go about carrying giant sets of bolt croppers. The answer is to buy a really good quality device that cannot be cut through, or broken. The best is probably the shackle type, a ½″ round section hardened steel, U-shaped lock that is closed by an even larger steel bar across its base. It is not enough to just clamp such a lock through the rear wheel and the frame as the bicycle can still be picked up and thrown into a van. The thieves would have a merry game breaking into a shackle lock, even in the privacy of their own home, or garage, but a laser cutter would probably overcome it – eventually.

The recommended method for securing bicycles is to remove the front wheel, which isn't difficult, – if you don't remove it somebody else will, and good wheels are expensive to replace – and, standing the front wheel alongside the frame, pass the U bend of the lock through both wheels and the frame, and then round an immovable object, such as the post of a parking meter, or anything else handy up to 4″ in diameter, snap the bar across the base and lock it up. Don't lose the key. If the Suffragettes had used shackle locks they would still be chained up to the railings, and so will your bicycle be until you can find a spare.

The Citadel is typical of this type of lock. There are four versions; Models 1, 1L, 2 and 2L. The L models are larger and have quicker acting locks. Prices are from £20 to £30.

The only drawback to a Citadel (a snag it shares with the similar Kryptonite, Crimefighter, and Cyclops locks) is that it is heavy and unwieldy, and to counter this objection Citadel now offer their smaller Micro model which costs £20.

The makers of all the locks mentioned above offer guarantees, from £100 up to £250, against having your bicycle stolen when properly secured with their respective products.

As a cheaper and lighter alternative, Trelock make a lockable steel cable in 3′ 0″ or 6′ 0″ lengths with a choice of combination or key operation. With the longer version there is the advantage that you can lash up your bike as if it were Houdini, and it does usefully extend the range of objects to which it can be lashed. However, as the makers are offering no guarantee, it must be assumed that the cable system is not quite as good as the U-shaped hardened steel lock, although it is easier to carry and lighter on the pocket at approximately £4.75 or £8.50, according to length. The ultimate in cycle security is probably an eight foot length of hardened steel Chubb chain covered in old inner tube and wound round all the components and joined with a great big Chubb deadlock, but this would be dreadfully heavy.

Whichever system you use to lock up your bicycle, your troubles aren't over yet. Take the pump, saddle bag, spare 'tub', and absolutely everything easily removable with you, or the chances are that somebody will have removed them by the time you get back. Don't leave your bike in a quiet place for any length of time where a thief could work on it without attracting attention, or you will return to a securely locked frame and two wheels and not very much else. This especially applies if you have expensive equipment. A busy street with lots of pedestrian traffic is very much safer. If ever you leave your bike, even for only a minute or two, lock it up properly. 'Whippit Quick' is the bicycle thief's motto. This shouldn't be necessary outside the village shop but if you live in a big town, lock it up.

Apart from carefully locking up, or chaining up your bicycle, carrying away with you all items that are not actually brazed or bolted to the frame, not parking in areas known to be stiff with undesirables (difficult to define, as in towns the sobriety and moral rectitude of passers-by varies with the time of day), or giving up bikes altogether, the only other precautions that you can take are prayers, insurance, which we will cover shortly, and keeping a written description of your bicycle. Make a complete note of all equipment, the frame number and any distinguishing features that you can think of. It might even be worth having your intials deeply etched on all components. If your bicycle is stolen such marks and information do help the police in the unlikely event of it being recovered whole.

My earlier remarks about ordering a stolen bike from obliging 'tea leaves' were not a joke. Stealing bikes is a growth industry, a success story based on the traditional business principles of hard work and profiting from the misfortunes of others.

On the other hand there is no need to encourage theft, either by being so careless as to have your own bike 'pinched', or by knowingly buying a stolen bicycle. Buying a stolen bike can have its drawbacks, and if one day when you are locking it up outside the abbatoir or office, the rightful owner should lay violent hands on you whilst yelling for the 'Old Bill' to come and feel your collar, it could prove both embarrassing and expensive. Apart from having to make tedious statements and lame explanations, the least that can happen is that the resentful owner will get his bike back, leaving you 'permanently deprived', with no chance whatever of getting any money back from the gentleman, or syndicate, that sold it to you. It might well be safer not to ask, as such requests can be received unsympathetically.

Unfortunately the same sort of thing can happen if you unknowingly buy a stolen bike, although a few sensible precautions will minimize the chances. For instance, street markets are not good places for buying second-hand two wheelers. I am certainly not suggesting that all bike sellers in the market place are 'bent', but some are, and unless you are an unusually shrewd judge of character, or don't much care whether the bike you buy was nicked or not, it is best to keep away from markets.

The main outlets for stolen bikes in London are the street markets in Brick Lane and the Portobello Road. If you have had your bike stolen, I suppose it might just be worth having a look around the stalls. Some of the goods that you will see displayed were probably liberated in Truro, Chichester or Chester, and your 12-speed pride and joy is up for sale in Manchester. Or it may well have been dismantled, the frame resprayed and numbers altered, and the components reassembled into several untraceable and apparently 'kosher' bicycles, though this would only happen to high quality machines.

Even adverts from private addresses should be treated with a little caution. If the seller has a mum and dad or auntie Glad, or a wife and kids and pets and well kept gardens, or is surrounded by other evidence of permanence, then the bike for sale is probably not stolen. The advertiser may be a child molester, and the bike may have a broken frame bodged up and skilfully disguised, but there is a good chance that it's legal.

All this boils down to *caveat emptor* once again, and it is not possible to insure against buying a stolen bike. People will tell you that you can insure yourself against absolutely everything, but it isn't true. What you can insure against is having your own bike stolen, or vandalized, or hurting other people, and this last category is in fact the most important. Few bikes cost more than several hundred pounds but claims against you by injured and embittered parties that you have inadvertently run down can amount to many thousands. Pedestrians can walk straight into you, and still swear it was your fault, and if they are sly and

87

grasping they may sue.

I have one leg an inch shorter than the other because a female Peruvian solicitor in a car began a quick U-turn as I was passing on a bicycle, and persisted with it until she knocked me down, and she was very definite that it was all my fault. Luckily I had witnesses and on their evidence she was convicted. Not of attempted murder, or manslaughter or even GBH, but for 'driving without due care'. Revenge apart, I got what I wanted which was compensation. If I had had no witnesses, and they can be hard to come by, she would probably have sued me for shock, nervous debility, infertility, loss of earnings, and damage to her car. It is amazing what people will think up and sue you for, so be prepared.

Public Liability, Legal Liability and Third Party insurance are all different names for much the same thing, according to the type of policy involved. It is not expensive and with many Householder's Policies it is thrown in as part of the deal. My own policy calls it Legal Liability to the Public and covers me against claims of up to £500,000 for any one accident or series of accidents arising out of one event, and definitely covers me for cycling accidents. Writing all this had me worried and I rang up to check, and if you have a similar policy I suggest that you do the same. Cover for up to half a million pounds is standard for most Householder's Policies these days and it would only cost you a further £20 to increase it to a million. Remember that half a million pounds may sound like an awful lot of money but it is minimal for this kind of risk. Should you knock down and injure a young man so badly that he could never work again, a court could award him an enormous sum of money – settlements of three quarters of a million are not unusual – and if you are not carrying sufficient cover you could be expected to contribute whatever the court considered you could afford out of your own pocket. Most of these policies exclude cover for the United States and Canada, simply because claims in those two countries tend to be absolutely astronomical and if you intend to go touring in North America you would be wise to arrange special cover.

Householder's policies can also provide cover for bicycles against theft or accidental damage, but it is quite common for this kind of policy, and others, to exclude cover for accessories that are stolen if the thieves don't take the bicycle as well, and for cover to be limited to the UK, the Isle of Man, the Channel Islands and

Eire, whilst excluding insurance for racing or for pacemaking. If in doubt, find out just what you are covered for and amend as you think necessary.

General Accident offer a very reasonably priced 'all risks' policy for cyclists which covers loss or damage to bicycles – but does not cover accessories unless they are stolen with the bicycle – personal accident and personal liability. The minimum premium is £10 and for that you are covered for claims up to £150. Up to £300, they charge £3 for every extra £50 of cover. The rate then drops to £1.50 for every extra £100 up to £500 and after that it drops again to £1 per £100 of extra cover. As an example, under this scheme it would cost £22 to insure £500 worth of bicycle.

There are a number of companies offering insurance schemes for cyclists (you will find them listed under the heading of Useful Addresses). If you intend to take part in massed start races or track events, check the small print very carefully as most insurance companies specifically exclude cover for these types of competition. Insurance for racing men is best arranged through membership of the British Cycling Federation, to which all cycle racing clubs will be affiliated. For non-racing riders I would recommend insuring through an insurance broker to get the cover that will suit you best.

Alternatively, membership of the Cyclist's Touring Club entitles you to free legal aid and third party cover up to £500,000. The club can also arrange more comprehensive cover at competitive rates.

'All Risk' policies are the wisest investment as for very little extra money they give personal accident and public liability cover, by whatever name they choose to call the latter, as well as insuring your bike. Do bear in mind, though, that neither the householder's or the 'all risks' policies offer significant sums for serious injuries sustained in accidents where others are at fault and one must look to their insurance to pay adequate compensation. If they happen not to be insured you do have a problem.

There must be a good case for making public liability insurance compulsory for all. There is certainly a case for compulsory insurance for cyclists, but that would involve documentation, registration, carrying extremely un-aerodynamic number plates and paying out exorbitant sums for road fund licences so perhaps insurance is best left on a voluntary basis.

Chapter 6

SAFETY FIRST IN TOWN & COUNTRY

In spite of British Rail's expensive television advertising this is not the age of the train. Successive short sighted governments have been tearing up the tracks as fast as they could get away with it ever since the 1950s and BR's earlier slogan 'Let the train take the strain' was much more honest, acknowledging the truth that this is the age of the car and lorry and that travelling by train avoids the unpleasantness associated with those two anti-social forms of transport.

Avoiding unpleasantness with cars or lorries is very important to the cyclist. In the good old days – whenever they were (I suspect that caveman used to grunt on about them as he skinned a mammoth) – you bought a bike, probably fifth hand for five shillings, twiddled off on it to learn the hard way and lived happily ever after, but such a delightfully carefree attitude just isn't on today if you are intending to collect your old age pension. It is a sad fact that there are old cyclists and bold cyclists but very few who are both old and bold. Whilst I don't wish to be depressing or to trammel a freewheeling spirit a few words of caution are a must for an unwary beginner if they are to avoid being trammelled by a Scamell, or something daintier but just as dangerous, on a rather more permanent basis.

Before we go any further let me say that this chapter is not intended to be a tirade against the motor car. A tirade against a fair number of motorists, maybe, but one has to realize that the car is absolutely essential to many people, including many cyclists, and rather than carry on wildly about banning cars from towns it would be a lot more practical to campaign for better driver training and a stiffer, more realistic driving test. Ideally, it should be compulsory for those who are physically capable to have to pass a cycling proficiency test before they are allowed to learn to drive. It would give them a far greater awareness of road surfaces and other people's problems.

Any campaigner for true road safety will need a lot of patience. Governments don't care for road safety measures that are going to cost money, which was the great attraction of the crash helmet and seat belt compulsion laws – both dangerous precedents in a democracy. If governments did care that much about road safety, the country's freight would be carried by the comprehensive railway system that we once had, and not by many thousands of lethal lorries that make the motorways a nightmare, cause hideous accidents, waste enormous quantities of fuel, pound the road system to destruction and make life misery for thousands unfortunate enough to live beside main roads.

However. The first thing to remember about drivers of all kinds of motor vehicles – I don't include motor cyclists in this category as they have much in common with us and have far worse problems with car drivers than we ever do – is that most of them have never owned, or even ridden on a push bike and seem quite unable to see anything smaller than a car. If it makes you feel any better about being pushed up on the pavement, or having to brake like mad when a car comes zooming out of a side turning right in front of you, it isn't personal antagonism that makes them do it, but unawareness of your existence. 'I never saw him' is the favourite cry of the motorist who has just felled a two wheeler, and very probably he didn't, although he might have had he looked.

The answer to this apparent invisibility is to be as conspicuous as possible. Not to the point of looking like an American hunter loaded for a Moose or two, or Caribou, and having to wear a bright orange suit with MAN painted on it in luminous letters to avoid being slaughtered by other brave hunters – a thought that gives me considerable pleasure – but wearing a bright coloured cycling jacket in the winter and equally cheerful gear in the summer can't be a bad idea and it won't spoil one's enjoyment of cycling, in fact very much the reverse as it will keep you out of all kinds of trouble.

Whilst on the subject of being seen it is important to make sure that you have, in fact, been seen. Just because a motorist can see the whites of your eyes it doesn't necessarily mean that he or she

91

has actually registered you are there. They could just be staring sightlessly in your direction whilst pondering on their lack of sexual appetite, young Tristam's school fees, or what to have for supper, and still come whizzing out in front of you. Having tolerantly said all that, there can also be an element of piggishness in such behaviour, in so much that a bike simply isn't big enough to pose a threat to the driver of a big fat car. Motorcyclists also suffer from this kind of thing, but police motorcyclists never, ever, suffer from it. Which does suggest that it can be pure bloody-mindedness.

Important as it is to make sure of being seen in daylight, at night it is absolutely vital. More than three quarters of the accidents involving cyclists occur in built up areas and in roughly a third of these the rider is badly knocked about, but in accidents that occur in rural areas, half result in severe injury or death, always to the cyclists, obviously because cars are travelling so much faster. The risk of being involved in a serious accident is four times greater after dark than it is during the day, and even more horrible is the fact that at night the rural cyclist runs a very high risk of being run into from behind and killed unless he takes some sensible precautions.

The good news, if one can call it that, is that nearly every cyclist involved in a serious accident at night had poor lights and wore dark clothing, which means that one can do a lot to remedy the situation. One has to realize that it is very difficult, even for a highly skilled, considerate, ex-cyclist driver to see a rider on a country road at night, especially when driving on dipped headlights when a string of cars are passing in the opposite direction, and especially if the cyclist is stationary. If you break down or stop for any reason GET OFF THE ROAD IMMEDI-ATELY, no matter how visible you think you are.

One is, of course, legally obliged to have lighting on a bicycle. A white light at the front and a red light at the back, plus a reflector. Actually the idea of lighting on a bike is not so much so that you can see where you are going, but that other road users can see where you are going, and for this purpose the legal requirement is thoroughly inadequate. Experiments have shown that red isn't a good colour for being seen at night, and it is difficult to judge a distance from a single light, but don't for heaven's sake mount two red lights side by side to make yourself more noticeable. Drivers will only assume that you're another car a long way away.

Siting the legal lighting for maximum effectiveness is critical. The front light should be as high up and as far forward as possible and on the centre line of the machine. The rear light should also be on the centre line and as high up as possible. The seat pillar is a good place but do be careful that it isn't masked by flapping clothing or a cycle cape. If you think that it could happen, mount the light on the rear of a carrier, or the mudguard if it's strong enough, or in the middle of your saddlebag. DO NOT mount lights low down and to one side of your machine as they can then be difficult to see from certain angles.

Much more effective than your legal lighting is a flashing amber light which ironically is illegal, but I wouldn't let that worry you as they are very effective indeed, especially in rural areas, if worn on the back of a 'Sam Browne' retro-reflective belt, although rather less so on a lighted street, and you are very unlikely to be prosecuted for using one. These lights weigh very little and are not expensive. We have already discussed makes and costs in Chapter 4.

It is a very good idea to identify yourself as a cyclist. It gives drivers an idea of how quickly they will come upon you and how much room you need. Light coloured clothing is the best way of achieving this, and retro-reflective bands on arms and legs, particularly legs. Bright coloured clothing is no use at all at night and lots of white is best.

I know that all this seems a bit ridiculous but, sadly, it is nothing of the kind if you wish to see your grandchildren grow up, or even the middle of next week. I also know that I started out by saying that there is no need to dress up like an American hunter and then go on to suggest a rig-out that would make you look like an electrified Morris Dancer, but cycling at night is really very dangerous and the only reasonable alternative to wearing all the proper gear is not to do it. And just one more thing. Always carry spare bulbs and batteries.

The next thing in this depressing catalogue of perils is wet weather. A wet night is hell on wheels of course, and everything already said about night riding still applies but with the added hazard of being able to see even less than usual, and, for the rural rider, of running over mud or cow's nasty. Most farmers do not instruct their workers to clean their tractor's wheels before driving off the fields and mud is a constant winter hazard in the country. Town riders too should watch for mud near roadworks.

Mud is just as bad as ice for riding on, and all that one can say about riding bikes on ice is, DON'T DO IT. If you fall off you stand a very good chance of being run over.

Getting back to riding in the rain, the roads are at their very worst after a shower following a long dry spell. Cars, lorries and buses all deposit rubber, lubricating oil and diesel fuel onto the surface which gets washed away in long periods of constant rain. A shower turns it into a slippery paste, so do be careful that your wheels don't glissade off the edges of metal studs, manhole covers or those silly little roundabouts that look like collapsed toadstools.

The law says that you must use lights when daytime visibility is seriously reduced but all the cars will have their headlamps blazing in the slightest shower. Whether you think that lights are necessary or not, if you have lights, put them on. It won't do any harm and it might save you from some nasty moments.

Always, wet or dry, anticipate as best you can what the traffic ahead of you is likely to get up to, and plan your path ahead as early as you can amongst the obstacles, riding smoothly and avoiding violent swerves. If you have to ride across a manhole cover in the rain, or a metal stud, or catseye, go straight over it, keep still, don't brake and don't tense up and you will be alright.

Bicycle brakes don't work as well when wet, as all brakes work through friction and in the rain there is less of it about. Most bicycle brakes work on the rims and wet alloy provides a better grip for brake blocks than wet steel, but both take some little time to dry out. It is a good idea in rain to occasionally apply them lightly to keep them dry in circumstances where you think you'll need them. Always apply both brakes together and avoid panic breaking in the wet. For a moment nothing much will happen, then, suddenly, you'll have the lot and end up on your ear.

Another good thing to avoid is puddles. Not so much the obviously shallow ones, and not at all costs, but certainly if possible. Running into a deep puddle without being prepared for it will slow you up dramatically and can snatch the handlebars away. Apart from being wet, puddles are imponderable. There might not be a nameless horror lurking in the depths but there could be a nasty pothole to smash your wheels and fetch you off.

In heavy rain pedestrians are even sillier than usual. In dry weather it is quite common for them to walk into the road, and then stop and have a look. In wet weather they don't just walk, they dash headlong and never bother about stopping. The most important thing to remember about riding in the rain is that it's difficult to stop and the moral of that is not to go so quickly that you cannot stop if need be. I learned that lesson the hard way one wet morning when hurtling down a long hill in the Lincolnshire Wold, at about 50 mph, tucked away like Fausto Coppi zooming down an Alp. Suddenly, up ahead, a cow strolled into the road – just like a pedestrian, which in a way I suppose it was – paused to have a look around, to sniff the air and to admire the view, and saw me bearing down upon it behind a bow wave, both wheels locked. I went through underneath the poor thing's tail just as it was accelerating and nearly frightened us both to death. How I missed ending up as cold cow pie I can't imagine. Certainly there was no skill involved, just luck. I have been a lot more careful in the rain since then.

To avoid these obstacles and hazards it helps a lot if you can see where you are going which in almost any grade of rain, from drizzle to a downpour, can be difficult, particularly so if you wear glasses. The remedy is to wear a hat or cap which has a brim or peak and keeping your head down, squint out from underneath it. What sort of hat or cap is really up to you but I wouldn't worry too much about whether or not it suits you, just so long as it does the job and stays on your head. Caps with long peaks are definitely out as the wind gets under them and whips them off. A sort of engine driver's cap would do quite well, or a tweedy version of a posh kid's sun hat gives a good protection and will stay on if pulled down at the front. This sort of headgear will lend a little tone to the proceedings as they are madly 'county'. They encourage policemen to call one 'sir' instead of 'squire' or 'sunshine' and are very cosy in winter. In the summer it is rather like putting ones head in a pressure cooker and for warm weather a cotton racing cap is very good and marks you as a proper cyclist. All in all it is simply a matter of experiment and personal choice.

Fast and stylish cornering is an activity which, I think, is curtailed by rain and slippery roads, especially in Autumn when lots of leaves are lying about. I say 'I think' because there are some riders who can still 'earole' round bends on rainy days, and it isn't luck, it's skill, because they have been doing it for years and their luck would have run out long ago. Modern tyres are very good indeed but my advice is to go round bends and corners very gingerly in the rain, keeping the bike as upright as possible and leaning your body into the corner instead of the bicycle, unless you happen to be one of the fortunate few unaffected by centrifugal force or the laws of gravity.

Another golden rule to go on living by is never to go belting into blind downhill bends, or corners, or anywhere else where you can't see what is going on until it's much too late to do anything about it, exhilarating as living dangerously might be. Always, always, always assume the worst and that there is bound to be something large and nasty in the way, and you won't go far wrong, for nowadays there nearly always is.

Safe riding depends a lot on mental attitude and it is better to be a live pessimist than a dead optimist. Time and time again in towns you see the motoring optimist come roaring up to the main road, give a quick glance right and have to brake like hell because there is a stream of traffic coming. Surprise, surprise. How can they be so stupid? Britain has more cars per mile of road than any other country which must be pretty obvious, and yet these idiots can still assume that nothing will be coming. Ten to one if it is just a cyclist that's coming they will zoom out anyway and if the cyclist is also an optimist that's just too bad. This sort of behaviour is prevalent late at night and early in the morning.

Traffic lights provide excellent opportunities for optimists to have an accident. Green does NOT mean go. According to 'The Highway Code' green means that 'you may go on if the way is clear', a very sensible proviso as I discovered late one night in South East London. Just as the traffic lights where I was waiting turned to green, there came a strange loud noise that became much louder and a huge American car packed full of wailing Rastafarians shot across in front of me – upside down and sliding on its roof – disappearing from view in a cloud of sparks. I still think that they were pushing their faith in the Emperor Haile Selassie just a bit too far.

This may be an extreme example but jumping traffic lights is very common. Being hit sideways on by cars, even cars the right way up, is very painful and damages the bicycle so it is best not to be too quick off the mark, unless you are absolutely sure the way is clear. Very slow, incompetent drivers who have never had an accident in forty years, but have caused dozens, are the worst light jumpers. They creep up to a green light very carefully in case it changes, getting slower, ever slower, and driving other drivers frantic and when inevitably the light goes red they shoot across. Do not be in their way. Lack of any faith in drivers is a fundamental tenet of the good cyclist's religion.

Another 'no no' at the traffic lights is to go pounding up on the inside of the waiting cars and to charge across regardless if the lights should change as you approach. The queue that you have overtaken can mask a car, or cars, making a right turn from the opposite direction and accelerating hard across your bows, if you are lucky. Or accelerating over you if you're not.

One final word concerning traffic lights. If you have to stop, make sure that you select a gear low enough for a quick getaway. If you stay in a high gear you will be very slow off the mark when the lights do turn green. Apart from the effort required to turn too high a gear from a standstill you may be bumped into from behind by a dozy driver who assumed you'd get away much faster, especially if you struggle to change into a lower gear and wobble.

A good place for practising the wisdom of the unbeliever is at a road junction, or a crossroads, where with very little effort you can have a nasty accident. Joining the traffic flow by turning to the left does need care but is not so critical. But if you are proceeding straight ahead, or intending to turn right, then watch out. If there should be a stream of cars approaching from your right and all of them are indicating their intention to turn left into the road where you are waiting DO NOT ASSUME that they will all turn left and ride across in front of them. The first two cars probably will turn left but the third car may well have been indicating for the last four minutes, the driver completely unaware of it. He actually intends to make a right turn, not a left, and with no signals whatsoever about two miles further on. If you are in his way as he sails straight ahead you may lose your 'no claims' bonus.

There are a couple of other pitfalls associated with the same kind of situation that should be mentioned. The first is the Volvo, a ponderous tank of a motorcar that thinks that it is invisible unless it has its lights on in broad daylight. The minute the ignition key is turned the lights come on and stay on until the ignition is switched off again. This piece of safety-conscious idiocy is actually extremely dangerous. Let us go back for a moment to the road junction. Once again a stream of cars approaches from your right. All apparently indicating their intention to turn left into the road where you are waiting. In the middle of them is a great big Volvo, safe because it has got its silly sidelights on, which in fact isn't indicating to turn left but at a quick glance looks as though it is. If you end up on the bonnet don't bother banging on the windscreen to complain because you can hardly blame the driver.

The other 'Blameless Driver Slays Cyclist' scenario in this situation is the chap who is indicating left but isn't turning left. He intends to pull into the kerb beyond the side-turning to post a letter, drop his wife, or ask the way. He is doing the decent thing and if you are in his way when he drives past the turning it will be your fault, even though he will be slowing down, it will still hurt you more than it hurts him. In these circumstances he may still wing you quite painfully if you have only filtered to the left and kept into the gutter.

The moral to be drawn from this is really very simple. Do not trust the motorist, or anybody else. Expect the worst to happen and you will avoid the accident, and surprisingly easily at that, for though it must sound difficult and daunting, safe cycling is only a matter of experience and common sense, and cautious riding soon becomes a habit. The accident statistics bear this out, appalling as they are, for in half the accidents to cyclists, the victims are young children.

Your best defence is to pursue a straight and positive course, a yard or so out from the kerb wherever possible. This allows you to avoid drain covers, old Coca Cola tins, bottles and the odd pedestrian, and at the same time gives you more room for manoeuvre if pressed by passing vehicles cutting in too close, for whatever reason. If you are already in the gutter there is no place left to go, except up on the pavement.

Positioning yourself correctly at all times is most important in order to be seen. If you ride up on the inside of cars at traffic lights do not hang back in the blind spot of the leading car. Ride right up to the front so that the driver can see you: if he doesn't know that you are there he may turn left and knock you over. The same 'make sure you are seen' rule applies when overtaking slow moving cars that are queuing to turn right. If you are riding down on the outside of the traffic be careful that nobody gets impatient and pulls out into you as you ride past. Remember. Drivers do get exasperated in heavy traffic and may suddenly decide to do a rapid U-turn and go back the other way.

Part of this positive approach to cycling is giving positive hand signals and positioning yourself properly and positively when turning to the right from a main road. First of all make sure that nothing is close up behind you. Or, even more important, coming up fast from behind. When glancing over your shoulder for this purpose be careful not to drift into passing traffic. When all is clear put out your right hand as if you mean it and move onto the crown of the road, in good time before the actual turning and keeping your hand out until you start your turn. Watch out for traffic coming up towards you, making sure that any car that is coming from the opposite direction and that is indicating to turn left actually intends to do so. The best guide to a car driver's intentions are the front wheels of the car. When they turn the car must follow, no matter what the indicators say about it. When in doubt, or in need of confirmation, watch the front wheels.

There are, of course, exceptions to the positive riding rule as there are to any other kind of rule and one of these exceptions is turning right in fast-moving traffic. This can be positively dangerous. Rather than exercise your God-given right to cut across the traffic stream it's best to carry on to the next traffic light or crossing, which in town can't be far, nip off the bike, walk across with the pedestrians and then retrace your steps or revolutions.

Making a right turn on a busy main road in the country can be very dangerous indeed. The lorries may be doing a good 70mph or more and pulling across in front of them into the path of an overtaking sales rep in a Cortina belting home at 80mph plus cannot be a good idea, especially with a similar traffic combination hurtling the other way. The whole idea is too terrifying to contemplate and I wouldn't even try. Better by far to stop, get off the road if possible, and then to run across during a lull.

In fact these A-roads are absolutely lethal for a cyclist even in the daytime, and are best kept away from if possible. Apart from the likelihood of being killed or seriously injured, the turbulence and noise from cars and lorries makes a cyclist's life a misery, and in wet weather the spray and filth thrown up by lorries makes it almost impossible to see. One wonders why it is that adequate mudguards on lorries are not required by law.

These roads are slightly less unpleasant at the weekends as there are fewer lorries but then there is the weekend driver to content with. The weekend driver is a special menace anywhere. He regards the windscreen as a kind of 'telly'. He has no control over the programme going on outside and very little interest in it. He is easily recognized for he usually has some sort of grotesque doll dangling from his rear view mirror and the parcel shelf is often covered with stuffed animals and cushions obscuring the view from the mirror that he never looks in anyway. Keep well away from drivers like this, they are completely unpredictable, and if he also smokes a pipe get off the road and hide until he's gone, or had an accident.

Stationary cars with occupants, whether weekend drivers or normal human beings, need special care as there is a very real risk that a car door may be opened right in front of you. Long lines of parked or stationary cars are even worse as it is difficult to see if they are occupied or not. The best approach to the problem is to keep as far out from them as possible as it gives a potential door opener a better chance of seeing you in his mirror, and it also much improves your chances of not hitting a car door. Often in town it won't be possible, because of passing traffic, to ride at a safe distance so go more slowly and be watchful. Sometimes you get a warning when a door is opened just a little for a driver or a passenger to have a quick glance to the rear. If you think they haven't seen you don't hesitate to yell. No need for insults at this stage, a loud 'look out' will do. It may not be very dignified but neither is running smack into a door.

Whilst on the subject of stationary traffic, and having carried on at length about the thoughtlessness and bad habits of the motorist, it is only fair to mention that pedestrians too are very vulnerable, not just to motorists but to us as well. Pedestrians do have a perfect right to cross the road as best they can, and are apt to walk through traffic jams thinking that everything has stopped, unaware that a silent cyclist is bearing down upon them. When threading your way skilfully and smugly through the snarled-up cars, and their irritable drivers, remember that pedestrians may pop out suddenly from between the cars, and although you are in control of nothing more lethal than a bicycle if you knock somebody down you will still hurt them quite badly, and hurt yourself at the same time.

Dogs are another threat to a cyclist's happiness and safety. Not on a par with the motorists or the rogue pedestrians but sometimes more aggressive. I have yet to meet a cyclist who has been bitten by a driver or a rambler but I do know one or two who have been nipped quite nastily by dogs, and are now definitely against them to the point of being rabidly anti-dog. I am very fond of dogs but could go off them, I suppose, if a wolf-hound had loped along beside me and yaffled my right ear. Most dogs have a sense of humour and when chasing you are very likely to be only joking, or at worst just seeing you through their territory. In these circumstances a good natured 'Gerroff yer furry loon!' will usually be enough to send the dog home chuckling, but one or two can be quite nasty. The thing to remember then is that dogs, with the exception of Doberman Pinschers, are thorough cowards and if you dismount, disguise fair nature with hard favoured rage, and threaten to shove your cycle pump right up its nose it will exhibit signs of 'lack of moral fibre' – a military term for a sensible disinclination to be killed or maimed – and remember that it left its breakfast to go cold. The trick is to mean it. If you should be attacked by Dobermans I don't know what to recommend.

One final word of warning. If you are deliberately and dangerously carved up by a car take the number and report it to the police. Do not pursue the driver and insult him, bang upon his roof and threaten violence. There are some very vicious people about who enjoy this sort of thing and you may get badly beaten up. So, unless the driver is only four feet high and wearing thick and heavy spectacles and you are a Bloodstained Belt in Judo, leave it to the law.

That really is enough about external dangers. Dismal as it all must sound, please let me reiterate that provided you ride defensively and sensibly there is no reason at all why you shouldn't live it up and die in bed. Caution soon becomes second nature and your cycling safe and enjoyable.

Safety on a bicycle is not entirely dependent on anticipating other people's idiocy. Your own acts of carelessness and folly can just as easily contribute to your literal downfall. Tucking in behind a coach or lorry to take advantage of its slipstream and get effortlessly towed along at speed is absolutely crazy, although very tempting in a strong headwind when you are tiring, and still miles from home. If a suitably large lorry goes past slowly enough to give you an opportunity to jump in close behind it, don't be tempted. These vehicles are very fast indeed and before you know it you will be twiddling your biggest gear and moving very quickly with two urgent problems to solve. The first is how to stop if the lorry should brake suddenly. This problem will resolve itself, for should the lorry brake hard you will run into the back of it. Lorry brakes aren't all that clever and take ages to actually bring a huge load to a halt, but they will slow it very rapidly and you won't stand a chance. Secondly, unless you let the lorry go and drop off before it really gets into its stride you will have a frightening problem controlling your bike in the turbulence as the lorry gets away from you.

I once jumped in behind a lorry because I was tired and had a long way still to go and then realized that there was a trailer close behind me. Luckily lorries were not so fast in those days and I just managed to get out in time.

Lastly, always look after your bicycle. There is little point in riding sensibly and safely, conspicuous by night and day, reading the road ahead and anticipating all contingencies if a brake cable snaps just when you need it most, or you slide off in the rain due to a worn out tyre. Keeping your bike clean makes it easier to spot potential failures before they cause you trouble.

Chapter 7

IN STYLE AND COMFORT

I am quite sure that there are more empty saddles in the shed at the bottom of the garden than there ever were in the old corral simply because people buy the wrong kind of bicycles and consequently and quickly decide that cycling is both uncomfortable and extremely hard work.

I once had an uncle who honestly believed that bikes were all much of a muchness – except that some had dropped handlebars of which he strongly disapproved – and that when you had ridden one bicycle you had ridden the lot. A staggering concept maybe, but I suspect that it's a widely held view. The bike buyer's motto should be 'Engage brain before opening wallet' but members of the 'a bike's only a bike, innit' school may find this difficult and end up with a roadster with a 3-speed hub and a mattress saddle on which to ride ten miles to work. It is the sort of thing that can easily happen to a beginner if he doesn't mention his intentions to the man in the cycle shop. 'I don't want nothing fancy' isn't really a help.

I recently rode seven miles on a roadster with a mattress saddle, not from choice but necessity, on a wet and windy day and I now know why the would-be 'nothing fancy' cyclist hobbles grimly down the garden, a disillusioned if temporary cripple after a couple of rides to work, shoves the new bike into the shed and slams the door on it.

This is not intended to be a vicious attack on the roadster. For going just up the road to the shops, or the post, they are splendid. If you need a reliable bike just for that purpose it would be silly to spend lots more money, but for anything other than short rides

103

the roadster is misery. I am aware that battles have been won by such bicycles. The Japanese used them to take Singapore and the Vietminh rode them to Dien Bein Phu – or was it Dein Bein, Phew! – whilst removing the French from French Indo China, but nobody has recorded how much the Japanese, or the Vietnamese, enjoyed the ride and enjoying the ride is just what this chapter is all about.

Apart from a diabolically uncomfortable saddle, the roadster has handlebars that are much too close to the saddle, leaving the rider sticking up in the airstream like a huge sore thumb and creating almost twice the wind resistance of a rider of the same stature leaning forward on drop handlebars. When you take into account the fact that, at 25 mph, around 90% of a rider's energy goes into overcoming wind resistance you can see that the roadster rider will soon run out of steam, and enthusiasm, if he is the sort who thinks that all bikes are very similar.

Changing the saddle and handlebars isn't really the answer. The unresponsive frame, the terrific weight and the lack of gear ratios are all against you. The roadster is a lovely old job for very short journeys but you can only make a dog's breakfast out of a sow's ear. The roadster might be voted the bike most likely to be bunged into the shed and abandoned but it doesn't necessarily follow that because you realize that one bike can be better than another and you have bought an altogether nicer class of bicycle that you are going to be ecstatically happy with it unless it, and the rider, are set up correctly.

Cycling can be hard work. It is, after all, excellent exercise and that does imply a degree of effort. What it does not imply is suffering and the avoidance of suffering is fundamental to enjoyable cycling, unless of course, you enjoy it.

SADDLES

Nothing to do with a bicycle can be more fundamental than saddles, in more senses than one. The most comfortable saddles would appear to be pretty uncompromising things, narrow and hard looking. Brooks were the high priests of bicycle saddlery a few years ago when all good saddles were made of leather. The Brooks B17 was the saddle to have, and is still to be had, in widths broad and narrow, but not now as top of the range. Brooks now make five leather saddles all with steel frames at prices from £34 for their Select with a tension adjuster down to £15 for the B17, a considerable loss of status. Leather is wonderfully comfortable when broken in to your shape, which takes at a minimum about 500 soul-searing miles. It is supposed to be possible to speed up the process a little before using the saddle by skilfully bashing it against a bench or a tree instead of your own buttocks, but this softening up needs to be done very carefully to avoid distorting or damaging the leather. Stoically suffering the breaking in period is probably better for the saddle and the soul.

The Italian Cinelli company offer an elegant steel framed saddle for £17.20 and the same saddle on an alloy frame for an additional £6. Covered in good quality leather over rubber padding, they need very little breaking in.

From Concor there is an aerodynamic design known as the Profil, in blue, black, beige or red leather on a nylon base that is faired in beneath the saddle nose and which costs just under £19.

Madison have successfully resurrected the old anatomical saddle idea with an effective system of varying thicknesses of foam padding to cushion the rider's pelvic bones. They, like Brooks, make a ladies' saddle that is slightly shorter and broader in the beam. Both ladies' and gentlemen's version of the popular G11 are priced at £15 and can be highly recommended. The most expensive Madison is the seamless, calf leather covered Pro-Am which offers instant comfort for around £27.50 while the suede covered Strada saddle costs less than half that price.

Other makers of padded, leather covered saddles are Selle Italia, Bernard Hinault and Milremo. The ladies' and gentlemen's models from Selle Italia are priced in the region of £12. The Hinault Turbo costs nearly £22, and the Milremo Pro is very similar to the stylish Cinelli lightweight saddles but is a great deal less expensive at a modest £9.50.

All the saddles mentioned will provide a rider with peace of mind and behind, but Brooks saddles with their thicker leather, and their handsome copper rivet and steel frame construction are much heavier than the nylon based saddles. The demoted B17 Narrow is the lightest of the range at 510gms. The Concor Profil weighs 360gms, regardless of colour, the Madison GII weighs 415gms. The lightest of the lot is the Cinelli L alloy framed model which weighs only 240gms. The Madison GII is the best value in lightweight touring saddles but for longevity and ultimately comfort, the two top of the range Brooks saddles are probably the best, provided that the extra expense, and the extra 120gms, don't bother you.

I have mentioned the best makes of saddles at some length because if you are building a bicycle you should have the best anyway, and an otherwise adequate ready-made commuter or sports bicycle may well be fitted with a cheap and inferior saddle that looks the part but actually isn't, and could well ruin the pleasure of riding. Quite a number of commuter bikes include a wide saddle in the specification, and a number of quite decent sports machines in the £200 price bracket have some nameless horror as standard equipment. It is ridiculous to spend that sort of money for a good bike with a bad saddle when for another £20 at most you could have comfort. In fact, you should be able to do an exchange deal with the shop before you part with your money.

SEAT PINS, OR POSTS

Seat pins have become scientific, and elegant, with polished flutings, or aerodynamic profiles, and micro adjusters for fine saddle adjustments by Allen key headed bolts. There is even one called a Shock Post which has a built in shock absorber but which is still remarkably light. Campagnolo, Shimano, SR, SunTour Simplex, Milremo and San Marco all make exceedingly good seat pins, or seat posts as they are sometimes called. Most makers offer alternative diameters from 26mm to 27.2mm to cope with the variations of the inner measurements of different tube sets. The SR Laprade model is excellent value at only £8.20. The Campagnolo Super Record, as well made and as beautifully finished as all the Campagnolo products costs around £28, and the aerodynamic Shimano Dura-Ace is also most attractive. This costs a little less at just over £20. The average weight for all makes is in the region of 250gms.

The discussion of saddles and seat pins naturally brings us to the subject of correct saddle heights and positioning, both of which are crucial to comfortable riding and also determine the length of the handlebar stem.

SADDLE HEIGHT

Whilst there is bitter controversy in the cycling world on the subject of frame sizing there is no more than mild disagreement about correct saddle height. The consensus of opinion is that the height of the saddle is right when, with both heels on the pedals and the cranks in line with the seat tube, one leg should be straight but not stretched. This system does have a serious flaw, for if ordinary walking shoes are worn the height of the heel can be most misleading. Also many cycle touring shoes now have a slight heel so I would suggest that placing the ball of the foot on the pedal is a more reliable method. In this position there should be a slight bend at the knee. To check that the seat height is right get someone to hold the bike steady while you pedal backwards with the balls of both feet on the pedals. If your buttocks then sway, or wobble alluringly, the saddle is somewhat too high for efficiency and comfort for any length of time. For maximum power output for very short periods the slightly too-high-for-comfort position is thought to be the best. A preference for high or low gears also affects the ideal height of the saddle. If you would much rather twiddle than push, try a lowish position. Some people seem to get things right straightaway, others take weeks. When you do find the right position for Heaven's sake take measurements and notes so that if you have to dismantle the bicycle you can easily put it back as it was.

When it comes to saddle angle and fore and aft positioning there is less unanimity. There is an American school of thought that advocates that the nose of the saddle should tilt slightly upwards. Others insist that the saddle should either be horizontal, or tilt slightly nose down, a matter of trial and error, which is where the micro adjuster type seat pin comes in, but I will lower myself down gently on the side of the flat saddle theory. Saddles that are tilted up at the front can be dreadfully painful.

Fore and aft positioning depends to a degree on preference and purpose, but as a general rule a shortish rider would need the nose of the saddle to be one inch behind an imaginary vertical line passing through the centre of the bottom bracket, a tall rider would need the nose to be 3" behind the same line and medium sized riders should adjust their saddles accordingly. Bear in mind however that if you go in for brief bursts of acceleration and power the saddle should be set slightly further forward and for a comfortable touring position it should be set a bit further back.

HANDLEBARS, STEMS, OR EXTENSIONS

It is necessary to have the saddle height and positioning absolutely right before deciding on the length of the handlebar stem and here we do come to a difficulty, as the only way to be sure that they are absolutely right is to ride the bike some considerable distance – which can hardly be done without handlebars.

However, the length of the handlebar stem can be determined empirically and pretty accurately by placing your arm horizontally in line with the bicycle's top tube. With your elbow against the saddle nose and your fingers outstretched, the tip of the middle finger marks the spot where the back of the handlebars should be. The length of a handle stem extension is measured from the centre of the hole for the expander bolt, so the distance from the fingertip back to a point where the centre of the expander bolt would be, plus approximately 12mm – just over half the diameter of handlebars – will give you the length of a stem that will be comfortable for touring.

As a rough guide to the ideal length of a stem to give a position suitable for racing, try adding 2″ to the measurement obtained by the above method.

Fitting the stem into the headset so that the tops of the handlebars are an inch or so below the level of the saddle nose is a good place to start to find a comfortable position for touring and general riding. For racing, try adjusting the stem so that it sits about two inches lower in the headset. Trial and error is the only way.

In order that a rider can adopt the optimum riding position, handlebar stems are available in a variety of lengths from a variety of manufacturers. Lengths vary from 5cms (about 2″) up to 14cms (about 5½″); the big names are Cinelli, TTT, Ambrosio, SR, Shimano and GB.

The two most popular are SR and Cinelli. SR offer three types of stem; the lightweight Aero in 6, 8 and 10cm lengths at £5.90; the polished SR Alloy in 5, 6, 8 and 10cm lengths at £5.65, and the aptly named SR Stumpneck with a 4.5 cm extension in stainless steel for £5.50.

Cinelli are rather more expensive, offering two very elegant designs. Their Cinelli I.A. model costs around £14 in sizes from 7-14cms and their slightly shorter Record model with a 13cm maximum, costs nearly £20.

Only handlebars from Cinelli and TTT will fit Cinelli stems.

TYPES OF DROPPED HANDLEBAR

One can say quite a lot on the subject of dropped handlebars. They are by far the most practical pattern of handlebar as they allow a rider to adopt a variety of comfortable and comparatively wind cheating positions against the one uncomfortable and laborious posture enforced by the flat or upswept type of bar. Drops also distribute a rider's weight more evenly instead of concentrating most of it onto the saddle. As a result, the spine is not subjected to road shocks as is the case with the upright position. Drop handlebars are in fact so superior in every way that it is hard to understand why anyone uses anything else although there is still an unreasoning prejudice against them amongst the non cycling public. This may have to do with half-baked notions of dignity and even I find it difficult to envisage the Vicar flashing past crouched over a racing bicycle.

There are three basic types of dropped handlebars, the Maes, the Pista and the Randonneur. I find that the Pista pattern has the most attractive shape but the forward curve begins close to the centre of the bars and the drops are deep and sudden, offering fewer alternative hand positions, so really they are only suitable for track racing. The Maes have a straight centre section and that, combined with the shallower drop makes them more suited to a tourist's needs. The Randonneur are a variation on the touring theme with a centre section that curves forwards and gently upwards.

Only the cheaper type of bicycle will have steel handlebars. As a rough guide, bars should be much the same width as a riders shoulders. They usually come between 16" and 17" wide and cost anything from £4.50 to £20. Good makes are Cinelli, SR, TTT and Ambrosio. Cinelli are probably the nicest.

SETTING UP BARS AND BRAKE LEVERS

When fitting the handlebars, set them up carefully so that the bottom straights, or drop ends, fall naturally to hand. If you set them level there will be an awkward kink in your wrists that will cause an ache. Clamp the bars lightly in the extension, push the ends down until you are comfortable, tighten the clamp and see how you get on.

The same sort of experimental approach is needed when fitting the brake levers. Remember that a great deal of time is spent, touring or racing, with the hands resting lightly on top of the levers, which is why most of them have moulded rubber or plastic covers, or hoods, and that most braking is done from this same position, with the thumbs looped over the hoods, so it is very important to site them correctly. The best place to start is just above the halfway mark on the downward bend of the bars which will leave the hoods inclined slightly upwards, and with any luck falling comfortably to hand, providing both a hand grip and something to lean on.

If you are going to use a handlebar gear control then fit that as well, but don't cover the bars properly until you are sure that everything is in the best possible place. Even quite small adjustments can make a considerable difference to comfort, and a considerable mess of your handlebar coverings.

SAFETY LEVERS

Some manufacturers offer brake levers with extensions that can be operated from the top of the bars and these are called 'safety levers', a bit of a delusion as they can be quite dangerous. They need rather more movement than the normal brake levers and if your brake shoes aren't adjusted up close to the rims, the 'safety levers' can end up uselessly level with the handlebars before the business end of the brake is properly applied, drastically increasing your braking distance, and your chances of a shunt. Although it is true that most brakes work better with a minimum of movement between being on or off, it is probably best not to use such extensions, especially as to use them at all the hands have to be in poor position for controlling a bike in an emergency.

Speaking of emergencies, do plug the end of your handlebars.

Plugs cost 50p a pair, or less, and could save you from getting the open end of the bars in your groin, or ear, which might do you a nasty mischief.

HANDLEBAR COVERINGS

When you are quite sure that everything is in its place and all's right with the handlebars then you can cover them, either with a woven cloth tape or a plastic tape, both of which are sold in a variety of cheerful colours. Better than tape but a great deal more expensive is a product called 'Grab On', a thick handlebar padding that comes as a set of four tubular pieces, two for the tops and two for the drops, fitting close up on either side of the brake levers. 'Grab On' not only soaks up road shocks, it also absorbs sweat, but washes up like new. It is very comfortable, but does give a bike a flat, clumsy appearance that I don't much like. Nevertheless, it is very durable and practical, so if you don't mind the chunky look it isn't really all that expensive at a fiver a set. Less comfortable but still softer than tape is the Ultra Thin version of 'Grab On' which looks very handsome and sells at the very same price. Both types are available in red, blue, black and brown. There are cheaper but similar makes available but they are not quite as good as original 'Grab On'.

BRAKE CABLES AND BLOCKS

There is now a regulation that states that the front brake should be operated by the right hand lever, a little bit of harmless standardization which cannot be a bad idea.

Getting the cable runs right is important, not just for the sake of appearance, although a pair of brake cables with graceful curves of identical height do look very crisp, but also for smooth operation. Sharp bends in a cable are death to efficiency and can ruin the pleasure of riding a bicycle.

Brake cables of good quality are most important as for much of the time your state of health will depend on them. Aztec make excellent cables that don't require lubrication but are especially smooth to use. If you like to add lightness Aztec also make an alloy Superlight brake cable set which works out at around £5.75.

111

Whichever cables you use it is a good idea to always carry a spare.

Brake blocks are a very important part of any brake set, and a lot of thought and development has gone into them in recent years, mostly with the aim of improving wet weather braking. There are several makes now on the market that perform well in all conditions.

Those made by Aztec and Scott Matthauser are the most popular and the only ones recommended for use with both steel and alloy rims. Aztec make two versions, both with integrally moulded attachment bolts that dispense with brake shoes. Their normal length blocks cost £2.65 a pair, and not only do they give improved wet weather braking, they also last longer than most ordinary brake blocks. The longer, aerodynamic, Aztec Super Blocks cost £3.50 for a pair, and have pivoting washers on the integral bolts that allow perfect alignment with almost any shape of rim, which is most important for efficient braking.

The Matthauser blocks are bonded to finned alloy shoes and come in several versions intended for HP, or for Sprint rims, all priced at £15.50 for a set of four. Matthauser also make standard brake blocks to fit almost every make of brake for just over £3 for a pair. Mafac blocks cost £1.20 a pair, and Campagnolo 'secret formula' blocks cost £1.40 each.

MUDGUARDS

Now a quick word about mudguards which are essential for touring, and for commuting, especially so if you ride to work in your working clothes. They are not a bad thing to have by you anyway in case they are needed. There are three types available at present in plastic, stainless steel and aluminium coated with plastic. The brightly coloured plastic mudguards are the cheapest, the lightest and by far the best looking, but they do tend to be flimsy and have short muddy lives, although perfectly adequate if you only intend to fit them occasionally. The stainless steel guards are heavier but handsome, and they live a lot longer, but as one would expect they are much more expensive. The most durable are the plastic coated aluminium variety of which ESGE are the dearest and best. They are extraordinarily flexible and come in silver or bronze finish at around £12 a pair.

An unfolded Bickerton bicycle.
(*Bickerton Rowlinson Ltd*)

A folded Bickerton bicycle.
(*Bickerton Rowlinson Ltd*)

A nice example of a traditional heavy roadster by Pashley.
(*W.R. Pashley Ltd*)

Excellent value for money: the mid-price, mid-weight, 10-speed Raleigh Royal tourer with good quality Japanese components.

The superb Cinelli Laser. Note the aerodynamic brakes behind forks and bottom bracket. Even the brake cables are hidden away.
(*IRB (Import Export) Ltd*)

A useful shopping 'trike' from Pashley. Here the small wheels are an advantage as they lower the centre of gravity, which improves cornering stability. Large wheeled tricycles are more easily inverted.
(*W.R. Pashley Ltd*)

Lugless bottom bracket of the aerodynamic Cinelli Laser.
(*IRB (Import Export) Ltd*)

An ultra-light time trial bicycle with a short wheelbase, steep angled TitaLite titanium frame. Total weight 7½ kgs. Note the radially spoked front wheel.

A Sun Manx TT of 1946 – very much in its original condition with a Sturmey Archer 3-speed hub. A surprisingly rakish bicycle for a short wheelbase design.

The tasteful lugwork of a lightweight racing frame in Reynolds 531 SL by Every. Note the semi-sloping fork crown.

The most rigid if not quite the most expensive chainset on the market – the Dura-Ace AX Aerodynamic, sold complete with special pedal, viewed here from below.

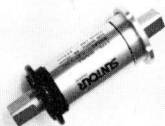

A sealed bottom bracket unit from SunTour.

Campagnolo Record large flange hub and Campagnolo Tipo small flange hub.

Left: topside of the Dura-Ace AX Aerodynamic pedal.
Right: the Ofmega Aerodynamic pedal from high density nylon. Note the difference in diameters at the crank end of the pedal spindles.

A graceful but aptly named Boneshaker of 1869.
(*Mark Hall Cycle Museum*)

John Collins, curator of Harlow's
Mark Hall Cycle Museum
demonstrating a 100-year-old 'Royal
Mail' Ordinary with a 52″ wheel. Note
the headlamp hanging from the hub.
(*John Collins*)

A 1905 Dursley Pedersen with a rare
and original 3-speed hub gear. This
bicycle was exceedingly light and very
comfortable.
(*Mark Hall Cycle Museum*)

The peculiar but charming Velocino.
(*Mark Hall Cycle Museum*)

Ken Kilvington of the Mark Hall
Cycle Museum shows off the
collection's 1935 Cyclo-Ratio
recumbent. The author, longer in both
leg and tooth, found it impossible to
ride.
(*Mark Hall Cycle Museum*)

Introducing "THE SUCCESS" *dual-line*
bicycle frame!

For Racing and Touring Enthusiasts!

* RESILIENCE gives COMFORT ! (Road shocks at front wheel absorbed by frame curves.)
* GIRDER CONSTRUCTION ELIMINATES WHIP !
* STREAMLINED FOR GRACE AND BEAUTY !
* CHOOSE YOUR OWN MATERIAL ! We supply in 531, Kromo SAQ, or Grade A Steel.
* FRAME WEIGHTS (as illustrated) 6 to 7 lbs.
* NAME YOUR OWN ANGLES AND WHEEL SIZES !
* WHEELBASE TO ORDER from 39 ins.
* DELIVERY ONE to FOUR WEEKS according to finish requested.
* CHOOSE YOUR OWN FINISH AND MARKINGS !
* 50 YEARS GUARANTEE !
* HANDBUILT TO SPECIFICATION.

A modern 'cross frame' – the Paris Galibier of 1947. Intended as an anti-whip design, it was less rigid than a conventional machine.
(*John Collins*)

A geared Facile of 1888 by Ellis & Company of Fleet Street. It was safer than the elegant Ordinary, but no match for the Safety bicycle.
(*Mark Hall Cycle Museum*)

A modern racing 'trike' by Higgins. Such devices take a lot of getting used to.

A Salvo quadricycle of 1878, for which James Starley invented the differential.
(*Harold Jones*)

CADENCE PEDALLING

Although we looked at gears and gearing in Chapter 3 (a briefing on makes and varieties of front and rear derailleurs would be a bit meaningless to a layman or layperson without a short lecture on gear ratios and how they are calculated), what we didn't go into was the theory of cadence pedalling. A quick look in a dictionary will tell you that cadence means a rhythm, or measured movement. The theory propounds keeping up a constant rhythm of rapid pedalling up hill and down hill and adjusting your gear ratios to suit your natural cadence by frequent swopping of cogs, it being thought more efficient to spin over a lowish gear rather than push on a higher one.

One would imagine that multi-speed gears were developed as a result of such theorizing but what seems to have happened is that the 5-speed block and the double chainwheel arrived first and the theory was thought up later to dictate actual use of the gears. Certainly 10-speed gears were prevalent in the early 1950s but nobody talked about cadence pedalling.

The theory that one did hear discussed was 'ankling', a technique of flexing the ankle whilst pedalling in such a way as to help push the cranks over top dead centre. One doesn't hear much about it nowadays and I have the feeling that there is a strong fashion factor in all such theories.

The current, common and almost religious belief that to keep up a pedalling rate approaching one hundred revolutions per minute is the most efficient way of getting along on a bicycle is not born out by scientific experiment, although it may be the most efficient way of wearing out trousers. According to Messrs Frank Rowland Whitt and David Gordon Wilson in the second edition of their paperback tome *Bicycling Science* maximum muscle efficiency is achieved at something like half the number of recommended revs per minute and that to pedal at a high rate 'is appropriate only for maximum-speed, maximum-output sprinting'. In other words, it is more efficient to push than to twiddle.

Backing up my own uninformed prejudices by quoting from such an impressively learned source does give me some pleasure but it is not intended to knock or denigrate the use of multi-speed gears. The great thing about having a wide choice of fairly close ratios is that you can please yourself about gearing. You will soon settle down to your own natural rhythm and if your legs aren't a mere blur, don't let it worry you. My own preference is for the lightness and simplicity of a fixed gear but when I do use a 10-speed I don't want to go thrashing along like a frenetic mechanical toy. The point I have laboured to make is simply that rapid pedalling techniques are only a fashionable dogma that may or may not suit you. Cycling should be enjoyable and not a form of time and motion study.

TOE CLIPS

Before passing on from pedalling techniques to other matters, a non-contentious word concerning toe clips. Amongst non-cyclists – and people who only ride bikes instead of cycling – toe clips, like dropped handlebars, have a baseless reputation for being dangerous. If anything, toe clips make cycling much safer because it is impossible for feet to slip from pedals, which can be very frightening and nasty. There is no need to tighten up the straps until your feet are one piece with the pedals and completely trapped, especially in town, and it might be best if you ride to work in walking shoes not to wear a shoe with a heavily treaded type of sole as I suppose it could just catch up on a 'rat trap' pedal pattern and cause undignified collapse, but the straps have quick release type buckles so this would not be very likely. Proper smooth-soled cycling shoes can be easily removed from toe clips even when the straps are done up moderately tightly. Toe clips can virtually double your pedalling efficiency as it is possible to pull the pedal upwards on the upward stroke which makes for smoother riding and more power.

Don't worry about having difficulty in getting your feet into the clips. A quick tap with the toe on the back edge of the pedal when you are under way and slip the shoe into the rising clip, then just lean down and give a quick tug on the strap. It is dead easy, and will become second nature to you in no time at all. You will feel much more secure and at one with the bicycle.

Toe clips are now available in plastic, guaranteed not to break in normal use (a good idea as toe clips tend to have hard lives, frequently being kicked and trodden on, and heaved at), at around £2 a pair. Galli, G.B. and Christophe and several other makers all offer spring steel clips in varying lengths costing between £2.50 and £4. Straps can cost from £2 up to £7. Toe clips can damage shoes, so if you ride to work in smart shoes, tape the clips, or buy clips that feature shoe protectors. The plastic 'Styrene' clips are probably kinder to the shoes than are the spring steel models.

CLOTHING

One of life's great mysteries is how some people can spend a great deal of money on a beautiful bicycle and very little money on suitable clothing. The human skin is wonderfully waterproof but for comfort it needs to be sensibly covered. 'To be well dressed is to be suitably dressed' may be a Victorian truism, but if you are not well dressed riding a bike can be misery.   Strangely, the Victorians seemed to go out of their way to be unsuitably dressed for almost anything other than formal occasions and the clothes they considered suitable for cycling were an extreme example, although in Victorian times it was only the horse that sweated. Gentlemen perspired and ladies glowed, and nobody used deodorants. The arrival of a cycling club at a hostelry on a hot summer day; the men in heavy Norfolk jackets and breeches buttoned at the knee and the ladies in hats and long dresses, or long jackets and knickerbockers, must have been a memorably smelly event.

Perspiration only becomes a problem when you stop. Ironically when you are on the move the heat generated by your efforts to overcome wind resistance will to a great extent be dissipated by the very wind that you are struggling against acting as a cooling fan. Overheating is a problem when training on a set of rollers, or when using an exercise bicycle, and what conditions must be like inside those lovely streamliners used in the Human Powered Vehicle Championships does not bear thinking about. When riding on a normal bicycle overheating occurs only when you stop riding it, for this also stops the fan and leaves you with an internal furnace of residual heat that has to be disposed of by perspiring heavily. This may be unpleasant, but is natural, and it has to happen. The thing is to remember this and to cool off quietly where it doesn't matter and won't cause you embarrassment. Don't, for example go scorching down to the bank on your Claud Butler and rush straight in to see the manager to coolly reassure him that your apparent poverty is only temporary, and break out in a muck sweat while you are talking. Dripping beads of perspiration on his blotter might be misunderstood.

There is not much that you can do to cool off gently in the summer; it isn't decently possible to wear much less than shorts and shirt and all you can do is coast along and take it easy for the last part of your journey. In the winter things are a little better. A cyclist's clothing has to cope with extremes of temperature. A zipped jacket over several layers is probably the most effective so, once again, take it easy for the last part of your journey but this time with the jacket zip undone, and remove your hat, or cap, if you are wearing one, as hats were invented to retain body heat when necessary. Just as the rabbit uses its huge ears for losing heat so the human head will disperse up to a third of excess body heat. The poor rabbit doesn't have much choice in the matter and it would be interesting to know what evolution will ultimately do with cyclist's ears.

However gently you may go about it cycling is bound to cause you to perspire, and for this reason it is a good idea not to wear your working clothes for riding into work. There must be somewhere for you to keep working clothes at work, and to change in and out of them. Much better to start work feeling crisp and cool than a crumpled clammy wreck, and it will make the riding to and fro so much more enjoyable.

We will have a quick glance at summer clothing first as it is a fairly straightforward subject. Shorts are a must, at least for gentlemen. Get proper cycling shorts, no matter how smart other kinds may be, the purpose made article will have the seams arranged so that you don't sit on them which can be most uncomfortable. Shorts are not the laughable baggy articles that they used to be. The fashionable cycling shorts are very smooth indeed, fitting neatly round the legs in some cases to within 6″ to 9″ above the knee. The sporting shorts are mostly black and have no pockets, and the more expensive models have a Chamois leather lining. Prices range from £12 to £16.

For girls not anxious to drive male commuters mad with lust, or to attract coarse comment, there are always culottes. It is true that both skirts and dresses can be cool enough but they do tend to blow about, and they can get caught in wheels and chains.

For your top half wear a garment made of natural fibre next to the skin to absorb any sweat, or 'glow'. Over that, it doesn't matter much, a shirt, a blouse, or whatever – so long as it isn't tight enough to restrict your movements or loose enough to flap about. In hot sunny weather be careful not to wear dark colours as they absorb the heat. I once set off to ride from London down to the Isle of Wight wearing a black shirt and nearly collapsed in Petersfield from heat exhaustion and had to stop and buy another shirt. And that was embarrassing as I was absolutely wringing wet with sweat. Top layer garments should be long enough to keep the kidneys covered as this area is very vulnerable to chills. Even though you may be steaming gently when climbing up long hills you will get quite chilly dropping down the other side. If you are riding any distance always take a jersey with you to slip over your blouse or shirt if the weather should turn cooler as it is most unhealthy to let sweat go cold on you. As an alternative to a shirt the most gorgeous cycling jerseys are available in stunning colours. They are very smart and practical and can't fail to make the wearer look like an 'ace', but are not recommended to be worn with a 'beer gut' if cyclists have such things, as they are rather close fitting. These jerseys can be worn next to the skin, and have useful pockets in the back.

Rain, hot or cold, is difficult to cope with on a bike. I don't like capes – who does? – but on balance I prefer them to waterproof suiting. They are cooler for a start, less restricting in some ways and much, much cheaper. A good quality lightweight 'Pakit' cape costs nearly £18 with a further £12.50 for leggings, whereas a good quality waterproof jacket and trousers such as the Caldo suit, in Gore-Tex condensation free material, costs over £100. There are cheaper makes using the same material but even they will cost you getting on for £60 or more. These are very attractive and smart but a major tragedy if torn or damaged in the slightest accident, or minor fall. Cheap waterproof suits are horrible to ride about in as they do not breathe and it is more pleasant to get soaking wet from without rather than from within. You hardly need waterproof trousers in the summer anyway, when the best thing to wear are shorts. Legs are more waterproof than any garment and one can buy specially made galoshes that fit over toe clips to keep your shoes dry, or even proper overshoes.

Cycling shoes are not the least bit of good for keeping feet warm in the winter, they are in fact designed to keep feet cool in summer. Socks are the best defence against cold feet. If you are into breeches that end above the knee, make sure to buy socks long enough to meet up with them and so cover the knee. There are all sorts of attractive, brightly coloured winter cycling gear to be had; pricey, but nice, and very practical. For keeping legs warm there are, not only breeches, but garments known as 'longs' which are ankle length shorts, of sorts. There is long thermal underwear, tights to be worn over shorts, trousers designed specially for cycling, and track suits also specially designed. There must be something that will suit your needs amongst such a choice.

As a quick and very approximate guide to the cost of such winter clothing, long socks sell at around £5; breeches £15.50; longs £19.50; thermal underwear or 'long johns' £7.50; tights £12; cycling trousers £17 and track suits £17 – £30.

For your upper half, a vest to absorb moisture is very necessary, then a shirt or cycling jersey, or both, with a shower-proof jacket, or even a Gore-Tex waterproof jacket covering the lot if you can afford it. The great thing is that the top layer must be windproof and have a zip for temperature control. Polo neck sweaters are not a good idea for cycling. If you get too hot there is nothing you can do about it except remove the sweater, which can be a great production, very irritating for companions, and no sooner have you taken the thing off you will feel cold and have to put it on again. Better to wear a low necked proper cycling jersey with a zipped collar combined with a scarf that can be easily undone. Jerseys cost from £15 – £25 and jackets from £20 – £60.

CLOTHING FOR RACING

Racing clothing is becoming very specialized although the shorts, longs, jerseys, training tops etc. mentioned above are perfectly adequate for training. At one time they were also considered suitable to wear when racing but with the introduction of aero-dynamic bicycles the racing man and woman has caught on quickly to the need to streamline themselves as well and 'skin clothing' is now very fashionable, especially for time trialling where wind resistance is the greatest adversary. These skin tight garments seem mostly to be made of Lycra, a lightweight nylon material or of Hi-Shine acrylics and are available as skin vests, skin tops, skin tights or complete skinsuits. Their visual effect is rather similar to that of the Victorian or Edwardian bathing costume only shinier, and the wet look is very popular. Approximate prices for skinsuits are around £27. Long sleeve skinsuits with hoods for streamlining the head cost around £33 and have a very sinister appearance. Skin vests cost £11 and skintights about £18.

CYCLING SHOES

There was at one time only two kinds of cycling shoe, but recently it has been recognized that some cyclists occasionally put one foot before the other on the ground and walk, so now there are three basic kinds of cycling shoe. The main feature of pure cycling shoes are still thick soles, the purpose of which are to stop the edge of the pedal from digging into the arch of a rider's foot which can cause great discomfort on long rides. Pure cycling shoes have no heels and that, with the stiff unyielding sole, makes them misery to walk in. For this reason, the latest breed of dual purpose shoe has a heel combined with a more flexible sole. The more that you intend to walk, the more heel you will need for comfort, within reason.

Racing shoes are naturally the most extreme example of the special cycling shoe. The soles are very thick where they press down on the pedals and taper off towards the back, which is why grounded racing cyclists don't walk normally but waddle. Most such shoes have laminated leather soles, with stiffening metal inserts in some cases. Racing shoes have a shoe plate or cleat; if these aren't fitted you have to buy and fit them separately. These plates, which have a fore and aft adjustment, have a slot across the middle that locates onto the back edge of the pedal cage and keeps the shoe in place. The uppers of a racing shoe are either perforated leather, to let the sweat run out, or made of a nylon mesh reinforced with leather that serves the same purpose and also keeps the foot cool. Sidi, Vittoria and Rivat are amongst the leading makers and prices range from £20 up to £30.

The second category, the sensible leather touring shoe has a thinner and more flexible sole than the racing shoe and all have heels of a sort. If you do intend to walk in them for any distance buy the type with higher heels. Cumbria make a very handsome shoe with a soft leather upper at nearly £22. Other makes are Rivat, Sidi, Patrick, Dalesman, Caratti, Ziffiro and Arturo. The Ziffiro Randonneur is the cheapest at £11. Prices go up to around £30.

The newcomers, the dual purpose cycling and walking shoes mostly look like training shoes in the usual rather gaudy two tone colours, and in some cases training shoes with stiffened soles is exactly what they are. Some are better for walking than they are for cycling but those made by Rivat at about £20 seem to be the best compromise. Sidi go the other way with their two touring/walking shoes which are better on a bike than on the ground. Madison and Adidas have the most flexible soles of all. Prices range from £15 up to £28.50.

Even with the dual purpose shoes I think it is fair to say that if you do intend to do as much walking as cycling you would be better off taking a pair of purpose-built shoes along with you.

HEADGEAR

Headgear for cyclists is very specialized because of the difficulty of keeping hats in place at speed. For this reason there are really only two types that are practical. The cap and the convertible Balaclava. There are two kinds of cap, the cotton racing cap to keep the sun off the head in the summer, and the training cap that has a flap to keep the cold wind off the ears in winter. The Balaclava becomes an instant woollen hat if full protection isn't needed. These are all very useful for temperature control as discussed above.

DIET

Just as important as the external essentials of bicycles and bicycling is the inner you. The lightest, most elegant racing bicycle without a rider is like a Ferrari without an engine – beautiful to look at but very little use. You are the engine of your bicycle, and if when you first start riding you find that you perform more like a rather tired old side valve twin than a twin overhead cam vee 12, don't let it worry you.

No matter how much money you may have spent upon your bicycle and cycling gear, the 'all things light and beautiful' rule applies to you as well, and if you smoke heavily, live on fourteen pints of beer a day, and hamburgers and chips, stay up half the night and eat Mars bars between meals I doubt if you will enjoy, or survive, even a short ride to the office, never mind a longish ride. Of course, such self-inflicted extremes of physical abuse are hardly likely if you are at all interested in cycling, unless you are taking it up to recover from a misspent middle age, but I am trying to emphasize that to enjoy your cycling you must be reasonably fit, and even if you are but haven't cycled much before, do not expect to be an Easy Rider straight away. Laborious Rider will be much nearer to the truth. Don't give up and advertise your nice new bicycle for sale, or shut it in the shed. Go into training and you'll soon get over it.

Not that I am advocating a diet of Ribena and nut cutlets, early nights and total abstinence from everything enjoyable, excepting smoking, but then smoking isn't actually enjoyable. It just hurts the smoker if he or she doesn't smoke. What I am advocating is moderation in all things, even moderation.

At the most basic, non-gourmet level, food is fuel which can be stored, but don't take on board more fuel than you need, or the storage compartments will begin to bulge. Eating too much is merely habit. The more you eat the more you want to eat. Fortunately the reverse is also true. Keep away from too much butter and cakes, buns and pastries, and also lots of sugar. There is no doubt that such foods are bad for you. Fruit and vegetables are good for you. Beyond that I won't offer any more advice on diet. There are too many opposing theories fiercely held by doctors, dieticians and slimming experts, some of them quite obviously dotty. But listening even to the saner prophets will soon convince you that all known foods will get you in the end, and some more quickly and nastily than others. You cannot eat your way to fitness as one TV advert claims, but eating sensibly does help.

Serious racing cyclists like to finish a good meal at least three hours before a race. This isn't practical for a touring rider off on a day's longish run. It isn't reasonable to have a nourishing breakfast at four in the morning and then sit about in a digestive torpor until the time comes to leave, especially if you are staying in a hotel or guest house. Do have a nourishing breakfast though, but don't make a beast of yourself. Little and often is a good rule for eating when cycling. If you stop for lunch at a pub or restaurant don't order rich food, but have grilled fish or meat, with vegetables as this will be digested more easily. And keep off the wine with your meal – it will make you thirsty and listless later on in the day. I have a weakness for good beer, and that has exactly the same effect. Don't have iced drinks in hot weather, they are not truly thirst quenching and can upset your stomach.

If you eat sensible food at regular intervals you should not suffer the 'bonk', a sudden and terrible feeling of weakness brought on by not having taken enough fuel on board for powering your muscles. If you are going to ride far and fast take some high energy food with you. The 'bonk' is the most ghastly feeling a long way from food, in the wind and the rain.

GET FIT, KEEP FIT

Being unfit is a feeling well known to western man, and the most common symptoms are shortness of breath, a thumping heart and aching muscles. Shortness of breath when taking unaccustomed exercise is caused by rapid burning up of the oxygen in the blood that is carrying it round the system, and the inability of the lungs to replace it fast enough, which is why we heave and gasp for breath. Even top athletes heave and gasp for breath, but not after a gentle cycle ride. Given regular exercise the lungs, which tend to be as lazy as the rest of us, will soon increase their capacity for breathing and gulping in more oxygen. The heart beats rapidly as it tries to keep up the supply of blood to muscles sending irate messages for more and more, and the muscles ache because the capillary tubes which carry their supplies of blood have become dispirited and closed up due to lack of use. What is the point in staying open all the hours God sends, if no rush of blood comes roaring through? Exercise will change these conditions too. The capillaries will start to take an interest in their work, and the heart will soon get stronger, matching the supply of blood to the increased demand. It won't happen overnight. However, as soon as your heart gets used to the idea of working for a living, cycling will become easier.

Running, cycling and swimming are all exercises that promote a general fitness but cyclists do have advantages. It is hardly practical to run ten miles to work each day because it would take so long, even less practical to swim to work, or go on a swimming tour of Ireland. Moreover cyclists rarely drown, although it can be said with equal truth that swimmers are not often chased by dogs, when swimming. Cycling does have the edge over other

122

forms of sport and exercise because it is such useful transport, and for that reason can be incorporated into all sorts of activities. It is the flexibility that makes cycling the best kind of exercise for people with a limited amount of spare time at their disposal, which seems to include most of us.

Whilst there is nothing to be said against daily exercises such as press-ups, sit-ups and knees full bend, except that they are very boring, the best training for a cyclist is cycling, but don't expect to lose much weight. You will get rid of excess fat and be a better shape accordingly but will exchange weight of fat for weight of muscle in its place, which is fair enough. When people speak of losing weight what they actually mean is losing flabby, uncomfortable, and unsightly fat. If they were lean and hard their weight would not be bothering them one bit.

The least painful, most efficient way of toning up your body, and getting it used to the idea that it is going to have to exert itself a little from now on and that you intend to keep it at it, is to ride regularly every day. This is where the ride to work can be so useful. It is training after all, and you can always ride home by a longer route if you feel you want to put in some extra miles. Try to ride about ten miles a day at first. It is no good at all just riding at the weekends, even if you do ride much longer distances. The heart, lungs, and muscles will have become slack and bored again in the meantime and you will suffer, not enjoy your riding, and achieve nothing in the process.

If you have never cycled any distance, or you are returning to cycling after a lapse of many years, as so many people are doing at the present time, I'm afraid you're going to suffer a bit anyway. How much you suffer will depend on your general physical condition and how sensibly you go about things. If you are fairly streamlined and in your teens or twenties you shouldn't suffer very much unless you seriously overdo it and try to ride too far, too fast, and too soon. If you are older, obviously it is going to be rather more difficult. There is no hurry, take it easy. If you find ten miles a day too much at first then only do five miles instead. You will soon find that you are breathing much more easily, your aches are diminishing, or have disappeared entirely, and you are beginning to enjoy your cycling. If you are middle-aged don't be unduly disappointed if you don't enjoy it much at first. It will inevitably be slightly painful. Don't punish yourself. If you persevere with daily riding the painful period will quickly pass.

123

Build up your daily mileage until you find you are riding without effort. At the weekends try some longer rides, say twenty or thirty miles or so, but don't be too ambitious. A circular route so that you are never all that far from home is quite a good idea at first and build up from that, until you are fit enough to ride as far as you feel you want to. Even then, ride every day if possible.

During this initial period the gears you use are most important. Don't heave and struggle with big gears. In fact keeping in one gear is a good idea, even if you do have lots of them. Select something in the region of 66" to 70" and stick to it until you can turn it easily and rapidly without distressing yourself. Single gears are very good for this early training but I don't think I would advise riding a fixed wheel at this stage in case you should get cramp.

RACING

All the above advice on training – perhaps 'running in' might describe it better – has been directed at the cyclist whose only need is to be fit enough to ride to work, or potter round the lanes, or go for long rides at the weekends, all at a reasonable pace and without feeling undue strain. If you are interested in going racing then training is another thing entirely, although the early stages for a complete beginner are quite similar.

The first thing to say about racing is, are you sure that you are all that interested? Racing hurts like hell and goes on hurting, no matter how good at it you may become. The second thing is that there is no point in my advising a racing training programme because until you are regularly putting in two or three hundred miles every week at an average speed of at least 15mph you won't be ready to start racing, and by that time you will know more about the subject from experience than I can begin to tell you. Suffice to say that even to do well in a club time trial you need to live a fairly spartan sort of life, with lots of early nights and very little time for anything else except concentrating on riding.

The dedication of the top professional riders is almost unbelievable. Phil Bayton, who won the National Criterium championship, and the Raleigh Riband series in 1982, trains very hard. In the winter he rides the fifteen miles to work each day and extends the homeward run to last about two hours. After that he goes weight training and swimming, and at the weekends puts in between three and four hours rapid road riding on both days, and still manages to find time to do some press ups, and some running, and a little cyclo-cross practice to keep him supple. In the racing season he has been known to win a 100 mile race, change into his training clothes and go out and do another seventy or eighty miles. He is thought to be a trifle over-enthusiastic, even by other professional riders, but his system works, he wins.

You don't, of course, need to go to such extremes to do well in ten and twenty-five mile time trials, but you do need to get the miles in every day, and at such speeds that give you little time to look around you and enjoy the scenery, or to feel a part of what's going on around you in the countryside. You certainly won't have time to stop to admire a view, a church, have a few words with a horse, or have a leisurely pub lunch. You will need to be up very early on most Sunday mornings to thrash yourself along against the clock on some very boring bits of main road, and all to feel elated or dejected at the time you have achieved.

If it seems as though I'm trying to put you off, honestly, I'm not. All of it is true enough and if it sounds good fun to you no doubt you will enjoy taking part in cycle racing. Hundreds of riders do enjoy hard training and the self-inflicted discipline and pain of racing, so obviously it has to be enjoyable. You need to be a tough, fit, and above all a competitive kind of person. I very much enjoy watching massed start, closed circuit and track racing, but lack the interest or the dedication essential to compete.

If you are keen to take up racing then it is best to join a cycling club. Apart from all the advice and help that you will get from experienced racing men who have been around the game for years, racing cyclists are very likeable and entertaining and you will have a lot of fun. Most clubs are affiliated to the Road Time Trials Council and to the British Cycling Federation. It is the latter who control track, massed start and closed circuit events in this country and it is possible to be a private member of the BCF and compete in all their races without being a member of a club, but you will miss a lot of laughs and your lonely evening training runs will be comparatively dreary.

Let us take a quick look at the various types of cycle racing. There are two kinds of road racing, one sort of off road racing known as Cyclo-cross, and six types of track event. Time trials are the most popular form of road racing in Britain (most popular, that is, from the competitor's point of view, because they are exceedingly boring to watch), a peculiarly English sport that derived from police hostility to road racing back in the 1890s. In fact it was the only form of cycle racing allowed on the roads of this country for fifty years, and probably still would be but for the British League of Racing Cyclists (BLRC) who, in the late 1930s got fed up with the National Cyclist's Union's subservient attitude to authority and pushed and pushed and campaigned for massed start races to be held on the road. Time trials are held on 'out and back' courses – which means a head wind in one direction, at least – over ten, twenty-five, thirty, fifty and 100 miles. Riders start at one minute intervals and race against the clock and not each other, although it is possible to catch the man ahead, or get caught by the man behind. The season starts in February and finishes in October. The short distance events are the most popular early in the season, but as the participants get fitter and the weather gets better so the races get longer, even to the point of holding twelve and twenty-four hour events.

The record time for a twenty-five mile race stands at fifty-one minutes exactly. Fifty-eight minutes is considered a good 'club' time. The average speeds fall very little for the longer events. One of our local riders recently covered the last ten miles of a 100 mile event in twenty-two minutes. In decent conditions an average club rider would expect to cover 250 miles in twelve hours. Now you know what you are up against.

Hill climbs come into the same 'lonesome road' category, taking place on very steep hills towards the end of the season. A ride rarely lasts more than two or three minutes and that is quite long enough as it can be very exhausting. Very light track bikes with fixed gears and steep angles are commonly used.

Then there is massed start racing, the national sport of France, Belgium and Italy. As the name suggests, all the competitors start off together, an exciting and colourful spectacle. Massed start races can be held on closed circuits or on the road. Closed circuit races are mostly one day events, with distances varying from ten miles to 200. The Americans are very keen on short circuit massed start races that they call Criteriums. The Continentals go in for city to city races. The longest and the oldest of these single day classics for professional riders is the 382 miles Bordeaux to Paris. When this race was first held in 1891, British riders took the first four places and the leading Frenchman was fifth, six hours behind them. Things have changed a bit since then. Then there are the 'stage' races. The greatest of all is the Tour de France, twenty or more stages of 2,500 miles. The Giro d'Italia is a similar affair and so to a lesser extent is our own Milk Race, which is tough enough but lacks the atmosphere.

The number of riders in a race varies from thirty to 300. In Britain the number of competitors in minor road races is limited to forty, but up to sixty are allowed in major events. Massed start racing is tough, skilful, very fast and fairly dangerous; in the absence of protective clothing you can leave quite a lot of skin on the road. Most of the racing is carried on in a bunch which whistles along on the flat and absolutely hurtles down hills and round corners. One mistake can bring down a whole heap of riders. It's exciting to ride in, and just as exciting to watch.

Cyclo-cross is a massed start race held in the winter through woods, bogs and ditches, which is muddy rather than colourful, and like most muddy things, not very glamorous. Riders can ride their bicycles, or carry them – the riders who do the least carrying usually win – and the events are so tough that they rarely last more than an hour. They are mostly held over closed circuits in parks or woodland, but there are one or two point-to-point cross country races, which are a good way of keeping fit for the road racing season and do not require much special equipment – just big heart, lungs, and muscles, and knobbly tyres.

From a spectator's point of view, track racing is the most interesting of all forms of cycle racing because it is possible to see all of the action. It makes excellent television viewing – just as good as snooker and a lot healthier. Most track racing in this country takes place on fairly large outdoor tracks with rather shallow banking on the corners. The bicycles used are the most functional and beautiful of all racing bicycles, uncluttered by gears, brakes or cables. They have very steep frame angles, almost straight forks, short wheelbases, high saddles, low handlebars and weigh almost nothing.

There are six forms of track racing. The oldest and oddest is sprinting. Usually held over 1,000 metre courses with only the last 200 metres timed. A race can take ages, as the competitors spend most of the time standing still watching each other. The idea is to make a sudden 'jump' and get clean away from your adversaries. If you don't get clean away they will sit in behind you letting you do the work and whizz past to win at the finishing line. The last

200 metres are a desperate business.

Then there is Pursuit racing – delightfully simple. Two teams start from opposite sides of the track and try to catch up with each other. The teams consist of four men or women – never a mixture – in either team, or two individual riders. Distances are 5,000 metres for professionals, 4,000 metres for amateurs and 3,000 for women. The races are very exciting for everybody and easily followed.

Thirdly, there is the Kilometre time trial, which has one rider on the track at a time, absolutely eyeballs out for the entire distance. The fastest time wins the event.

The fastest form of track racing, in fact the fastest form of cycle racing, is the Motor paced event. Up to six riders shelter behind a similar number of riders who sit bolt upright on the back of huge and peculiar motorcycles – between 1,000 and 2,000cc – that are belt driven and belt round with the cyclists behind them bellowing 'Faster, faster' or 'For God's sake slow down' as the case may be. These motorbikes have a roller attached to them behind the rear wheel and the cyclist keeps his front tyre as close to it as possible. Speeds are around 60mph and the best thing is to get out in front and stay there. This is less complicated and much safer, but just what everybody in the race will be trying for – making for keen competition.

The flamboyantly named Devil-take-the hindmost is an elimination race. A group of riders start and the last one over the line on every lap is eliminated. Eventually the last two or three fight it out in a final sprint for the line.

Lastly there is Madison racing, named after Madison Square Gardens where this kind of racing was invented, or evolved, in 1899. Two-man teams take part riding in relays. One rider races for one or two laps and then his or her partner takes over. Races can last from one hour to six days. The six day events take place on indoor tracks. These interminable races used to be known as 'wobbles' and are very difficult to follow. Spectacular accidents are common.

CYCLING CLUBS

The well known Kipling line that goes 'He travels the fastest who travels alone' may not be true of massed start racing but it is

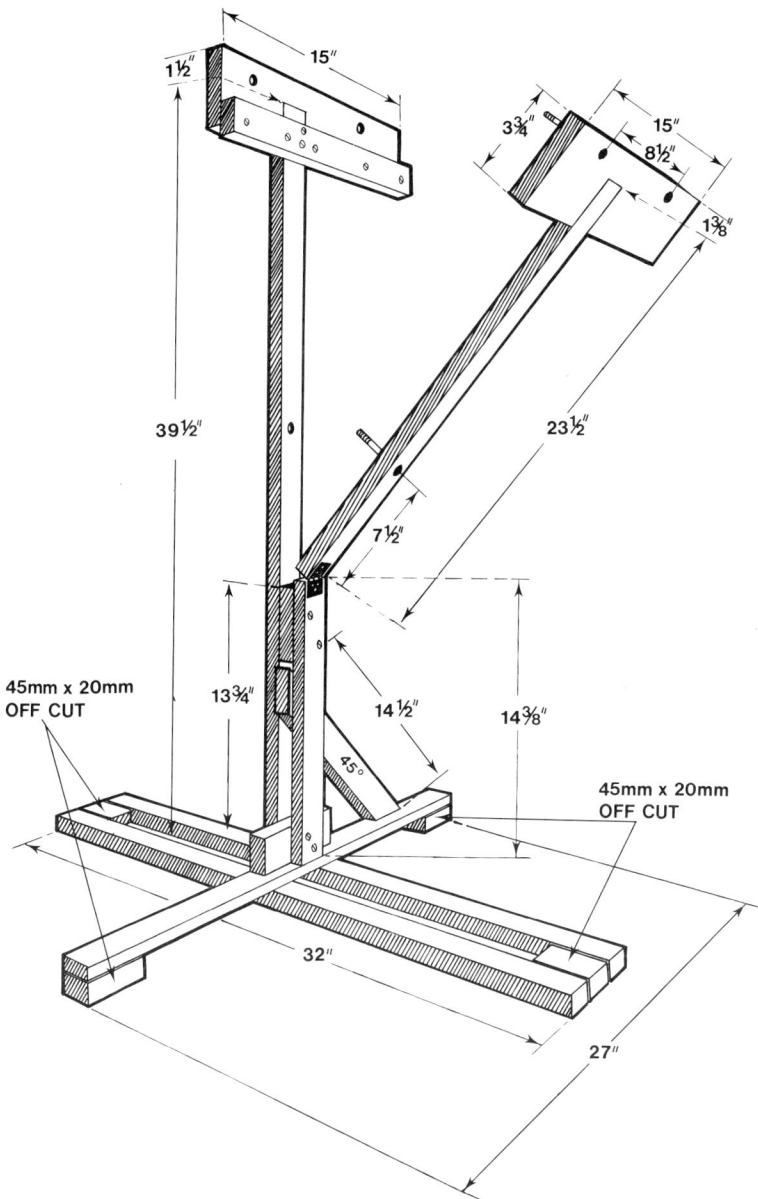

Fig. 1 The wooden workstand.

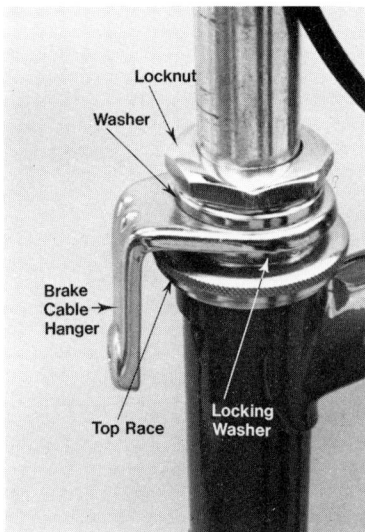

Fig. 2

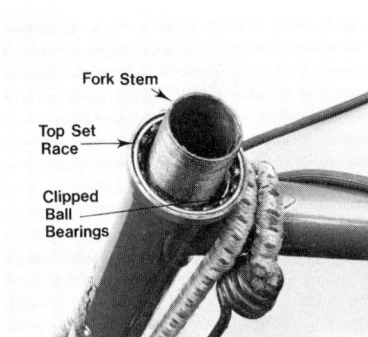

Fig. 3

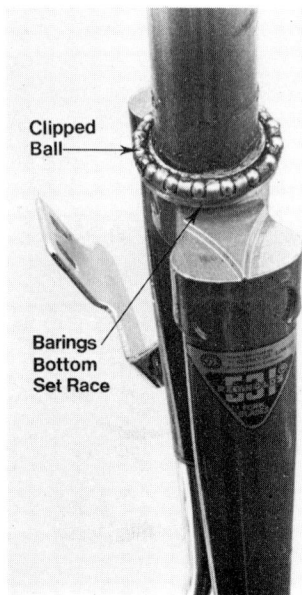

Fig. 4

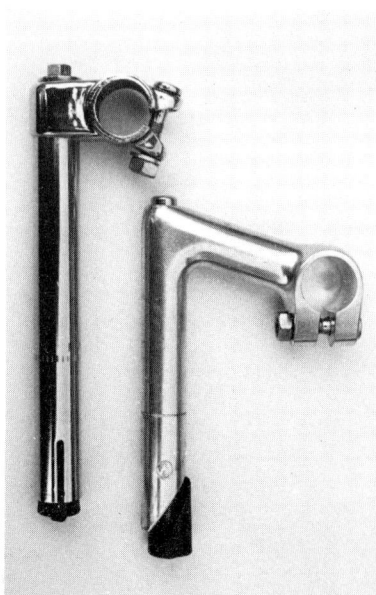

Fig. 5

Fig. 6

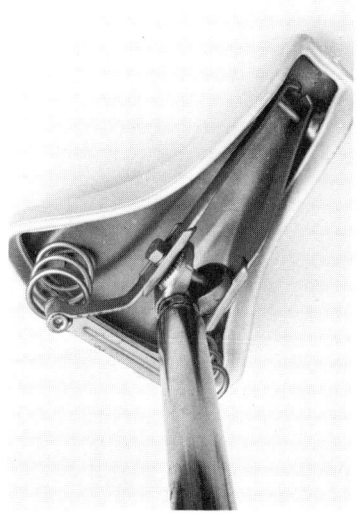

Fig. 7

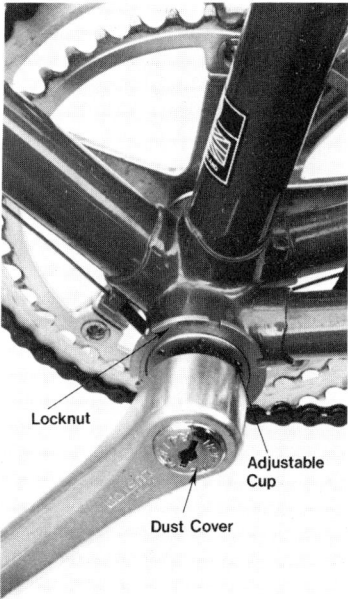

Locknut

Dust Cover

Adjustable Cup

Fig. 8

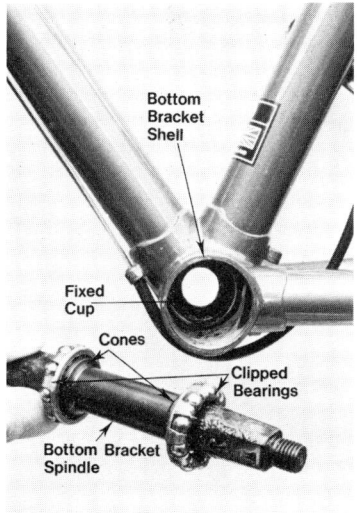

Bottom Bracket Shell

Fixed Cup

Cones

Clipped Bearings

Bottom Bracket Spindle

Fig. 9

Right Hand Cup

Clipped Ball Bearings

One Piece Crank

Locknut

Washer

Adjustable Cone

Left Hand Cup with Bearings

Fig. 10

Cotter Pin, Nut and Washer removed

Fig. 11

Crank Extractor

Fig. 12

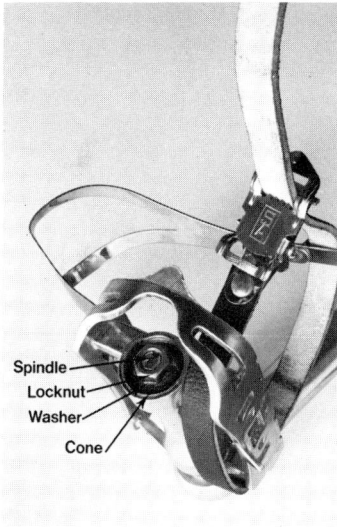

Spindle
Locknut
Washer
Cone

Fig. 13

Fig. 14

Fig. 15

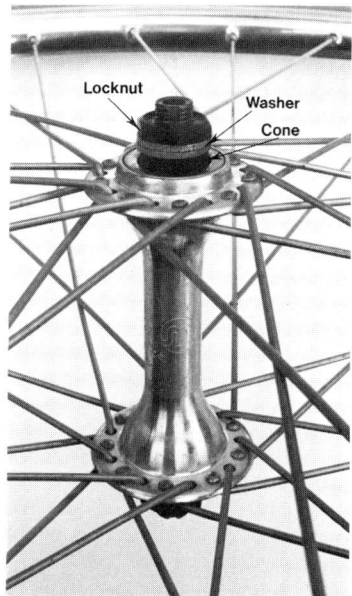

Locknut
Washer
Cone

Fig. 16

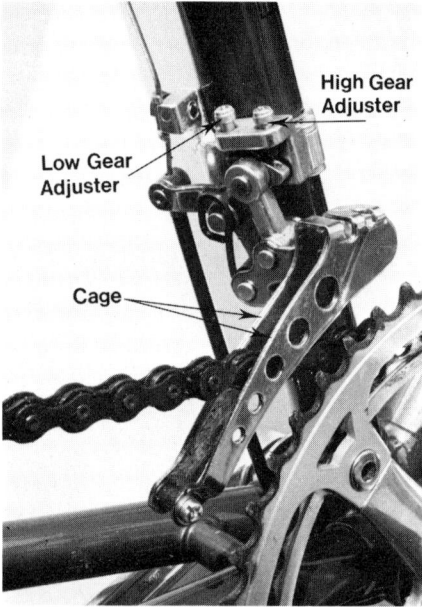

High Gear
Adjuster

Low Gear
Adjuster

Cage

Fig. 17

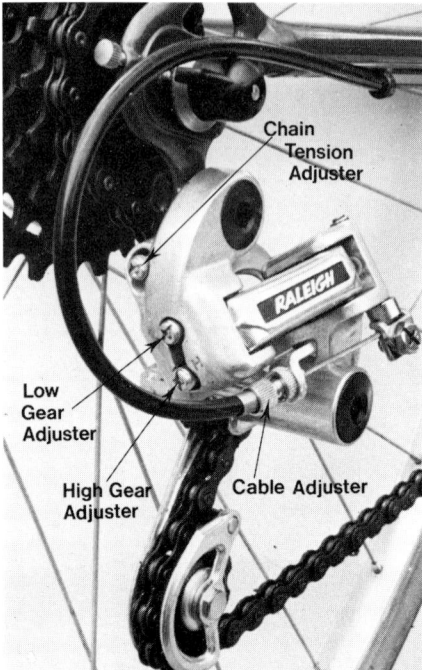

Chain
Tension
Adjuster

RALEIGH

Low
Gear
Adjuster

High Gear
Adjuster

Cable Adjuster

Fig. 18

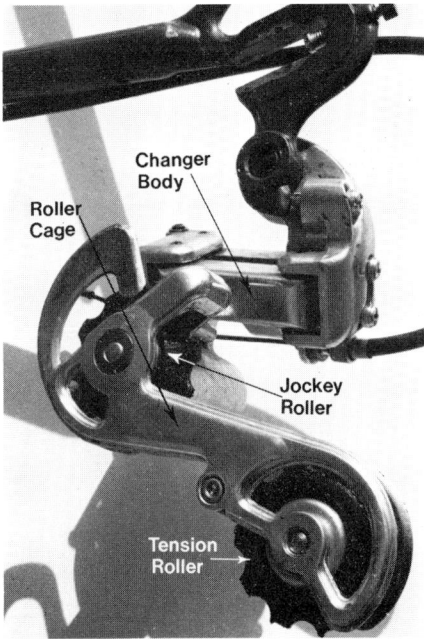

Fig. 19

Fig. 20

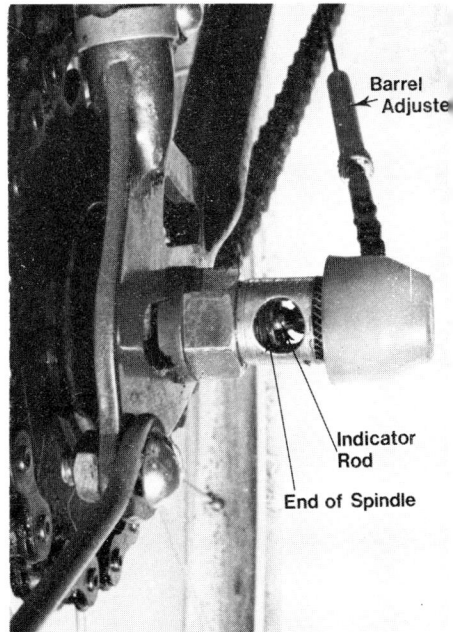

Fig. 21

Fig. 22

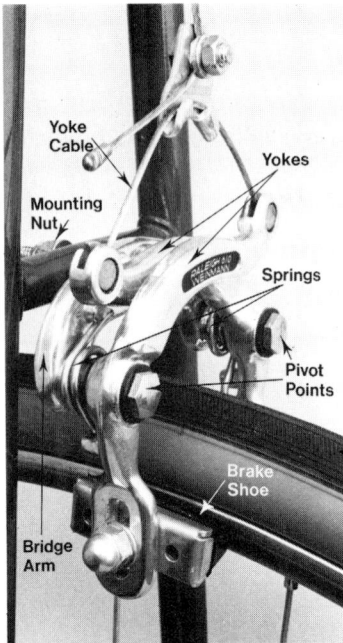

Fig. 23

Fig. 24

certainly true of weekend cycle rides and for this reason I hesitate to suggest membership of a cycling club for such a purpose. Not that tourists are any less good company than racing men, or that speed is an essential ingredient for a successful club run, but waiting around for late arrivals and non-arrivers, stopping every few minutes for adjustments, elevenses, lunch, tea, public lavatories, puncture repairs, and to find out yet again where 'Old George' has got to, can be a frustrating and time-wasting pain. Being a considerate soul yourself you wouldn't dream of stopping just when you want to and will consequently miss out on views, photography, and all sorts of things that interest you, but not the other club members. This is a pity for one of the great advantages of bike riding is that you can stop just when you feel like it without having a parking problem. Nevertheless, on balance, it is worth being patient and putting up with the inconveniences and irritations of group riding for the pleasures of the social side of cycling and the feeling of being amongst good friends.

Even if you are a loner preferring to pedal a lonely cycle path, joining the Cyclists Touring Club is a very good idea. The CTC was founded in 1878 under the name of the Bicycle Touring Club to protect cyclists – a term which then applied to anybody who pedalled a two, three, four, or even more, wheeled vehicle – from their enemies which, broadly speaking, was the police, the magistrates, and every strata of society, and to provide cyclists with information about roads, dangerous hills, hotels and things of general interest. The Club changed its name because the word bicyclists had come to mean the elitist riders of the 'Ordinary' or Penny Farthing bicycle.

The CTC is still there to protect our interests, which it might do even more effectively if it wasn't quite so nice, and it provides a range of useful services for every kind of cyclist. These include free legal aid and third party insurance, a handbook containing all sorts of information and addresses indispensable to tourists, a very comprehensive and efficient advisory service, with a library of maps and recommended routes, on touring holidays in the UK and abroad, and six free issues of *Cycletouring*, a charmingly old-fashioned club magazine full of pre-war atmosphere and pictures of thatched cottages, which also carries some pretty straight-forward and outspoken reviews on new equipment. It's well worth the £10 a year subscription fee, even if only for the free third party cover up to £500,000.

MAPS AND TOOL KITS

It would be boring and repetitive for all of us to discuss cycle touring as a separate and distinct activity for much of what has already been said in other chapters is as applicable to touring as it is to general riding. However there are a couple of important things we have not touched on and these are tool kits and good maps.

It is always a good thing to carry a tool kit of sorts, even when riding to work. The additional weight will be minimal and can save you a long and bad-tempered walk. For local riding a few bare essentials suffice. A puncture outfit and tyre levers, a small screw driver, all the appropriate Allen keys, and one of those cheap, flat and nasty multi-purpose spanners which come free with new bicycles. Horrible as they are these spanners are easily carried and useful in emergencies but shouldn't be used in the workshop where better tools are to hand as they do tend to damage bolt heads and nuts, and so give a bike an uncared for appearance. For long weekend rides take spare brake and gear cables – it isn't a bad idea to carry these items with you at all times as they weigh very little – and take a few spokes, nipples, and a spoke spanner. If you intend touring abroad take all the spares, within reason, that you might not be able to buy in the countries through which you will ride. This only really applies to places like Kurdistan and Albania, as bicycle spares are readily available throughout Western Europe. The only exception to this are 27" high pressure tyres which are difficult, if not impossible, to get as the continentals use 700C. A worn tyre that can be folded up more or less flat is the best thing to take in these circumstances along with a good spare tube. Always take some thin wire and some cutters for 'bodge up' repairs and if you are really going into the outback take all the tools needed to strip down your bicycle. Above all, service your bicycle thoroughly before you set off and replace any worn parts such as cables and brake blocks, take spare brake blocks with you anyway, and fit a new chain if the old one has done a few miles. You can always keep it and put it back on for commuting so nothing will be wasted.

Maps are a delight at all times except perhaps when lost, in pouring rain and semi-darkness, and struggling with an Ordnance Survey map, roughly a yard square, in a rising gale. It isn't always possible to avoid this situation but you can minimize the chances

130

of it happening by working out a route beforehand. There are people who actually enjoy getting lost, and then finding themselves again miles from where they thought they were, and whilst this can be tremendous fun and lead to all sorts of discoveries the spontaneity and charm of exploration can wear thin when you're a long way from dinner, on a cold wet night – and even thinner if you haven't got a map.

The best sort of maps for a cyclist are Bartholomews and the Ordnance Survey series. The Bartholomews used to be ½-inch to the mile before metrification but are now to a scale of 1 to 10,000 or about ⅝-inch to the mile. The same thing has happened to the Ordnance Survey and these are now 1 to 50,000 or approximately 1¼-inches to the mile, and 1 in 25,000 or 2½-inches to the mile. The 1 to 50,000 maps (or 2cm to 1km scale if that's any help to you), cover an area 40km by 40km.

Both the smaller scale maps are excellent for route planning, whilst recording the land, and man's influence on it, in absorbing detail, but for closer exploration of a much smaller area the 2½-inch to the mile maps are superb, they even give pub names, and are a much more manageable size being approximately 18½-inches square, although they only cover a quarter of the area, or 10km by 10km, and so are not much use for planning long journeys that avoid main roads.

Major roads are hell on earth during the week, although they calm down to be mere purgatory at the weekends. How people have the courage to ride bicycles along them at any time I shall never know. Apart from the ever present and real danger of being run down by speeding cars, the turbulence created by vast lorries with enormous trailers, unstoppable as ocean going tankers, doing 60mph and more, is absolutely terrifying and will hurl a cyclist helplessly about. Apart from the appalling danger of it all riding on these roads is so unpleasant, the terrific battering of noise, the dust, the stink of fuel and fumes, make cycling a nightmare. On wet days conditions are made quite unbearable by spray thrown up by lorries pounding past. As an aside, if you want a yardstick of how much our cynical masters really care about road safety, drive a car along a motorway on a wet day. The speed limit is 70mph, the lorries, some of them unladen 'artics' that will jack knife under heavy braking, are cruising between 75 and 80mph, bullying slower motorists in the slow lane or belting along nose to tail in the centre lane, creating a maelstrom of spray from hundreds of virtually un-mudguarded wheels that completely obscures the view for overtaking, and overtaken drivers. This state of affairs is nerve-racking and lethally dangerous, but it has been going on for years and nothing has been done about it.

Unfortunately it just isn't possible to avoid main roads entirely, but with the help of the smaller scale maps already mentioned it is possible to reduce main road mileage to a minimum and plan to travel on quiet and peaceful minor roads. Most motorists seem never to have seen a map, and would feel nervous anyway if separated from the herd, so at weekends while the main roads hum with car loads hurrying from 'illiberal lives' in suburbs to something very similar at the crowded seaside, the minor roads carry little else but local traffic which leaves them free for civilized enjoyment.

A half hour or so with a good map before a ride, jotting down place names and road numbers, if any, on a piece of card will be rewarding, allowing you to avoid busy roads as much as possible, without constantly stopping to struggle with a largish map which can be irritating and quite time consuming, leaving less time to enjoy the scenery, or have a leisurely lunch.

Maps are the most use to cyclists when read correctly. If you are touring the wilder regions of Scotland, Wales or the Upper Niger, a compass can be a true friend and comforter, especially if the terrain is a bit featureless and the weather misty. They can also be a help on overcast afternoons in Sussex when children have turned signposts round.

Something else that might be of use for working out distances to destinations, or for finding out how far you have ridden in the day, is an instrument for map measuring. Some very grand and complicated devices can be bought in stationers for a small fortune but just as good, much lighter, and much cheaper, is a small kind of cog wheel thing on a threaded axle carried in a small brass handle. Run the cog wheel up against the stop, then run it over the map following your route, and then back along the scale that you will find printed on your map, and there you are. They are easy to carry, and easy to lose if you aren't careful as they are very tiny. They are very accurate if used correctly, and yield some interesting results. Mine cost 68p and has settled many arguments. Stationers will try not to sell you one, trotting out shiny plastic geegaws that do the same job but cost about £8. If you insist they will say 'Oh, you mean those old things' and reluctantly discover several in a drawer.

One sure way of avoiding traffic is to get away from roads completely and this can be done by using the 'green lanes' and bridle paths that can easily be found on maps. In fact, maps are absolutely indispensable for seeking out such tracks for 'green lanes' are rarely signposted as bridle ways are, and apart from the ancient and well-known Peddars Way, Icknield Way, much of which is now main road, Ridgeway and many others, Britain is criss-crossed with public rights of way. Some are prehistoric, some Roman and some date from the Dark Ages, some connect with metalled roads and some peter out some miles from anywhere. Many happy hours can be spent with maps discovering such tracks and their history can make fascinating reading.

The Ordnance Survey maps list green lanes as RUPPs or 'roads used as public paths' and they are in fact un-metalled roads legally useable by all kinds of traffic. Not that you will meet cars or lorries but the odd tractor is a likelihood and near towns at weekends the suburban cavalry will be out in horsey force. I find it best to stop and let them pass. Most horsey people are polite and appreciate such consideration, but there is a modicum of enlightened self-interest in allowing them right of way as, for the most part, horses don't have a lot between their ears and are apt to shy and rear up at all sorts of things including whirring bicycles, and you could get very well kicked in such excitements.

It may be heresy to say so but horses are a menace in the winter as their hooves cut the surface of the tracks to pieces, but they are a traditional, if no longer very natural, part of rural life and one cannot reasonably complain about them. Tractors make a much worse mess anyway, and if it wasn't for horsey-minded landowners and farmers there probably would not be any trackways or bridleways left to use. Like many footpaths they would have been ploughed up long ago.

A less traditional and natural menace in the winter are 'trail riding' motorcyclists. Many of them are civilized people out to enjoy the countryside, but sadly there is a strong 'rock ape' element of thick, if basically decent, lads who regard 'green laning' as a kind of moto cross event and they are best watched out for. Not that they'll creep up on you. You will hear them coming from a long way off.

During weekdays in the summer, and further away from towns these off road excursions can be pure delight and relaxation but I wouldn't recommend riding a decent bicycle along them in the winter. If you have an old bike especially for such riding and enjoy a bit of unorganized cyclo cross then such riding can be a lot of fun, and as it is such hard work you will get very fit, if muddy.

For anyone interested in the subject of ancient tracks 'Roads & Tracks of Britain' by Christopher Taylor published by J. M. Dent is a must, and the Ordnance Survey offer a series of Archaeological and Historical maps.

Chapter 8

A BRIEF LOOK AT BICYCLE HISTORY

Although cherubims and seraphims appeared in medieval stained glass windows riding on monocycles of fire the church did not develop the idea and it was left to a M de Sivrac of Paris to bring a primitive form of cycling to the ordinary mortal, although he used two wheels and dispensed with the fire.

His machine, which he called a Célérifère, looked much like a child's rocking horse on wheels instead of rockers and caused great excitement. While célérifèreing became a fashionable Parisian pastime for a number of years, by the early 1800s the novelty was rather wearing off as the célérifère, apart from changing its name to vélocifère, had developed hardly at all and still had several fundamental drawbacks that prevented it from becoming a serious means of transport. Basically it was a pair of unsprung wheels connected by a heavy beam of wood, or iron, the rider uncomfortably straddling the beam and paddling himself along at some risk of a hernia. Although quite fast, especially downhill with a following wind, anything more than a walking pace only served to highlight its design defects which were simply that no provisions had been made for steering or stopping a vélocifère, and as they weighed something around fifty pounds or more there must have been a great number of painful and spectacular accidents.

The vélocifère had smooth iron tyres, probably flattish in section, and whilst it was supposed to be possible to steer one by banking it over I doubt very much if it was, even if the rider was brave enough to try. A more practical method of steering would have been to heave the front wheel into the air and wrench it over to point, more or less, in the desired direction before the wheel crashed back to earth, but for those already ruptured by over-exertion in an awkward posture it was probably better just to let events take their course.

Vélocifèreing became popular again in 1818 after Baron Von Drais de Sauerbrun (who actually used a vélocifère as everyday transport for his work), tired of running into things and built one with a steerable front wheel, and eased the pain of paddling himself along by padding the beam that he straddled, although he still retained the rocking horse appearance. Von Drais took his improved machine to Paris, announced it to be a Draisienne and demonstrated it in the Luxembourg Gardens where it created an enormous impression and started off another craze which this time spread to Britain and America.

Incidentally, the French discovered years later that a French-man, Nicephore Niepce, had invented the steerable vélocifère long before Von Drais had come up with the idea.

In England the Prince Regent and the Regency bucks and beaux enthusiastically took up the new sport and the Draisienne soon lost is nice French name and became known as the hobby-horse, which was odd as by this time it had completely lost its horsey appearance and become rather elegant in a functional sort of way, the solid spoked wheels looking very like the magnesium alloy wheels of a modern motorcycle, although they must have been much heavier.

Such was the popularity of the hobby-horse amongst the smart and well-to-do that riding schools opened and prospered but the craze only lasted for a few years. The cartoonists had a lot of cruel fun at the expense of the portly prince and his chubby chums; they really must have looked ridiculous as they paddled themselves along, and the conservative British public generally disapproved of such an elitist fad. What really killed off the hobby-horse were much the same things that had killed off the vélocifère twenty years earlier. Discomfort, a high incidence of hernias, and the fact that nobody had yet thought of a practical means of propulsion, or retardation, other than the soles of the riders' feet.

In the early 1840s the evolution of the bicycle took a turn for the better when a Scottish blacksmith named Kirkpatrick Macmillan virtually invented it by building an improved hobby-horse for his own use which he propelled by treadles attached to rods that turned cranks on a large rear wheel. This system worked well enough for him to treadle the 140 miles from his home in Courthill to Glasgow and back, a tremendous achievement considering the primitive state of the roads at that time, particularly as he is reported to have covered forty miles in five hours – which says a lot for the muscles on his brawny legs.

This machine still had some way to go as a practical means of transport; it was only steerable to a very limited degree as the treadles moved backwards and forwards beside the front wheel. Also it had no brakes other than, presumably, applying pressure against the returning treadle and these shortcomings may have contributed to an accident in the Gorbals where Macmillan knocked over a child, which in turn contributed to the sensation that he was already causing.

In spite of the success of his design, Macmillan passed up the chance of becoming the world's first bicycle manufacturer and development stagnated for another twenty years, although one or two people built copies of Macmillan's machine, and Thomas McCall of Kilmarnock built several with brakes and improved steering. Inventors interest centred on the treadle-propelled horseless carriage with three or four wheels in a wondrous variety of arrangements, and which years later bore fruit with the introduction of the pedal powered ricksaw.

Oddly enough it was Pierre and Ernest Michaux, a Parisian firm of three-wheeled velocipede manufacturers who gave the development of the two-wheeler a much needed boost when with a typically French preference for front wheel drive they converted an old Draisienne to 'traction avant'. By fitting cranks to the front axle and pedals to the cranks they superseded Kirkpatrick Macmillan's treadle and rod rear wheel drive, which must have achieved some saving in weight, although the Michaux machine still weighed something in the region of 60lbs or more. It does seem doubtful if this early form of pedalling was ergonomically any happier than treadling.

Nevertheless, the pedals were a great success that sparked off another boom in bicycles and the Michauxs, who knew a good thing when they saw it, were quick to capitalize on their invention. By 1863 they had built and sold 143 machines and increased production every year until by 1868 they were producing 1,500 units a year in a new factory employing three hundred people.

It is difficult to understand quite why the Michaux's machines were so popular. True, they had pedals, were made of a combination of wood and metal, and could be steered. They could also be stopped, eventually, by a crude back brake but essentially they were little different from the hobby-horse. Whatever their attractions, the Michauxs must have hit upon the idea of pedals just at the right moment and were hard put to keep up with demand, and other firms were quick to take advantage and move into the profitable business of making velocipedes for the bourgeoisie.

It was not only in France that the craze took hold. Americans, hungry then as now for novelty, took up velocipeding or bicycling in a big way and the inhabitants of New York and Boston soon had a number of bicycle manufacturers catering for their enthusiasm. By 1869 the New York firm of Pickering & Davis were exporting their products to England. However, the craze soon collapsed. The Americans had never considered the bicycle to be a serious means of transport and by 1871 they had all returned to the horse, leaving the field free for the English and French, although by that time the French were pre-occupied with losing the Franco-Prussian war.

Ten busy years of money and bicycle making had seen a slow but steady improvement in the design of the two wheeler. Early in the boom the bicycle had acquired the name 'bone-shaker' and much thought and effort had been expended with the aim of making the name less apt. By 1869, when the world's first cycle show was held in Paris, many machines had spoked wheels made of metal rather than wood and some of these metal wheels wore rubber tyres. True, these tyres were only solid rubber, but nevertheless they were a great step forward in terms of road holding and comfort, and no doubt made a lot less noise than the iron rims previously used.

The ten years of intense activity that had furthered the long drawn out development of the bicycle also saw the introduction of cycle racing. Although bicycling, or boneshaking, had died a death in America before anybody there had thought or organized competition, the French had found time to invent cycle racing before getting involved once again in the age-old European sport of killing large numbers of people as unpleasantly as possible. In 1868 they held a 1,200 metre cycle race on a purpose-built track in the suburbs of Paris and the following year organized the first long distance road race between Paris and Rouen. Both races were won by James Moore, an Englishman who covered the eighty-three mile road course in ten hours twenty-five minutes – good going considering the horrible state of the roads and that his racing machine must have weighed at least half a hundredweight.

Up to this time the makers of bicycles had been amateur mechanics making machines for themselves, but in 1869 the Coventry Sewing Machine Company changed its name and product and, as the Coventry Machinist's Company, began to make bicycles for export to France which were very similar to the Michaux's machines. The Franco-Prussian war soon put a stop to that as it also put a stop to bicycle production in France itself, leaving the English, however unfairly, to the forefront of manufacturing and technical development.

Possibly due, in part, to the antagonism of large sections of the public there was no mass market for bicycles. To be a bicyclist in Britain was much like being an early Christian in Ancient Rome and one had to be keen to continue with it. One also had to be fairly well off. A typical British boneshaker cost about £20 which may not sound much until one remembers that in 1869 a well paid railway 'navvy' was earning twenty-seven shillings a week and an agricultural labourer about a third of that sum, and the volume of trade was obviously limited by the high cost of machines.

Nevertheless, there was a sufficiently profitable home market to be found amongst the moderately well-to-do to support a healthy British bicycle industry and to encourage the struggle for a larger share of that market by constantly improving the product, although not all the ideas that manufacturers came up with could honestly be described as improvements. The Carriage Wheel Company actually produced a prototype with hinges in the middle of the frame, claiming that it would prove easier to manoeuvre than a rigid boneshaker. The job of test pilot in a cycle factory must have been fraught with hazard, for this theory was not borne out in practice.

The most noticeable change was in the size and construction of bicycle wheels which by the early seventies were mostly wire spoked, the rear wheel becoming smaller and the front wheel much larger. Direct drive was still the order of the day and with the cranks and pedals attached to the hub the bigger the wheel the greater the distance covered with one turn of the pedals, allowing the rider to get along faster, at least on the flat and downhill. The larger front wheel also gave an improvement in comfort as it rode more easily over bad road surfaces and was less prone to drop into potholes, but the size of the wheel was limited by the rider's inside leg measurement.

By the mid 1870s, the 'Ordinary', later to be called the penny farthing, had superseded the boneshaker. The better off riders moved up, quite literally onto the new high wheelers and there was soon an estimated 50,000 or so of these machines rolling along the roads of Britain, although probably not all at the same time. This of course brought many second-hand boneshakers onto the market bringing the pleasures and excitements of bicycling to a wider public, and reinforcements to the bicycle clubs that had sprung up in towns around the country.

The machine that popularized the 'Ordinary' in England was the 'Ariel', a name perpetuated until the mid-1960s when bad management and the Mini Minor killed off the British motorcycle industry. The 'Ariel' was the design of James Starley who had been with the Coventry Machinists Company but had left in 1871 to form a company with William Hillman, another name destined to become famous in the motor industry. In many ways Starley was the founder of the British cycle industry, a remarkable man whose many inventions for the bicycle and the tricycle did so much to advance the day when personal transport became a practical proposition for almost everybody. The 'Ariel' had metal wheels with tangential wire spokes adjustable 'en masse' by levers on the hubs, another leap forward in the evolution of the bicycle and one which shortly afterwards led to Starley perfecting and patenting the system of spoking still in use today.

Another of Starley's innovations was the 'speed gear' which enabled a strong rider to turn his pedals once for two revolutions of the wheel but this gear was expensive. A standard 'Ariel' sold for £8 but the geared model was half as much again.

The size of the front wheel of an 'Ordinary', which tended to be between four and five feet in diameter, could also be limited by a rider's courage, for the saddle was situated on top of the wheel and the taller the wheel the further one fell. Falls were frequent, for these large wheeled machines were quite dangerous. They might be unwieldy and heavy but they were capable of high speeds downhill and headers over the handlebars were a common and painful occurrence. Getting on and off could also have its moments. To climb aboard, one scooted away with one foot on a step on the frame just above the tiny rear wheel and from there swung the other leg gracefully, or just any old how, hopefully over the saddle. Dismounting was equally exciting. The minute one stopped, or slightly before, one let go of the handlebars, sprang lightly backwards off the saddle, dropped or fell the five or so feet to the road and then grabbed the machine from behind before it toppled over.

In England bicycling had gone beyond a craze and had become established amongst a growing band of enthusiasts if certainly not with the public in general. A great deal of hostility was shown towards the bicyclist especially by coachmen, cabmen, carters, draymen, huntsmen, and indeed almost everybody who had anything to do with the horse, which at the time represented a considerable body of opinion often violently expressed. Not only did the bicyclists frighten the horses; bicycling also frightened the horsey community by posing a possible threat to their livelihood, and as this community was not noted for being delicately nurtured, bicyclists were frequently attacked and in some cases nearly killed by resentful horse operators. If the riders of 'boneshakers' had not been at all popular with the public in general it seems that the 'Ordinary' rider was hated, and this hatred may well have been brought on by the huge front wheels, the observer confusing altitude with arrogance and reacting instinctively.

Apart from the danger of assault, the heavy horse-drawn traffic in towns was chaotic and the highway code of the day was very neatly summed up by the Satanist Aleister Crowley when he said 'Do what you will, it is the only law'. The roads were so hazardous for bicyclists that they often took to the pavements which were not only safer but smoother and this, not unnaturally, upset the pedestrian population who joined in the verbal and physical attacks. Small boys delighted to thrust sticks through the spokes of tall front wheels and whether this was done in a spirit of mischief or enquiry the result was equally disastrous; dogs savaged the fallen, and to cap it all the police happily persecuted the bicyclist as he had no legal status, as nobody had yet decided whether or not the bicycle was a vehicle. It seems very likely that the cycle club had its origins in a desire for mutual protection from public and police as from any great wish for companionship.

The use of the name 'Ordinary' seems very peculiar and requires explanation. The reasons for the derisory term Penny Farthing which came in at a later date are obvious enough but

141

'Ordinary' is an unlikely name for such an extraordinary looking machine. There is a theory that at the height of its popularity it was just called a 'bicycle' and that the name 'Ordinary' only came into contemporary use to distinguish the high wheeler from the later and much more appropriately named 'Safety Bicycle', and this seems to make some sense. But, in 1878 the Singer Company introduced a model they called the 'Xtraordinary' which suggests that the name 'Ordinary' was in common use for some time before the 'Safety' came on the scene. I think the truth must be that no one really knows. Many people hold strong views about it but none of them agree.

The Singer Xtraordinary was an interesting machine, partly because it had lever cranks instead of pedals to allow the saddle to be placed further back (which lessened the chances of being hurled over the handlebars), but mainly because it had front forks that sloped backwards up to the steering head, giving the front wheel a self-centering action and imparting directional stability to the Xtraordinary. Directional stability, or the lack of it, was one of the drawbacks of the ordinary 'Ordinary' whose vertical front fork arrangement made them very sensitive and difficult, if not impossible, to ride 'hands off'. Riders of 'Ordinary' bicycles were recommended to take their feet off the pedals and to hang their legs over the handlebars when going downhill at high speed, so that in the likely event of a 'header' they at least had a nice clean take-off unencumbered by 50lbs of machinery that might well come down upon their heads, and one can imagine that any improvement in stability was welcome indeed. The rearward inclination of the fork also contributed to the rearward positioning of the saddle and as much of the design work of the day was done on the principle of 'suck it and see' it is perfectly possible that this was the reason for the angled fork set up and that the improvements in the steering department were a fortunate spin off.

Hanging ones legs over the handlebars was a difficult thing to accomplish and some makers of 'Ordinaries' brazed footrests onto the forks, but if there was the slightest chance of having to stop on the way downhill the wise rider dismounted and walked down, for brakes were another problem associated with the large front wheel.

The average 'Ordinary' brake was a stout piece of metal some two inches long, shaped to follow the sectional profile of the solid rubber front tyre, and hovering above it in front of the steering head. This shoe was connected to a handlebar lever that was only for use in a case of emergency, for when the lever was used, the metal shoe grabbed hold of the tyre and stopped the wheel dead in its tracks. Sadly this didn't stop the rest of the machine, or the rider, and whilst it was obvious to everyone that a brake was needed that stopped all three together in a dignified and controllable manner this was impossible to achieve when most of the weight was carried high in the air and nearest to the accident. Even a modern and sensitive hub brake would have been a dangerous thing to use in these circumstances.

By the late 1870s the design of the bicycle was more or less in the doldrums and interest had shifted back to the development of three- and four-wheeled vehicles, which we will examine in Chapter 9. However, good ideas are seldom wasted and several inventions that got off the ground on the tricycle and quadricycle were later applied to the bicycle and eventually to the motorcar.

Two final flings, and interesting dead ends, in the search for a more stable 'Ordinary' were the 'Star' and the 'Facile'. The 'Star' was designed by an American named Kelly and finally introduced in 1885 by the Smith Machine Company of New Jersey. On Kelly's machine, the rider still sat tall in the saddle on the top of the big wheel, but the big wheel had become the back wheel, the small wheel having been moved forward to become the front wheel. This machine had all the advantages of the 'Ordinary' but, with his weight placed well to the rear, the rider was a lot less likely to be thrown over the top in a 'header' a 'cropper' an 'imperial crowner' or whatever else it was that the Americans called this kind of accident. Braking also was much improved and far more controllable as the long steering head, and the short reversed front fork, acted as a torque tube that stopped the machine from revolving around the axle of the braked wheel. In later models the frame was most unusual because the steering head tube was the only substantial frame member, the rest of it being an early kind of space frame bent up from small diameter rods. These handsome bicycles became popular in America and were very successful in competition, but strangely they never caught on over here.

The 'Facile' was another, less graceful attempt to place the weight of the rider further to the rear where it could do less harm, though not nearly so far to the rear as was possible with the novel wheel arrangement of the 'Star'. Some measure of improvement was achieved by using a smaller front wheel driven by a complicated system of cranks and levers, or chains and sprockets, that raised the gearing and lowered the pedals and the centre of gravity all at the same time, but it was only a partial solution, although the 'Faciles' were extremely stable.

A late development of the Facile theme was the Kangaroo, which came to be called the dwarf Ordinary, an unattractive name that suited it very well. These ungainly machines had a geared pedal drive allowing the use of an even smaller front wheel, and although they achieved a measure of popularity – the various manufacturers employed professional riders to advertise the new models by record breaking rides and endurance events – they never really challenged the supremacy of the stately 'Ordinary', and the success of the Safety bicycle soon killed them off.

By 1885, it has been estimated, there were two hundred firms making 'Ordinaries'. The worst of these 'Ordinaries' were unspeakably heavy and crude, being cobbled together from old lumps of iron by the village blacksmith, but the best of them were remarkably refined machines with ball bearings in the hubs in place of the old brass bushes, proper ball bearing 'Stanley' steering heads, frames made of steel tubing, and hollow drawn front forks. The racing 'Ordinary' had got down to around 25lbs in weight and a weight of only 22lbs was claimed by the Surrey Machinist Co. Ltd. for their racing 'Invincible'. If the claimed weight was correct the machine must have been dangerously flimsy. Apart from fitting epicyclic gears and 'adding lightness' the penny farthing format had gone as far as it could go and there was nothing more that could be done with it.

In spite of the undoubted popularity of the 'Ordinary' and to a lesser extent the 'dwarf Ordinary', and the number of people engaged in making them, the time had come for the bizarre tall wheeler to give way to a more rational type of machine that was to bring about the last, and the greatest, cycling boom. This new type of machine was known as the 'Safety', the very name implying a criticism of the 'Ordinary' as it was self evidently much safer to ride.

Once again a Starley was in the vanguard of technical progress but this time it was John Starley whose Uncle James, the man responsible for the innovative 'Ariel' had died in 1881 at the age of fifty.

144

John Starley introduced his 'Rover' Safety in 1884 but it was by no means the first 'Safety' bicycle. H. J. Lawson, the Manager of the Tangent & Coventry Tricycle Co., had been experimenting with smaller front wheels and rear wheel drive in 1876 but his first machine was really only a refined version of Kirkpatrick Macmillan's velocipede of thirty years before. His second attempt in 1879 was infinitely better and looked rather rakish with its 40″ front wheel and 24″ rear joined by a straight backbone frame, with the bracket for the pedal and chainwheel that supplied the rear wheel drive, suspended from a tube descending from the frame and lightly stayed to the bottom of what could be called the seat stays, although in fact the seat was mounted on a curved leaf spring that sprang from the top of the same tube that held the bottom bracket. Lawson called it the 'Bicyclette' but everybody else called it the 'Crocodile'.

'Despite its nickname the 'Bicyclette' was a good deal more attractive than either Starley's first 'Safety' or its BSA equivalent which came out in the same year. All three designs had indirect steering with the handlebars set well back towards the saddle and connected to the forks with rods, a system that may have been intended to minimize the road shocks to the riders' arms as there seems little other point in using it. The 'Bicyclette' had forks that raked back stylishly to form a right angle with the downward sloping frame, but both the 'Rover' and the 'Beesa' had vertical forks and a shortish wheelbase and were somehow knobbly to look at. The BSA made extensive use of rifle cleaning rods and bits of tricycle, and had wheels of different sizes, 20″ at the front and 32″″ at the rear, while Starley, who also used wheels of differing sizes on his Rover, placed the larger wheel in front.

Humber also introduced their Safety model in 1885 and this was different again. It had a very small front wheel and very short front forks connected to a raked back steering head of enormous length, with handlebars directly on the top, and pedal and chainwheel drive to a large back wheel. This was probably the first bicycle to have a diamond frame, with the down tube curved upwards and the top tube curved downwards. The saddle perched rather perkily on top of a short piece of tubing sprouting vertically from the frame but there was no seat tube as such, which meant that all the back end bracing was done by the seat stays and the chain stays. The Humber really was very pretty and it sold quite well, and although with its lack of a seat tube it looked rather delicate, it certainly was not. In his second attempt at a 'Safety', Starley used a curving backbone frame which also lacked a seat tube although this may have been strengthened to some degree by an elaborate saddle mounting that bridged that gap where one might have expected a top tube to be. The answer no doubt lay in the use of heavy gauge tubing, a theory borne out by the weight of Starley's machine which looked light but in fact weighed 37lbs.

This second attempt of Starley's was much more successful. It employed straight forks, raked back this time, with direct steering and with the larger wheel up front. This format was well received by the public but Starley couldn't have been very happy with it for shortly afterwards he introduced his third design. This machine had a top tube, but still no seat tube, and although the front wheel remained the larger, the rear wheel was increased in size. The saddle looked a great deal more modern, with coil springs front and rear on a small neat frame. In all, Rovers produced eight different models to Starley's designs over the next few years but it is in this third version of his 'Safety' with its diamond frame and more or less equal sized wheels that one can first recognize the prototype of the modern standard bicycle.

The fact that John Kemp Starley had virtually set the pattern for the twentieth century standard pedal cycle was not recognized at the time by the other manufacturers and they continued to experiment. In the days before the perfection and general adoption of the pneumatic tyre a lot of energy was expended, and very largely wasted, on attempts to produce a practical sprung frame, a very difficult thing to contrive for any kind of two wheeler. Applied to a pedal cycle there is a tendency for much of the rider's effort to be absorbed by the springing and any lack of lateral rigidity, which would have been impossible to avoid at that time, brings with it serious steering and handling problems. In a powered two wheeler the handling problems are even more acute and the large and prosperous British motorcycle industry didn't properly overcome them until 1950.

At least half a dozen makers listed a 'spring frame' Safety model, all referred to as 'Whippets', a generic and probably appropriate title, like 'Hoover' brought about by the name of the first of the breed catalogued in 1885 by Linley & Briggs of London's Clerkenwell Road. In spite of their peculiar appearance they were no doubt more comfortable than the rigid framed 'Safety' and they all enjoyed some brief measure of success until the market for them collapsed and died when a reliable inflatable rubber tyre became available.

Outside this interesting backwater the search for the ideal frame format went on. Rudge for example, and Singer, went in for the 'cross frame' which was not dissimilar to the 'backbone' frame of Lawson's 'Bicyclette' or 'Crocodile', except that the cross tube was set rather lower. Dan Albone, an agricultural engineer and publican from Biggleswade, made a 'cross frame' machine called the 'Ivel' after the river that runs past the town. He also listed a 'diamond frame' Safety model but the 'cross tube' model was so successful and popular that he later listed a version for Ladies, but in this he seems to have reverted to the 'bent spine' frame by replacing the straight central tube from the head to the seat tube, lightly braced to the bottom bracket, by a tube curving down from head to bracket.

As a passing aside on the pleasing continuance of local names, the Bedford & District telephone directory currently lists seventy-three Albones, all of them in the Biggleswade area. The Peterborough directory lists only two.

A truly remarkable example of the 'cross frame' Safety was made by Harry James who by way of blowing his own trumpet advertised his 'James Special' as the lightest machine in existence weighing 11lbs only when fully equipped. That was in 1889, long before Titania took up metallurgy, and if a 'James Special' exists today Harry's claim must be as true now as it was then, for the current 'Team Replica' Raleigh which retails at £580 and is generally regarded as good value, has a given weight of 22lbs.

J. S. Smith, the proprietor of the Surrey Machinist Company mentioned earlier, made an unusual 'cross frame' Safety. In this design the oblique main frame tube continued downwards to the centre of the rear wheel, the wheel being offset on a form of stub axle. The front wheel was also offset, but on the opposite side, from a single fork blade.

Four years before, Smith had used the same advanced features on his ultra light 'Ordinary', and a similar arrangement is currently used on a BMW motorcycle.

In 1890 Humbers introduced the first true diamond frame and it was this frame that seems to have finally convinced most of the industry that the straight tubed diamond layout was the most functional, aesthetic and commercial compromise available and that there would be little profit in carrying on the search for an alternative.

147

By this time most of the people who were later to become famous as the makers of cars and motorcycles were on the scene and building bicycles, and it was the discoveries that they had made and applied to the developing bicycle, and the manufacturing lessons that they had been forced to learn that facilitated the rapid rise of the motor and motorcycle industries. The invention and perfection of the tangentially spoked wheel, the ball bearing and the ballrace, and the bush roller chain had all come about because of the bicycle and were absolutely crucial to these new industries, as was the pneumatic tyre shortly to become popular on the 'Safety' models, and even glued onto the rims of some surviving 'Ordinaries'.

The pneumatic tyre had in fact been invented and patented in 1845 by the young Robert Johnson, a Scottish engineer. Had he had the good fortune to have thought of it a few years later, his name instead of Dunlop's might have been a household word today, but he was a bit too early and his invention foundered from lack of interest and consequently lack of capital.

Johnson's tyre had not been intended for bicycles but for carts and carriages, and had his idea been taken up commercially the world would have been a much quieter place. The roar of the thousands of iron clad wheels and iron shod hooves made the streets of the nineteenth century city much noisier than the streets today. It is surprising that no one invented a hard rubber horseshoe. Johnson also invented a solid rubber tyre for use on railway rolling stock, an idea that Michelin experimented with on a French built railcar in the 1930s, so it does seem a pity that his ingenuity and foresight were not rewarded with financial success.

Hollow, but non-inflatable rubber tyres were experimented with for a while but the idea of the pneumatic tyre occurred again and quite spontaneously some forty years later, not this time to an engineer but to a Dublin vet, although the re-inventor was also of Scottish descent. This, of course, was John Boyd Dunlop. He fitted his first tyre to his young son's bicycle and the lad had the honour of testing the prototype. Dunlop was granted a patent for an inflatable inner tube and a separate outer cover which had to be glued on, or taped to the rim. His ideas were taken up by Harvey du Cros and the Pneumatic Tyre Company was formed, as were many other tyre companies who jumped onto the rubber tired bandwagon. The rather sausage like tyres were at first ridiculed by the sporting cyclists until they quickly proved their superiority over the narrow section solid. In fact, the new tyres were a tremendous success in competition which greatly increased their popularity and spurred on development. At first they were much more expensive than the solid tyres and also difficult and tedious to mend in the frequent event of punctures, and it wasn't until the introduction of the wired-edged tyre, that could be quickly and easily removed, that they really came into their own.

Of the many tyre makers the two most successful were Dunlop's own company and the Michelin Company of France, both household names still with us today and in the same line of business. Very few of the bicycle makers of that era continued to make bicycles as the great majority of them switched over to car and motorcycle production in the first few years of the following century. Most of today's cycle manufacturers are comparative newcomers.

At the beginning of the 1880s there was a curious outbreak of oddities that were well outside the mainstream of bicycle and tricycle development and contributed nothing towards it. Quite the oddest of these was a unicycle designed by Richard Hemming of New Haven, Connecticut in 1882 which was reminiscent of the three-legged emblem of the Isle of Man enclosed in an enormous wheel, with the rider sitting inside the wheel and propelling it with hands and feet. No provision had been made for steering other than leaning over, and the motto of the Isle of Man 'Whichever way you throw me I stand' could not have been appropriately applied as it looked likely to fall over at any moment. 1882 must have been the year of the unicycle as a gentleman from Hammersmith designed and built an even bigger one which was driven by two men, one on either side, which really must have been a menace to other road users.

Almost as peculiar was the Otto Dicycle in which two wheels of 'Ordinary' size revolved side by side with the rider sitting in between. On the early models there was absolutely nothing, except his sense of balance, to prevent a rider tipping backwards, or falling forwards in danger of being run over by his own machine. And the Dicycle was designed, believe it or not, to get away from the risks attendant on riding an 'Ordinary' bicycle. Funnily enough they cannot have been as difficult to ride as one would imagine for BSA made, and sold, nearly a thousand of them and the owners formed a club and called themselves the 'Ottoists'. The drive was by belts from a suspended crank axle running over spring loaded pulleys and steering was a delicate matter of slackening off the drive belt with a lever on the side towards which one wanted to turn. Club runs must have been like 'dicycling' with death.

In 1885 it was estimated that there were forty thousand bicycles in Britain and this number soon increased dramatically with the amalgamation of the various elements that made the new 'Safety' bicycle a practical and attractive proposition for the ordinary man and woman. This almost universal appeal brought about the great cycling boom of the 1890s when the bicycle really was King of the Road bringing with it a mobility and freedom never before known to the masses.

The aristocratic 'Ordinary' and the humbler 'dwarf Ordinary' lingered on for a while, their athletic and strong-minded admirers sternly resisting the change, but when the racing 'Safety' consistently proved to be faster than the fastest 'Ordinary' even they had to climb down. The 'Ordinary' gradually faded away and an exciting era was over.

Cycling, which had certainly started out as an essentially lower middle class movement and had for years remained the province of the fairly well off and well educated, was enthusiastically taken up in every strata of society in Britain, in Europe and in America and this included the upper classes and the aristocracy.

Not that an interest in common brought the classes closer together in any way, and it is doubtful if the nobility and gentry joined the proliferating cycling clubs, unless Boodles or the Athenaeum had a cycling section, but the clubs thrived nevertheless. The Cyclist's Touring Club or CTC more than doubled its membership in twelve months, from 16,000 in 1895 to 34,000 in the following year – and these members were only the keen cycle tourists. The ranks of the many other clubs and the completely unaffiliated probably ran into millions.

Up to the mid-1880s, bicycling had been a little undignified and, although a little genteel tricycling seems to have been socially acceptable, for the most part women had left it to the men. With the advent of the 'Safety' bicycle, however, women took to two wheels in great numbers and most manufacturers listed a Ladies' model. The clothing industry also profited greatly from this new mass market for fashionable and suitable garments for cycling ladies and the ready availability of such attractive clothes probably attracted some women to take up the sport.

150

The bicycle boom of the 1890s was in reality two movements in one. The less well-off were delighted to have, at last, the freedom of their own personal transport and their acceptance of the bicycle for sport and transport was a lasting if diminishing phenomenon, for the bicycle was more popular during this period than it ever has been since and its following gradually fell away over the years. This erosion was greatly accelerated in the early twenties by the availability of the 'nice little car' which was actually nothing of the kind, for under £100, and the mass-produced but much more exciting motorbike for a great deal less. However, there always remained a substantial core of roadster riders and a hardcore of enthusiasts sufficient to keep a healthy if smaller cycle industry alive over the next few decades.

The defection of the upper classes was much more sudden. For them the bicycle had been a charming and fashionable toy but riding it did require a certain amount of work that couldn't be done by a servant and the novelty of that quickly palled. The middle classes watched them go and then they gradually began to drift away.

During the boom period the bicycle was to become much improved and refined in every way but there was only one serious attempt to improve on the diamond frame layout. This was the Dursley Pederson; Dursley because that is where it was made, and Pederson after Mikail Pederson, the Danish engineer who designed it. One of the most scientifically constructed bicycles ever built and one of the most delightfully different, it was made of very small section tubes triangulated in pairs and so thin that they had to be soft soldered together, but so strong that there are many Dursley Pedersons still with us today.

This fascinating machine had a revolutionary hammock saddle made of silk cords which was slung between the top of the steering head and the seat pillar by an adjustable strap at the front and by a number of spiral springs at the rear. Like the rest of the bicycle this saddle looked most unusual and took some time to get used to, but the late A. W. Rumney, the keen clubman and writer on cycling topics at the time of the cycling boom, toured Europe and North Africa on a Dursley Pederson and it was his opinion that the saddle was the most comfortable available at the time and he, after all, had been in a position to know. There is a theory that Pederson had designed his 'space frame' solely as a vehicle for his hammock saddle but this does not seem likely as a diamond frame with a lowered top would have done just as well.

The only other notable diversion in frame design and one that was different for different's sake was the bamboo frame, and even that stuck to the diamond frame format. Solid male bamboo was used in place of steel tubes although the machine still had frame lugs to hold the bamboos together. The makers, who had the marvellous name 'The Bamboo Cycle Company' advertised it as 'better than steel' but didn't go on to say why and the cycling public was not bamboozled, but it did have a certain charm. Interestingly, an unrestored example of a Bamboo bicycle hangs from the ceiling of the Museum of British Road Transport in Coventry – according to their records the frame weighs 8½lbs – and another one was recently sold at auction for £1,150. One or two makers of racing bicycles experimented with wooden framed racers but didn't persevere with the idea. The motoring writer L. J. K. Setright neatly summed up the use of wood in engineering when he remarked that it 'was an excellent material for trees'.

By the turn of the century frame design was well advanced, and had been helped on the road to strength with lightness when in 1897 the young Alfred Reynolds invented the thin walled seamless steel tube with 'butted' or internally thickened ends and began the Reynolds' long association with the bicycle industry, although the industry had to wait another thirty eight years for Reynolds 531 tubing.

It was in the field of brakes and gears that there remained the most room for improvement. The most practical way of stopping any vehicle is to progressively slow down the rotation of its wheels, and on a bicycle this can best be done by pressing something onto the wheel rim. Until the pneumatic tyre came on the cycle scene, tyres had been very narrow and consequently rims were also narrow, leaving insufficient room for brakes to act upon, and these rims were not only too narrow, they were also the wrong shape due to the U or V section used for solid tyres. That only left the tyres themselves to provide a braking surface and what brakes there were just grabbed hold of them, leaving a lot to luck, and whatever extra retardation the rider could exert on the fixed wheel drive via the soles of his feet.

When pneumatic tyres came into general use they soon led to a solution of the braking problem as they were so much fatter than the solid, or the hollow tyres they superseded, and wheel rims became wider, leaving surface to spare for brake blocks to be pressed against, although for a while some manufacturers continued using the old fashioned spoon brake. One would have thought that such a practice would have led to immediate and spectacular tyre failure, but the spoon brake was so ineffective on this type of tyre that it caused very few problems, other than those usually associated with being unable to stop. By the early years of the twentieth century rim brakes were as efficient as they were commonplace.

Lack of interest may have been another factor that slowed the development of brakes, as most manufacturers' energies went into ways of making bicycles go faster, rather than means of arresting their progress. This was certainly true of the early motor industry which was, after all, made up mostly of ex-bicycle makers. Some work had been done on the 'back pedal' brake; a few manufacturers favoured it, whilst others preferred both types of brake to the same machine, but the back pedal brake was never very satisfactory as it was, and still is, difficult to control with any finesse. A Mr Kitchen of Manchester patented an air brake that was worked by a rubber bulb attached to the handlebars but there is no record of its being taken up commercially, and it is the rim brake and its derivatives that have come through to the present day, although the back pedal brake has made a comeback on the BMX bicycle.

In spite of James Starley's 'speed gear' on his 'Ariel' Ordinary of 1871 and some early 2-speed epicyclic gears on one or two of the other big wheelers it wasn't until the beginning of the 1900s that reliable multi-speed gears became available and the most successful of these was the Sturmey Archer hub gear of 1902, a 3-speed hub gear with free wheel on all gears that was straight away taken up by Raleighs and put into production.

The derailleur had been patented in 1899 but it wasn't a practical proposition until 1909. There had been some earlier attempts at this form of gearing, with Linley (of Linley & Briggs, the makers of the 'Whippet'), bringing out his 4-speed 'Protean' gear with an expanding chainwheel in 1894, and E. H. Hodgkinson's 3-speed 'Gradient' gear in 1896, both working on the principle of derailling the chain from one sprocket to another. For the time being, however, it was the hub gear that triumphed. There had of course been some previous attempts at that too, one as early on as 1883 with the Jay hub gear, followed by the Johnston hub gear twelve years later. As one might expect, Mikail

Pedersen offered a 3-speed hub gear on his Dursley Pederson in 1901 but it was left to Henry Sturmey and James Archer to perfect the system that is still with us today in 3- and 5-speed form.

A few of the 'up market' manufacturers, Rover and the Wilkinson Sword Company amongst them, offered shaft drive as an alternative to the chain, and Wilkinsons went so far as to claim that their shaft was a 'forged sword blade' although the advantages of that were not made clear. Nor were the advantages of shaft drives in general. It is true that they looked nice, were well lubricated, less messy and needed little adjustment, but on the other hand the machines were expensive, and heavier, and the shaft wasted power. The oilbath chain case was a cheaper, lighter and more efficient way of obtaining the same advantages. Had shaft drive been offered fifteen years earlier during the cycling boom it might have appealed to the nobility and gentry but by the early 1900s the nobility and gentry had lost interest in cycling.

By the outbreak of the First World War all the essential ingredients that go to make up the modern bicycle had been gathered together and vigorously stirred into various recipes that are still palatable today. And whilst it is true that the sports and racing bicycle has benefited from the appliance of science, it has been a gradual process – a steady improvement in design and materials along guide lines laid down all those years ago – the heavyweight roadster has changed very little. The 1983 version is only a little less dignified than its elegant Edwardian counterpart.

The mainstream of frame and component development may have been undramatic, though there have been many attempts to divert the course of that stream away from the diamond frame format, but even the Moulton bicycle with its 'cross frame' and novel suspension – the most recent and successful of all such attempts – was never a serious challenge to the supremacy of the conventional layout.

Nevertheless, over the last sixty years the quest for an alternative – and commercially viable – method of keeping a bicycle's wheels apart has exercised many keen minds, with the Italians and the French leading an upsurge of experimentation early in the 1930s.

The Italian effort was named Velocino, a short wheel based creation that looked a lot like a single tracked invalid carriage. The rider sat amongst the handlebars over a large rear wheel and progressed by turning the pedals that were placed over a tiny front wheel, an apparently unstable layout that had several drawbacks, offered no discernible advantages and contributed nothing to the advancement of bicycle design, although as a 'shopping' bicycle it achieved a certain popularity in Italy. There is a nicely restored Velocino in the superb Mark Hall Cycle Museum at Harlow, and despite its odd appearance, it is a very pleasant bicycle to ride.

The prime mover of the breakaway movement was the French Velocar, a recumbent design that featured 19″ wheels and a 69″ wheelbase that was road tested by *Cycling* in 1933. The tester remarked that whilst it was fast on the flat, it was sluggish uphill and tiring to ride, for instead of the legs hanging down in a naturally restful position they were stuck out in front of him in a manner that needed the constant support of the muscles.

In 1934 a French fast man named Faure gave the recumbent a boost when he covered an unpaced 27.75 miles in one hour on a very 'laid back' Velocar derivative. And Oscar Egg – the remarkable inventor of the ultra-light and vestigial Osgear derailleur still in use in the late 1940s – came out of retirement to break several records on a recumbent racer of his design.

All in all, 1934 was a good year for recumbents. The first English example, with 20″ wheels and a 62″ wheelbase was introduced by F. H. Grubb & Co. at the Motor Cycle and Cycle Show at Olympia, priced at £14/14 and *Cycling* printed a picture of Gracie Fields reclining on one. J. E. Sibbit, a well known Manchester sprinter built a recumbent, and another 'one-off' example appeared in the Southgate Club's '25', ridden by a time triallist named Frost. But Frost, or the recumbent, made a poor showing, covering less than half the distance before giving up.

There seems to have been a strange correlation between designing recumbents and gears, for the Cyclo Gear Company, makers of the effective and ingenious twin cable operated Cyclo derailleur, introduced their Cyclo-Ratio recumbent at the 1935 'Show'. Unlike the previous small wheeled design this had a 26″ rear wheel and the pedals were out on the end of the 'cross frame' that extended beyond the 20″ front wheel. The rider sat high in the air in a most relaxed posture, but the Cyclo-Ratio was anything but relaxing to ride for the rider's legs were inclined steeply uphill and the combination of a very high centre of gravity, a 36″ wheelbase and handlebars placed close to the rider's chest made it a difficult machine to control, and one that needed a strong nerve to get started.

The idea of seating the rider at more or less normal bicycle height may have been done to overcome the valid objection that road-going recumbents were difficult for other road users to see, an objection that is even more relevant today. There is an excellent example of the Cyclo-Ratio in the Mark Hall Museum together with two partially finished prototypes with 20″ wheels at either end and lower and more comfortable riding positions.

1935 also saw the introduction of the Triumph recumbent of which six were made, all still with us. The Triumph was a long, low, open framed bicycle with 20″ wheels, a raked back steering column with a steering wheel instead of handlebars, and a half saddle/half bucket seat arrangement. It was more of a recliner than a recumbent and the production figures suggest that it was not a commercial success. Neither was a short wheelbase 'Kneeler' that came out that same year. In this dangerously uncomfortable device, the pedals were on an outrigger well behind the back wheel, the rider lying along the machine holding onto a pair of extremely dropped handlebars. The saddle was agonizingly situated above the back wheel, and what shape it was is hard to imagine.

Not surprisingly, this freak posed no threat to the old diamond frame and it seems to have marked the end of an interesting era. The recumbent has recently surfaced again in America, but fascinating as they are, all the fifty-year-old objections to lying on one's back on a bicycle are as valid as they ever were.

In the late nineteen forties and early fifties, there was an outbreak of unconventional designs, of which the Baines 'Flying Gate', the Paris 'Galibier', and the 'Success' were the most innovative, all making use to some degree of small diameter twin tubes.

The 'Flying Gate' had a vertical tube from the bottom bracket to the top tube, and behind that a very short seat tube, attached at the top to the seat stays and at its base to two small twin tubes that ran diagonally from the rear dropouts to the junction of the vertical tube and top tube. It was said to be very rigid, yet at the same time very comfortable.

The Paris 'Galibier' was a short wheelbase design that had small diameter twin tubes in place of a single top tube, and a large diameter down tube that was, in fact, a cross tube bisecting the seat tube at its centre, leaving the bottom bracket out on a limb, relying only on the chain stays for any lateral stiffness. Needless to say the frame was rather 'whippy' although it was different and had a certain charm.

George Cushing's little known 'Success' was the most unusual of the three. It had a conventional head tube, and seat tube, connected by twin curving loops of tubing, $\frac{1}{2}''$ in diameter and cross braced at intervals, that also formed the seat stays and the chain stays. Road shocks were absorbed by the frame curves, and in terms of comfort and lateral rigidity the 'Success' was a success, but in spite of its title only twenty-six were ever made.

The only alternatives to the diamond frame that are presently available – 'folder' and 'shoppers' apart – are the Paris 'Galibier' from the recently reformed Paris Lightweight Cycle Company, and the triangulated twin tube frame from English Cycles, made of an unusual combination of Reynolds 531 and aero specification T45 tubing. Both are interesting, but it looks as though the diamond frame which has monopolized the market for almost 100 years will be with us for some time to come.

Chapter 9

A HISTORY OF TANDEMS &
TRICYCLES

Years ago, when children were not so much encouraged as expected to make their own amusements, a friend and I built a sort of temporary tricycle. It was constructed very quickly using my friend's father's nice new Rudge roadster and a nameless old iron of mine that we used for cycle speedway – which was to us what BMX is to little lads today. I say 'temporary' as it was rapidly dismantled the minute my mate's dad discovered it, and 'tricycle' because it had three wheels. True, the wheels were all in line instead of in the more conventional arrangement, but there were three of them and that, I suppose, must qualify it as a tricycle. It was astonishingly quick, and a most interesting thing to ride – the front forks of my old bike dropped onto the fortunately long rear spindle of the Rudge, so our 'trike' was all of 9′ long and had a pivot in the middle – and we got along much better after we'd thought of slackening off the expander bolt of the rear set of handlebars, which lessened a frightened back seat driver's contribution to the steering. This strange device was later the subject of a reader's letter to *Cycling* magazine – the writer, who seemed not to expect to be believed, mentioning that he had seen it being thrashed down Barnet Hill, flat out past the buses, with 'a charlie at the back, stoking'. That 'charlie' was me and I was very proud.

A little research reveals that we were by no means the first, the last, or the most ingenious of a long line of makers of unusual machines. Some of the things that people got up to a few years after the Battle of Waterloo quite beggar belief but many of these tricycles, or quadricycles, or whatever grandiose title the inventor had chosen, were in fact masterpieces of ingenuity and craftsmanship, however bizarre they may appear today.

The bicycle had already been paddled away slowly and unsteadily on the start of its 100 year journey to practicality, but to many people two wheels were not the answer. What they were striving for was a kind of horseless carriage, a pedal-powered version of the car, a versatile vehicle that was difficult to fall off, could be ridden or driven by both sexes with some degree of dignity, would carry people, pets and luggage and didn't kick, bite, shy or bolt, or consume huge quantities of hay.

To make a fair appraisal of their work one has to remember that these pioneers of personal transportation were badly hampered by the lack of many things. For instance they had no ball bearings, no chain drive, no gears, no light steel tubing, no means of welding things, no wire spoked wheels, no tyres, no aluminium alloys and no knowledge of steering geometry or aerodynamics. There was no fund of experience to draw upon, no one to turn to for advice, and to make things more difficult, the roads were terrible. All they had was a knowledge of wood and iron, and the crank axle, a tremendous enthusiasm, a capacity for work and a common desire to get rid of the horse.

In spite of all these handicaps their achievements were astonishing. The first essays on the lines of horseless carriages were absolutely vast and ridiculously heavy. Mr Revis of Cambridge – a good place for an inventor of horseless carriages to live, the countryside around being fairly flat – built a tricycle device that was 12' long with a pair of rear wheels 6' in diameter. This was tromped along by two large men trampling on treadles and Mr Revis claimed that it was capable of thirty miles an hour, which it might well have been, given luck and a fair wind, on a well surfaced road. According to a contemporary technical magazine this monster was called 'Aellopodes', and was exhibited in London in 1839 although it isn't made clear if it was driven from Cambridge to London and back. From all accounts it went well enough, but it was only an elaborate way of providing two men with a lot of hard work and very little else.

Also in 1839, a Mr Merryweather built a machine that he called a Pedomotive Carriage. It was much the same size as 'Aellopodes' but was propelled by only one man on a treadle. And in 1843 a Mr Williams produced his 'Passenger Propelled Locomotive Carriage'

– a contradictory sort of name – that he mysteriously claimed was suitable both for young men and for invalids. It was sheltered by rotating umbrella and was supposed to cruise at around 10mph.

Probably due to lack of communications, things happened more slowly in those days and ideas for such monstrous vehicles persisted, although one would have thought it obvious that the designers were flogging a dead horseless carriage. Some of the designs that appeared in the technical magazines devoted to DIY transport were quite fantastic but many of them were only designs and, sadly, were never made. None of them were quite as fantastic as the 'Celeremane' which was designed for fast running and looked a lot like an early lorry chassis with rear wheels five feet high. It was actually *rowed* along by four men, only two of whom faced forward – I wish I could truthfully say that they used oars and roared out shanties as they rumbled by – but the dull fact is that they used levers connected to a crank axle. The thing was steered from the back by a hardcase 'cox' and it all happened in 1869 by which time its builder really should have known better.

In fact by that late date many people did know better and the concept of the 'Manumotive' or 'Pedomotive Carriage' gradually died out as the realities of the power to weight ratio problem gradually sank in. One of these men was Willard Sawyer and he always had known better than to become involved with vast and lumbering contraptions.

Sawyer was a carpenter turned velocipede maker, the term velocipede encompassing not just the bicycle, but anything on wheels that was propelled by human feet. As early as 1845, seventeen years before the Michaux's came on the scene, he was established at 20, St James's Street, Dover as the world's first professional man powered vehicle maker. Sawyer was very successful and deservedly so. His machines were elegant, functional, and so nicely made that by 1858 he was able to advertise that he was 'under Royal and Imperial Patronage' having sold one to the Emperor of Russia and another to the Prince Imperial of France. He very nearly sold one to Prince Albert but Albert changed his mind at the last minute and bought a similar but inferior machine from Ward's of Leicester Square. What he paid for it isn't recorded but in 1851 a Sawyer Quadricycle cost £17/2/6 which can hardly have been too expensive for a man on a princely salary with bonuses and annual increments, so perhaps his wife just didn't like the colour. Whatever the reason, Willard

Sawyer must have been very disappointed to lose such a distinguished patron, but later on he did sell one to the young Prince of Wales.

Sawyer's speciality was single seater four wheelers with direct acting crank and treadle drive, and, to the modern mind accustomed to excellent roads and efficient bicycles, this might seem to be two wheels too many. One has to remember that the roads at that time were still poorly surfaced, bumpy and uneven, and that the bicycle had hardly progressed beyond the 'hobby horse'. It was still generally regarded, even by most of the makers, as little more than the toy from which it had sprung in the first place, and the kind of person who could afford a Sawyer velocipede was not keen to demean his social position.

In contrast to the bicycles of the day, Sawyer's machines were actually usable for quite long journeys. One was shown at the Great Exhibition of 1851 and Sawyer himself rode from Dover to Hyde Park for the occasion, an advertising exercise that paid off handsomely and attracted a lot of favourable attention. Sawyer sold quadricycles to buyers from all over the world, and when the exhibition buildings were taken down and re-erected as the Crystal Palace at Sydenham, Sawyer got the contract to supply machines to the Crystal Palace Company.

Some of Sawyer's customers covered enormous distances. The Honourable J. C. Skeffington for example rode 526 miles in twenty days on a tour of the West Midlands, the Peak District and East Anglia and was highly delighted with his machine, and a Henry Hill Hodgson rode his from London to Salisbury and back, covering sixty-two miles in one day.

On the debit side, in a letter to the *English Mechanic & Mirror of Science* magazine, another of Willard Sawyer's customers mentioned that in his opinion velocipedes were not much use for high speeds as the rattling and shaking over the poor roads would soon destroy the machine and that riding fast on a four wheeler 'requires the greatest attention' and 'sufficient road for safe steering'.

The problems of steering a speeding quadricycle did not just stem from the bad condition of the roads, although lurching and bouncing didn't help. Little was known about steering geometry, as self-centering steering on the principle soon to be advocated by a Mr Ackerman, and still in use on modern motorcars, had yet to be re-discovered. Actually, Ackerman the artist, famous for his prints, only held the English patents. The system had been invented in 1714 by George Lenkenburger, a German coach builder, but as being dragged along rather than driven does lend a vehicle some measure of directional stability, poor George had no success at all in selling the idea to his fellow coach builders and as nobody was interested the principle was shelved.

However, Sawyer's machines can't have been too nerve racking to ride quickly, and it wasn't instability that eroded their popularity but the introduction of the 'boneshaker' and the subsequent improvements to the bicycle.

From 1869 until 1877 the energies of bicycle builders and inventors were directed to developing the two wheeler but with the increase in the size of the front wheel and finally the introduction of the 'Ordinaries' with their gigantic front wheels, many peoples' interest turned to the tricycle and the tandem tricycle as being a safer and more dignified means of locomotion.

Unlike 'Aellopodes' and other early monsters the new generation of tricycles were for the most part not much bigger than bicycles and even the odd transitional model that appeared at this time looked lighter and less like a siege engine, but despite these advances the tricycle was still a breed apart. Tricycle makers seemed to be on the steering levers of a dilemma about the best way to arrange three wheels. Some had two wheels at the front, some had two wheels at the back, and the great James Starley's Coventry Lever Tricycle of 1876 had two steerable wheels in line, but some six feet apart, and a much larger wheel as an outrigger, whilst the rider or driver sat in the middle on what looked like a small park bench and operated the treadle drive to the big side wheel.

This layout looked odd and lopsided but having the advantage of only two tracks it only hit two thirds of the bumps and potholes, whereas a three tracked tricycle would seem to hit them all. What its other advantages were isn't clear but the design was an instant success and the Coventry Lever model was the first tricycle to be successfully put in production. This may explain why the Rudge Rotary, brought out two years later, looked very similar indeed, but with its superior chain drive it soon superseded the Starley machine.

When his Lever Tricycle was ousted from esteem, Starley, never a man to give up or waste a good idea, added another big wheel to the opposite side of the tricycle and invented the

'Sociable' quadricycle, on which two riders could sit sociably side by side, but it was not an unqualified success. With the two big wheels on a common crank axle revolving at the same speed, the machine was reluctant to turn into corners, but Starley cured this worrying tendency but cutting the crank axle in half. The new divided drive arrangement improved the cornering no end, but unless the riders synchronized their efforts very carefully, the modified 'Sociable' was then reluctant to go straight ahead, progressing in sickening swoops and upsets and the 'Thoroughly Irritating' might have been a more apt name for it.

One could be excused for thinking that the 'Sociable' wasn't one of Starley's better efforts, particularly as it had derived from a redundant tricycle that itself had been developed from a Ladies' model 'Ordinary' bicycle, that had a one-sided treadle drive to a markedly offset rear wheel. This was intended to be ridden side-saddle and definitely was not one of Starley's better efforts.

However, Starley cleverly overcame the steering problem by devising and patenting a form of differential that he called a 'double driving gear' and this system of drive was not only used by every subsequent tricycle but is still in use in the transmission of the modern car.

Starley introduced his differential gear in 1877 on his innovative and highly successful Salvoquadricycle which more than made up for past eccentricities. Not only did it have the new differential, it was the first machine ever to be fitted with continuous chain drive from a crank axle with pedals inserted in it, attached to a chain wheel, and steered via the small front wheel by a rack-and-pinion steering gear, another system still in use in the motor car.

Starley soon dropped the small back wheel, and the 'quad' from the title, and the Salvo became a tricycle, and when Queen Victoria bought one for her own use at Osborne, the firm of Starley Brothers became 'Tricycle Makers to Her Majesty the Queen' and their products the 'Royal Salvo Tricycles'.

This royal recognition was a fitting end to a distinguished career, for James Starley died shortly afterwards, leaving his sons and his now famous nephew John Kemp Starley to carry on with the prosperous business. Not only did the royal patronage benefit the Starleys, it benefited the whole tricycle industry, for if tricycling was good enough for our own dear Queen, it was good enough for the middle and the upper-middle classes. The upper class thought that both tricycles and the Queen were common.

The tricycle had three attractions for the middle classes.

Firstly, the 'fair sex' could ride them and this was important, and secondly, and even more important, was that tricycling was a pastime untainted by working class involvement as the working class simply couldn't afford to buy tricycles, a state of affairs that suited the new breed of tricyclists very nicely. The snootier of them took a very high moral tone and held the view that not only tricycles, but bicycles, and probably sex as well, were too good for the lower orders, and even the more liberal 'Don't call me Sir, my good man' kind of tricyclists regarded the bicyclists as a rough old lot and was all for having nothing at all to do with them. The bicyclists, who were largely upper-working and lower-middle class didn't think of themselves as untouchables and retaliated with mocking cries and accusations of spinelessness and toffee-nosed effeminacy. All in all, it was good clean class war fun of the kind that still goes on today in the Houses of Parliament.

The third attraction of the tricycle was that it was safer and easier to ride than the contemporary bicycle, which does go to show just how difficult and dangerous the 'Ordinary' bicycle was. Nowadays, the reverse is true and the tricycle, or 'trike' is thought of as difficult, and riding one quickly through corners can be an exciting business as they tend to tip over quite easily. To counteract the forces of gravity the rider needs to shift his weight to where it will do the most good and hang it over the side. It just was not possible to hang over the side of the big wheeled tricycles as the wheels would have got in the way, and there weren't any handlebars to hang on to. Also, it does seem doubtful whether the Victorian tricyclist went in for that kind of levity or that the wheels would have stood up to the strain if he had done so.

The reputation that the tricycle had for safety stemmed more from a staid style of riding than from any innate stability, and a lack of performance can only have helped. However pleasant it may have been to sit side by side on one's 'Sociable' with a heavily perspiring member of the 'fair sex' the seating arrangements were all wrong from an aerodynamicist's point of view, and the fact that no such profession existed at the time made not the least bit of difference. Most of the energy expended in cycling goes into overcoming wind resistance and it requires almost twice the input of energy to move an upright roadster along at 10mph as it does to move a sports model with drop handlebars along at the same speed, provided of course that the rider is using the drops and not sticking up like a sore thumb. This being the case, one can imagine the effort required to move a 'sociable', with its enormous frontal area, at anything above walking pace.

Aerodynamic efficiency or deficiency apart, the 'Sociable' also took up a lot of road and storage space but the thriving tricycle industry that had sprung up along with the popularity of the tricycle wasn't content to stick to any particular format until it had found the best one. There were twenty tricycle makers in Coventry alone and experiment and rapid advance was the order of the age.

The way round the problem of excessive wind resistance on a tricycle made for two was to place the riders in tandem. Many makers offered tandem tricycles which, whilst they were heavy (the Quadrant model weighed nearly a hundredweight), were much faster and required a lot less effort than the 'Sociable', although the riding position did inspire the old joke about the two chaps who were riding a tandem when a dog came out of a house and threw a bucket of water over them. In spite of such jibes, this form of tricycle worked very well and were capable of covering large mileages in a day. People even went on European tours on them.

It is interesting to speculate on the reasoning behind the introduction of the tandem arrangement, for while it is obvious to the present day observer that such an arrangement has considerable aerodynamic advantages, it is far from certain that this was realized at the time. If one looks at the shape of the early racing cars, which were mostly made by ex-bicycle makers, it is perfectly clear that not the slightest attempt has been made to cut down on frontal area, or to minimize drag. This suggests that twenty years earlier the significance of lessening wind resistance had not occurred to anyone.

The most probable reasons for the seating of riders one behind the other were that by doing so, one could then build a narrower machine which took up less road space, and – more important – would be easier to store. Several makers addressed themselves to the storage problem of tricycle ownership for people who had nowhere to put one, and Bayliss & Thomas came up with the solution of making one that could be folded. When it *was* folded, it looked like a bicycle with two big wheels well out of line, and this of course had no aerodynamic advantages at all. Another novel space saver was the dividable 'Sociable' quadricycle on which it was possible to halve the width by removing one of the large wheels thus reverting to the lighter Rotary layout for storage or solitary riding, and on many of the tandem tricycles it was possible to separate the front and rear halves to make them easier to store, although this of course made them shorter and not narrower and quite impossible to ride.

The solo tricycle was also immensely popular. There was no conventional layout, as no convention had yet been established and the numerous makers offered a plethora of models in a bewildering variety of forms. Some had one large wheel and two little ones in the Rotary layout, but most had two large wheels placed side by side. Some models pushed a small front wheel, some towed a small wheel along behind them and some had small wheels in both those places. Some had lever drive, some had a treadle drive, and some had pedals, a chainwheel and a chain. Some were front steerers and some were rear steerers. The only thing they all had in common was that they were all indirectly steered, until 1886 when the Starley brothers came up with their 'Psycho' model. This strange name for a tricycle implied, no doubt unintentionally, that one had to be funny in the head to ride one.

The 'Psycho' had handlebars directly connected to a large front wheel, and chain drive to the back axle. This machine is said to have been another Starley family 'first' and to have heralded the ultimate form of the modern tricycle but to some extent the very pretty 'Quadrant' of 1882 had beaten them to it with central chain drive to the rear axle, and handlebar, but indirect, steering to a single front wheel.

Another interesting machine was the Singer of 1879 which looked like, and indeed may have been, a three wheeled version of Lawson's first 'Safety' bicycle. The tricycle, like the bicycle, was still stuck with the huge driven wheel due to a lack of suitable gearing, but in this symmetrical and graceful design the large wheel was at the back, with two smaller wheels in front, and whereas the Lawson 'Crocodile' was not a visual triumph, the tricycle was most attractive, though it was soon superseded.

The passing over of the Lawson/Singer single rear wheel format was a great pity, for it may well have been the way that the tricycle should ideally have developed and it is hard to understand why it evolved as it did, with one wheel at the front and two at the back. One wheel at the back was, and is, ample for transmitting the power output available and doesn't require the complication,

166

weight, and expense of a divided drive or differential, while two wheels at the front give far greater stability. The Kendrick racing 'trike' of the 1930s was built on these lines but may not have been a commercial success as the layout never caught on, probably because it didn't look quite as attractive as what has come to be regarded as the conventional wheel arrangement.

By the early 1880s the ridiculous class war between cyclist and tricyclist was over. A common enthusiasm is a great leveller and they had forgotten their differing backgrounds. They belonged to the same clubs, competed against one another, and went on club runs together, but the tricycle faded away over the next decade. The success of the 'safety' bicycle that brought about the great cycling boom of the 1890s dictated the future form of the tricycle, and knocked the quadricycle on the head once and for all. Although each fresh development of the two wheeler was immediately mirrored in the three wheeler, ironically it was the success of the 'safety' bicycle that all but killed off the tricycle. Almost anybody of either sex could safely ride a 'safety' and no sooner had the tricycle been perfected – some of the tricycles of the 1890s were really beautiful – than it was virtually redundant, although it has always retained a small but enthusiastic following down to the present day. The only form of tricycle that continued to enjoy a ready, if specialized market was the heavy and durable commercial delivery machine which invariably had two wheels at the front. These were certainly in use long after the end of the Second World War, although I doubt if their riders could honestly be described as tricycle enthusiasts.

During the sad decline of the tricycle the two wheeled tandem was born, though it was never to be as popular as the tricycle had been during its elitist heyday. The tandem was a latecomer. It hadn't been practical to make a tandem version of the 'Ordinary' or Penny Farthing. It would have been a nightmarish machine for obvious reasons, and as far as is known nobody was silly enough to try, but in spite of being born into a good family with all the advantages of years of breeding, the tandem went through some unattractive phases before it grew up and settled down.

The first tandem two wheeler was the Beeston Humber, a strange device unsuitably based on a 'dwarf Ordinary' bicycle with the underslung 'Kangaroo' pedal and chain drive on either side of the wheel beneath the hub. One rider sat in front of the vertical forks and the other just behind them; the pedals had long extensions fore and aft so that both men could operate the same set, and the machine was probably quite fast with an excellent power to weight ratio. It is not known how many of these things were made, but I would have thought not many. It would have been difficult to control with all that weight over the front wheel, and the foremost rider was very precariously placed.

The first tandem to be based on the 'Safety' models appeared in 1885 when Dan Albone, the Biggleswade bicycle maker and publican, and his friend A. J. Wilson took one of John Kemp Starley's second series 'Safety' bicycles and fitted it with a saddle in front of the steering head and a 'dwarf Ordinary' front wheel with the same 'Kangaroo' drive arrangement that had been used on the earlier Beeston Humber. This creation had all the disadvantages of the Humber, plus an unsynchronized two wheel drive which must have added to the difficulties of controlling a machine with a heavy man sitting over the front wheel, like the groceries on a delivery boy's bicycle, exerting pressure first on one side then on the other. In fairness to Dan Albone, who was a clever engineer, this first 'Safety' tandem was only an experiment, and may in fact have been a joke, and when he built his own machine in the following year, he came much closer to the ultimate tandem format.

The hallmark of the early tandem was instability, brought on by a reluctance on the part of the manufacturer to make them any longer than a standard bicycle. This may have been a praiseworthy attempt to keep down weight and cost, but in practice it resulted in some very odd machines. This economy of length was taken to extremes in the Premier Tandem Dwarf Safety of 1887, a design that had a lot in common with American cars of the late 1940s, in as much as it was difficult to discover which way it was intended to travel. It had a much shorter wheelbase than a normal 'Safety' bicycle, with front forks at the back as well as at the front (the fork blades curving away in opposite directions). The wheels, which were of equal size, were placed so close together that it was only just possible to squeeze a bottom bracket in between them, and there was absolutely nowhere for the second man to sit, other than right up the sharp end, like a figurehead, a vulnerable position shared with a set of pedals that were suspended ahead of the front wheel. The impression that the Premier Tandem Dwarf Safety might suffer from bad weight distribution, unless ridden by two dwarfs was borne out by a small outrigger wheel under the foremost bottom bracket. Just to make things interesting it was steered by the back wheel.

It didn't take manufacturers long to realize that the short wheelbase tandem was a non-starter and the long wheelbase form, similar to the modern tandem, very soon evolved, although some makers rather over-reacted and made them much longer than was necessary. One of these was the Rudge Tandem of 1895 which was an enormous length and, like several similar models, was intended for a lady rider at the front. This was not an early warning of the erosion of male dominance, as these tandems could be steered from the back seat.

The long wheelbase tandem was unavoidably heavy. A modern lightweight built with Reynolds 531 tubing and all alloy components weighs around 40lbs, and the Victorian/Edwardian tourer which had none of these advantages must have weighed more than double that amount. Massive as they were, they weighed no more than two separate bicycles and had only half the wind resistance, so with two good men on board they could outrun a solo on an undulating road, and were a great deal faster downhill, although they were a burden going uphill.

As soon as the wind resistance and weight advantages were realized the way was open for all sorts of extravagances. Tandems built to carry three were not uncommon and were probably quite rapid and pleasant to ride, if a little unhandy in traffic, but some manufacturers literally went to ridiculous lengths and catalogued machines that would carry up to eight riders. In 1896 the American Orient Cycle Company actually made a bicycle capable of carrying ten which had the ugly title the 'Decemtuple' and could hardly have been a serious proposition even for a man with a large family, and this folly has only recently been surpassed by the 'Quatrodecimalopede', built in 1967 from large diameter tubes and bits of motorcycle. This absurdity took fourteen at one sitting and now occupies 30′ of wall space (that could be put to much better use) in The Museum of British Road Transport.

It was as a track-pacing machine that the multi-seater bicycle really came into its own and in 1898 Ariel's even went so far as to build a Quintuplet for this purpose, minimising the wheelbase as much as possible by placing the rearmost rider behind the centre of the back wheel. They must have been a stirring sight as they were thrashed around Herne Hill and other tracks but they only lasted until primitive large capacity motorcycles were available to take over their duties.

Even these extraordinary tandems were upstaged by Singer and their Military model, which was in fact two tandems fixed together to form a monstrous quadricycle and supposed to be capable of carrying large numbers of soldiers, although whether bravely into battle, or just back from the pub was not made clear. It would certainly have been of no use whatsoever over difficult terrain.

One or two manufacturers offered an alternative to the tandem by reviving the old 'sociable' system applied to two wheels and this involved the riders being suspended on either side of a central bicycle like rather tall loads slung over a donkey, with the difference that donkeys tend not to fall over and bicycles do. They must have been difficult machines to get started and even more difficult to ride solo, and with the same large frontal area problem of the three and four wheeled 'Sociables', it is not surprising that they never became popular.

Throughout the history of the bicycle, the tricycle and the quadricycle, there runs a rich vein of inventiveness and eccentricity directed to developing passenger carrying vehicles that never did catch on, fascinating to the historian but otherwise unsuccessful. This is because all the inventors of such machines came up against the fact that – with the power available for overcoming friction, wind resistance and the weights involved – there was no place, at least not in the Western Hemisphere, for passengers on man-powered vehicles. Anybody boarding a two, three, or four-wheeler in company with others must expect to do his or her share of the work.

The bicycle rickshaw apart, and arrangements for carrying children, the quest died out as soon as the motorcycle combination and the cheap car became available but as late as 1912 even reputable manufacturers were still striving for the unattainable.

In that year Triumph introduced their bicycle combination, an upright tourer with a sidecar. It wasn't a very big sidecar and, being made of wickerwork, didn't weigh a lot when used only as a shopping basket, but light sidecar outfits tip over very easily. This tendency to overturn on corners could be cured by carrying an adult passenger but hills and headwinds quickly killed enthusiasm for this lop sided kind of transport.

In much the same category was the Raleigh Carefree, another handsome and heavy tourer that came with a substantial two wheeled trailer complete with a wickerwork armchair on the top.

This is supposed to have been very popular with courting couples but dragging a well built young woman about the countryside wouldn't have been everyone's idea of love's young dream, so the intention may have been to sublimate a gentleman's desires. Perhaps love, and cyclists, were stronger in those days, but even so there was more than a remote possibility of the trailer getting out of hand on long descents, finally parting company with the bicycle, and an event like that would test the sweetest nature. The only good thing that can honestly be said for this ensemble is that when a romance ended, or the love object was in the cottage hospital recovering from its injuries, the trailer could be easily removed.

There was a brief resurgence of the 'Sociable' tricycle in 1914 bit it didn't survive the war for the shape that the tricycle was to take in the future had been established by 1895 or even ten years earlier. The successful tandem was only a development of the 'Safety' bicycle, and the same could be said of the tricycle. Certainly from 1895 onwards nothing really dramatic happened to either of them, and their subsequent history is a matter of refinement in parallel with the bicycle rather than radical change. Both have become lighter with the introduction of lightweight steel tubing and alloy fittings, and more efficient with the gradual improvement in gears, brakes and tyres. Both the tricycle and the tandem are with us today in a form that the late Victorian and Edwardian designer and rider would recognize and very much admire.

It might now be possible to successfully build a muscle-powered 2+2 car with three or four wheels that would carry two people, two children and luggage, and so achieve what the pioneers were striving after all those years ago. Mike Burrow's recumbent tricycle, the 'Windcheetah', is a step along the way, although I'm not sure that I'd want to pedal a streamliner, with wife, dogs and shopping, along a fast main road infested with huge lorries.

Nevertheless, when the oil runs out someone may resurrect the horseless carriage.

Chapter 10

AN OUTLINE OF THE SOCIAL HISTORY

Freedom of mobility, by whatever means, is so much taken for granted these days that it is hard to imagine what a profound, liberating and far-reaching effect the bicycle had on Victorian England and the rest of the more or less civilized world. The invention of the 'célérifère' at the end of the eighteenth century caused a tremendous sensation, for although it was only a toy a means of self-propelled transport, however primitive, was almost literally a significant step forward in a world that had hitherto been condemned to the limitations of walking, or the numerous inconveniences of the horse.

When the novelty had worn off, the inadequacies of the 'célérifère' began to be realized – an unsteerable, unstoppable, and uncomfortable vehicle does have its drawbacks as serious transport – and the craze soon died out, only to be revived strongly but briefly several times over the next sixty years in Britain, France and America, usually sparked off by some fresh innovation. These crazes were for the most part confined to the better off sections of society as the worse off were too occupied with scraping a living. Fashionable bicycling schools sprang up and made money for a few years until the machines were once more found wanting and the craze died away.

During those eighty years the two wheeler was called many things. In France it changed from 'célérifère' to 'vélocifère' to 'draisienne' and then to 'velocipede' whilst in England it went from 'celeripede' to 'dandy-horse' or 'hobby-horse' to 'bone-shaker' then to 'ordinary' and finally to the 'safety bicycle'. Each new name marked a fresh innovation in design or construction but it wasn't until the introduction of pedal drive in 1861 that the public, who had been dragging their feet for so long, began to take enough sustained interest in two wheeled machines for development to cease progressing in fits and starts and to steadily gather momentum.

Although there were buyers enough to make the manufacture of 'boneshakers' a viable proposition – profitable enough to create competition which in turn spurred development – it wasn't until the introduction of the 'Safety' models in the mid-1880s that the bicycle really took off and became a rather unlikely instrument of social and technical upheaval.

Before that, it went through the 'Ordinary' or 'Pennyfarthing' period which brought to a head a great deal of latent hostility, but which laid the foundations of club cycling and the cycle enthusiast movement, and brought personal transport and unprecedented freedom to anyone fit enough and brave enough to cope with the very real dangers of accident and assault.

The Pickwick Bicycle Club was formed in Hackney in the East End of London in 1870, starting a movement which very quickly snowballed so that by 1874 there were seven clubs in London alone and twenty-two in the rest of the country. Four years later that number had grown to sixty-four clubs in London and 125 elsewhere and by 1882 there were over 500 clubs centred in towns throughout the land.

The hostility shown to bicyclists by the non-bicycling public was a major factor in the rapid growth of cycling clubs – the old 'safety in numbers' theory being uppermost in riders' minds. But it is also true that the behaviour of many clubmen aggravated the public, particularly in the country districts. Country people still have a certain reserve about strangers and nineteenth-century rural England was much quieter and a lot more insular than it is today. Not that the cyclists were early Hell's Angels, but they were over exuberant. The sudden and noisy arrival of a cycling club on a Sunday afternoon must have been a startling event for a village, rather like being invaded by Martians. The members tended to be irritatingly pleased with themselves and instead of just turning up quietly they rode in at high speed perched high up on peculiar machines, and to make matters worse they wore uniforms and announced their arrival with rude noises from bugles, so it is really small wonder that they were not made welcome. Later on, in the 1870s as more and more people rode bicycles the country people became quite used to incursions of townees, the inns and the local shops did well and the antagonism quickly died away.

It was the Pickwick Club that started the uniforms and the idea spread rapidly. This rather unhealthy para-militarism seems more Prussian than English, but the uniforms were partly practical and partly an expression of a certain understandable pride and elitism, that bordered on arrogance, of the young men who rode the elegant high wheeled machines of the day. The 'Ordinary' bicycle was in fact very dangerous, and to master one needed both courage and style. With their twitchy handling, vestigial road holding and inefficient brakes they would have been dangerous on well made-up roads. On the roads of the time they were lethal, but that didn't bother the young men very much. It would be interesting, if ghoulish, to know what the accident figures were but no records were kept, although by all accounts the injury rate was high. In spite of the drawbacks there is no doubt that the 'Ordinary' was very exhilarating and satisfying to ride, so much so that long after the introduction of the greatly superior if much less impressive 'Safety' bicycle many riders carried on with the 'Ordinary', if only for the view.

To the pioneer cyclist each ride out into the country was high adventure. There were very few maps to be had and they literally rode off into the unknown, not quite like the crew of the Starship 'Enterprise' perhaps, boldly going where no man had gone before, but certainly to go where very few men on bicycles had been. There was very little information about the state of the roads. Near towns these were sometimes macadam – a solid foundation of broken stone that had been watered and rolled to form a smooth hard surface – but many were only tracks cut in the chalk, horribly dusty in the summer and rutted and horribly slippery in winter or wet weather, although not as slippery as the macadam. Riding high in the air on solid tyres in such conditions, especially on a windy day, required both nerve and skill. A loose gravelled surface must have been quite restful by comparision. There were a few good roads – the London to Portsmouth route for instance which was very popular with riders – but mostly they were terrible. The railways had all but killed the stagecoaches and as a consequence the roads had been neglected and were in a much worse state than they had been forty years before. It took the development of the motorcar to bring about a marked improvement. Nevertheless Britain was largely unspoilt and very beautiful and the riders revelled in their new found freedom to explore it.

In spite of the primitive state of the roads, and the similar state of the art of bicycle making, the riders of 'Ordinaries' covered great distances. As early as 1873 three members of the Middlesex club rode the 800 miles from Land's End to John O' Groats in exactly a fortnight, an average of nearly sixty miles a day, and met with surprisingly little unpleasantness along the way. This ride received a lot of publicity from the newspapers, all of it pro-bicycle, and the *Daily Telegraph* pointed out that it could not have been done in the time on horseback.

With the coming of the railways and then of the bicycle, the poor horse was having a very bad time, which seems rather unfair after centuries of service. An ordinary sort of a horse and an 'Ordinary' bicycle cost much the same to buy, but the bicycles cost much less to run and as an efficient means of getting about without fouling the streets the bicycle had the town dwellers' vote. Most cyclists lived in the new suburbs around the big towns and had nowhere to keep a horse anyway, even if they had been so inclined.

At weekends the clubs met and went for long rides. These were all-male affairs, for the ladies hadn't taken to the indignity and dangers of sitting high up astride a huge wheel, and this aversion helped to spur on the development of the tricycle so that they too could take part. During the week a gregarious clubman could enjoy a full social life that revolved round the bicycle. The antagonism of some magistrates, some policemen, and some of the general public turned cyclists into a new kind of brotherhood and that attracted new members. Many people joined clubs as much for the companionship as for the pleasure of riding, and cycling flourished.

Cycle racing was flourishing also. People had raced boneshakers. People had even raced 'célérifères' back in the late eighteenth century, but the rakish 'Ordinary' was a natural for racing.

The first official races, organized by both cycling and athletic clubs, took place on the road, not as massed start events (it was assumed that the police wouldn't tolerate that), but as handicap events with riders starting in handicap order. Naturally the back markers gradually caught up with the others, bunches were formed, and if the handicapper had got his sums right sixty or more riders went pounding across the finishing line all at the same time. The police weren't too keen on that, either, and neither were the public if they happened to get in the way.

These races attracted large crowds and special tracks were soon built, not so much to avoid provoking the police and other objectors, although they did have that fortunate effect, as to capitalize on the upsurge of interest in bicycle racing by enclosing a paying audience and excluding the non-paying public. 5,000 people paid to watch a fifty mile race at the Wolverhampton track in 1874, between two of the stars of the day, John Keen and David Stanton, and in October of that year, at the Lillie Bridge track in West London, a large crowd was present to see Stanton beat Keen in a 106 mile race. Stanton averaged just under $13\frac{1}{4}$mph, which may not sound very fast now, but which was thought to be fast at the time. One has to remember that at that early date the 'Ordinary' was still very heavy and in spite of the huge wheel the direct drive gave the effect of being very low geared. A 50inch wheel gave a 50inch gear, so to speak, and not many front wheels were larger than that.

Despite the success of track racing there were a great many racing cyclists who persisted with racing on the road, and the 'massed start' event became increasingly popular until in 1883 the police lost patience and began to turn ugly, prosecuting the participants for 'riding and driving furiously to the common danger', a charge that accurately summed up their sporting activities. As a result the NCU, the governing body of all cycle racing in Great Britain, decided to keep the peace and ban all road racing, a ban that was Britain's loss and the Isle of Man's gain. Time trialling crept back in the 1890s when the attitude of the authorities had changed for the better, but the ban on 'massed start' events on the road remained in force until the colourful British League of Racing Cyclists rebelled and held a 'massed start' race over open roads in 1942. Road racing proved to be just as popular as it had been sixty years earlier and by 1952 even the stuffy old NCU had been forced into organizing such races. In 1959 that conservative body merged with the flamboyant 'League' to form the British Cycling Federation, which has done so much to further the sport and organizes such events as the two week Tour of Britain.

The top riders of the 1870s were tremendously popular, their fame greatly enhanced by an enthusiast's press that sprang up with such titles as the *Bicycle Journal*, *Bicycling News* and *Bicycling Times*. Although these periodicals were rather short lived (the *Bicycle Journal* only lasted two years) they did a great deal to glamorize the riders and to stimulate the sport, and the sport stimulated the development of the bicycle.

Commercialism never crept into bicycle racing. It was there from the very beginning. Bicycle designers and manufacturers, many of whom were themselves enthusiastic cyclists, were quick to realize the beneficial effect on sales brought by racing successes and they hired riders to demonstrate their products in the best possible light. Here again the enthusiastic press helped to expand the cycling movement by reporting the races, which attracted newcomers, and by giving, or more accurately selling, the proud manufacturers somewhere to advertize their successes.

The bicycle makers were soon to discover that 'racing improves the breed' and that discovery hastened the end of the 'Ordinary'. It is true that racing first honed the 'Ordinary' to the peak of perfection, as 'Ordinary' bicycles went, and no sooner was it perfected than it had to go. The inconveniences and hazards attendant upon the huge wheel, and the perilous weight distribution could never be overcome and were holding cycling back from becoming a truly popular movement.

The true 'Ordinary' clubmen were scornful about all the ingenious and well meaning attempts to lower the bicycle's riding position. They could afford to be unimpressed when the rider of an Ellis 'Facile' with a 46″ front wheel rode 924 miles on the old 'end to end' proving ground in just under a week. His front wheel after all was only 4″ smaller, but what they thought about a 38″ wheeled 'Facile' completing the distance in only eight days and fifteen hours isn't recorded. They sneered at the 'Safety' bicycles and called their riders 'effeminate', but racing got the graceful 'Ordinary' in the end, for when the 'Safeties' defeated the 'Ordinaries' in all kinds of racing, and time after time, the diehards climbed down and the big wheel was dead.

By the time the 'Safety' bicycle was safely established and here to stay, the cyclist's lot had become a happy one (the riders of 'Safety' bicycles called themselves cyclists as 'bicyclists' were the riders of 'Ordinary' bicycles). The Bicycle Touring Club had changed its name to the Cyclist Touring Club for the very same reason, and although the roads were no better than before, the CTC, acting on information received from its numerous members, was able to advise riders about road conditions, and spent much time and money posting warning notices on dangerous hills, saving riders the trouble of discovering the dangers for themselves.

In 1878 the CTC had 144 members. In 1879 it went forth and multiplied and by the end of that year there were over 800, and by the middle of 1880 the membership had increased wonderfully to 2,629. It went on increasing until in 1887 there were 22,000 card-carrying cyclists. 1887 also marked the occasion of the CTC becoming a registered company, an event that strengthened its hand in the courts and empowered it to issue writs, a useful weapon in the fight against persecution. The breakthrough came in the following year when the Club influenced an amendment in a local government bill, inserting a clause that gave the bicycle legal status as a 'carriage', subject to the same laws as all other carriages, which at least put a stop to the invocations of repressive medieval laws by pompous policemen and malevolent magistrates.

The Club had arrangements with hotels throughout the country to provide respectable accommodation at reasonable rates, and similar arrangements with restaurants to provide cyclists with wholesome meals at predictable and acceptable prices. There were literally hundreds of cycling clubs keen to welcome new members and cycling was fashionable, exciting and innovative with new models appearing almost weekly. Never before in the history of mankind had so many people such astonishing freedom to go where they pleased – and so cheaply.

As cycling became increasingly widespread in the social sense – up to the advent of the 'Safety' bicycle it had been an almost exclusively middle class movement in which men had pre-dominated, although some nicely brought up middle class girls had become quite keen about tricycles – so the opposition to it diminished. The shape of the 'Safety' bicycle, which kept a long low profile in contrast to the arrogant image of the 'Ordinary' helped a great deal, as did the fact that almost anyone with their full complement of limbs and faculties could easily learn to ride a 'Safety'.

By the 1890s the great cycling boom was in full swing with both sexes of all classes, although competitive cycling for women was not encouraged – and was in fact further away than the franchise – and *Cycling* magazine complained that there were very few racing men of good social position. On the continent cyclists were free to hold road races that had established cycle racing as the national sports of France, Belgium and Italy but in Britain the ban on all road racing had given track racing, and football, a boost and ultimately spared us from the cycling hooligan. Many of the first generation of cycle tracks had been small, flat and inadequate but the new tracks that were coming along were suitable for much higher speeds, being larger and well surfaced, with banked corners.

One of the few racing men of good social position was the Honourable C. S. Rolls who won his half blue whilst at Trinity College, Cambridge, for his wholehearted efforts at cycle racing and who was later to become half of the firm of Rolls Royce Ltd. He often graced the track at Herne with his presence at the handlebars of a pacing triplet as late as 1896 when the craze for a little languid cycling was dying out amongst the upper classes.

There was nothing languid about C. S. Rolls's honourable efforts at the helm of a track bike or 'triplet', although he was soon to desert two wheels in favour of four. The pacing 'triplet', 'quadruplet' and even the 'quintet' was a phenomenon of late Victorian and early Edwardian track racing and were extensively used for paced events until the perfecting of suitable rapid and reliable motorcycles changed the name of the game to Motor Paced racing. A few of these enormous, primitive and powerful machines, or some very similar, were still to be seen at Herne Hill long after the end of the Second World War.

The replacement of muscles by motorcycles was a great shame, particularly so in an environment dedicated to cycling. These lengthy two wheelers must have been very spectacular, powered along as they were by teams of professional riders sponsored by such firms as Dunlop, and others. It is well known that a good sporting tandem energetically ridden will see off most solo riders, simply because of the power to weight and wind resistance ratio, and it is easy enough to imagine the staggering performance of a stark 'quintet' stoked by five well built young men in a hurry, and the sight and sound of several 'quintets' on the track at one time providing shelter for a similar number of famous 'crack' riders must have been a stirring experience that it would be difficult to forget.

In this chapter I have skipped over the great bicycle boom of the 1890s as we went into it briefly in chapter 8. Triggered off by the introduction of the 'Safety' bicycle and encouraged by the re-invention of the pneumatic tyre, the boom had run out of steam by the turn of the century and over the next ten years interest in cycling dwindled. In America, where the boom had boomed more loudly if not quite for so long, and a million bicycles were made each year, things were also in decline. At Crystal Palace, Herne Hill and other tracks racing went on much the same as usual, the competitors as keen as ever but the huge crowds that had made large cash prizes possible had begun to melt away. The sales of bicycles fell steadily and far too many bicycles chased too few buyers and many manufacturers were forced into liquidation or moved on to making cars. The excitement of it all was definitely over and the bicycle had become mundane.

The backbone of the bicycle clubs had been the middle classes, but it turned out not to be bicycles that they were keen on so much as the freedom and convenience of having their own transport, and they defected to the motor car as soon as cars became available. The middle class had had the time and money to go cycle touring, the working class had neither. With low wages and the twelve hour day, and not much in the way of holidays, they had few opportunities for lengthy rides and although they continued cycling it was only to the works, and back, with jaunts into the country on a Sunday. Bicycles were no longer 'smart', and had begun to acquire an 'image' of being more suited for cheap transport than for pleasure.

The membership of the CTC accurately reflected the trends. There was a bit of a hiccup between 1887 and 1894 when membership had fallen – nobody could quite work out why for the bicycle was on the up and up – but from 1894 the Club gathered momentum and new members until five years later there were some 60,000 cyclists on the books. From 1899 the rot set in again and renewals and applications fell away until in 1918 the numbers had reached a record low at 8,546, although that figure is a misleading indication of its state of health as many of the 50,000 members it had lost had been killed in the First World War.

With the abolition of the twelve-hour day which gave the working man more freedom, leisure cycling picked up again so that by 1927 the CTC was well again with 25,000 and more members, but the peaceful days of pre-war cycling on empty roads had gone forever.

However, the clubman of the 1920s did have one great advantage not enjoyed by his pre-war counterparts and that advantage was the roads, which were so much better surfaced, and although the riders of the day complained about the stink and noise of cars and lorries, traffic was in fact minimal by modern standards and speeds were low, and it was the demands of the motoring public and the lorry owners that brought about better roads.

Cycling in this country in between the wars was fun, by all accounts – photographs of cyclists on a club run, innocently enjoying the rural peace of an English countryside still to a large extent unspoiled, always show the riders smiling happily – and yet the social history of cycling in that period seems extremely dull. Historians gloss over it with a few facts and lots of figures, performances in time trials by riders long since dead or faded from the scene. They mention the Road Traffic Acts of 1930 and of 1934 which eroded cyclists' freedom by forbidding them to ride more than two abreast, made it unlawful to carry more than one person on a bicycle unless specifically constructed for that purpose, and required a cyclist using a red reflector instead of a rear lamp to carry a white patch on the rear mudguard. These measures were thought very shocking. They finish off by mentioning that the first cycle-path in Britain, all $2\frac{1}{2}$ miles of it was built beside the Western Avenue, in the suburbs of West London, in 1935, and then pass on gratefully to something more interesting.

There must have been much more to it than that 'quiet enjoyment' on a simple private level. The great days of the bicycle were over. All the thought, hard work and ingenuity that had gone into developing the tricycle and bicycle, the wire spoked wheel, the free wheel clutch, ball bearings, variable speed gears, the differential and live axle, seamless steel tubing, the re-discovery of the Ackerman principal of steering three and four wheeled vehicles, and much, much more were being applied to developing the car and motorcycle, and to some extent the aeroplane. Many of these machines were very beautiful indeed. Motor racing in the 1930s had an atmosphere of glamour never experienced before or since. In the air the disasters and excitements of the Schneider Trophy races caught the public's fancy. The railways brought in even faster streamlined trains and huge Ocean liners raced each other to America. There were airship disasters, record breaking flights, jazz, wars, depression.

In contrast to all that the ordinary bicycle was very ordinary. The machine that had brought unprecedented freedom to the masses and hastened technical advance was taken very much for granted and considered *passé*. For all that, 1.6 million bicycles were sold in Britain during 1935, a record only recently surpassed, so cycling wasn't in decline, it simply wasn't fashionable. But millions rode their bikes to work and keen cyclists went on cycling, enjoying their racing, touring, or pottering about the lanes, trying not to dwell too much on international events and prophecies of doom and gloom. The black tights and the black alpaca jackets of the pre-war time triallist seem to typify the period.

When most of the gloomy prophecies did come to pass and war broke out in Europe yet again, the bicycle saw little active service on the British side, even less than in the First World War – not surprisingly in view of the greatly increased use of motor vehicles.

Use was also made of cycle orderlies to carry messages, a thankless and a dangerous form of cyclo-cross, but the half-baked strategist's vision of regiments of cyclists riding down the enemy on roadster bicycles was never put into practice. By the late twenties even the 25th Cyclists Battalion were serving in Afghanistan without their bicycles.

Nevertheless, the idea did give rise to the folding military bicycle. BSA won the contract to supply the army and in 1915 began producing an uncouth looking machine capable of surviving all abuse, except, perhaps, a direct hit. The same idea was trotted out again in 1940 and once again the British Small Arms Company obliged, this time with a lighter version for use by paratroopers, amongst others. With its curved tube construction it was almost graceful. There was also a heavyweight non-folding military machine that was in fact a trademan's bicycle painted khaki. Many of them were lugged ashore on D-Day and did see some kind of service, if not in the 'Death or Glory, Charge of the Bike Brigade' situations originally envisaged when the cyclists units were first formed back in the 1880s.

There seems nowadays to be a notion that cycling turned up its toes and went into a coma immediately the war had ended. Certainly it went into a decline as soon as people could afford to buy cheap cars but in the late 1940s and the early fifties cycling was booming once again. Dismal as parts of the industrial north had been in the depression, they had not been as depressing as the general dreariness of post-war Britain. When Orwell wrote *1984*, his intention was to call it *1948* – his contention was that 'Big

Brother' was already with us – and so exactly did the book catch the general atmosphere that his publishers, for sound commercial reasons, didn't like the title and pleaded with Orwell to reverse the order of the last two digits.

As if in rebellion against all officially fostered drabness the British League of Racing Cyclists, who had been active in the war years, began to exert their influence for brighter cycling, pushing the NCU – which had been tugging its forelock to authority for far too long, even insisting that clubs held time trials at ungodly hours in order not to attract too much attention – into organizing massed start racing on the road after the continental pattern. The 'League' also went in for brightly coloured clothing and happily that caught on; to see a group of BLRC riders on a training run was rather like watching the Tour de France thrash by. The big names in lightweight bicycles began to paint their products in some pretty striking colours, and some – Paris Cycles were the ones that set the fashion – began to use 'flamboyant' finishes, all the colours of the rainbow merging into one another in a lovely, vulgar, vibrant riot.

At the weekends the roads were full of cycling clubs, and not much else. Supporters of the 'League' and of the NCU yelling good natured insults at each other, and both groups yelling 'tuggo' at members of the CTC, many of whom were elderly and not amused. Most weekday evenings groups of racing men – spare tubes and cycle pump rolled up inside a cape, or the previous week's *Cycling* – went pounding round the lanes on their own chosen training loops, often finishing a rapid ride in company with several groups from other clubs as they converged on a cafe used as a meeting place by cyclists, sprinting the last half mile to determine who would buy the tea. On one occasion large numbers of us met by chance at Hatfield, then on the A1, the old Great North Road, and the 'tearup' for the Marshmoor cafe two miles up the road (now a private house, probably haunted and full of murmurings of gears and 'evens'), began immediately as there was obviously going to be a considerable queue. I can still remember the noise, the swishing of tyres and the whirr of chains and gears as two hundred or more riders using the entire road sprinted for the 'caff'. Fortunately we met no other traffic. Those were exciting times for a keen, young cyclist.

Apart from the sporting scene the bicycle was very much alive as a basic means of transport but the ambition to become a motorist or motorcyclist was ever present with the 'ride to workers' and it was only poverty that kept them cycling.

Several companies made attempts to tap this tempting market with small engines designed to be attached to pedal cycles. The average capacity was 25cc, the average price about the £25 mark and the occasional top speed, the rider pedalling like mad downhill, was pushing 25mph. Some, like the Powerpak, were mounted over the front wheel which they drove via a roller pressing on the tyre, and these were guaranteed – though not by their manufacturers – to wear a tyre out in a week.

The most efficient models were the Cyclemaster and the BSA Winged Wheel, both of which were complete motor units, petrol tank and all, contained inside a wheel. To keep the record straight, I never heard of a decent lightweight bike being motorized, not even as a joke. Several members of the Vintage Motor Cycle Club still ride such devices, presumably for pleasure.

As the 1950s wore on, prosperity, previously thought of as being much too good for people who knew no better than to use their skilful hands to earn a living, was allowed to filter down, just enough for working people to become 'consumers' and even enthusiastic cyclists began to be seduced away to the comforts of four wheels. At one time it had been a common sight to see groups of clubmen riding to events with sprint wheels, often with wooden rims, on either side of the front wheels of their bicycles. More and more one saw racing bikes upside down on top of cars, and then one saw them less and less. As the traffic increased dramatically one saw fewer and fewer cycling clubs on the roads at weekends, or at any other time and soon they too became a rarity. Many well known clubs gave up completely, and one heard pathetic stories of the last two members of once thriving clubs holding club meetings once a week in pubs and sobbing in their beer.

By the time all this had happened, the reluctant 'ride to worker' had been long gone to the inside of a cheap tin motor and the factory cycle racks stood rusting, forlorn and empty. After a few car mad years when even the policeman, gasman and the postman were pushed, or eagerly leapt into cars and vans, and which did incalculable harm to health, natural resources, the countryside, and many other things, the bicycle began to creep back again. In China and many of the Third World countries it had never been away, but the situation in those countries is similar to that in Great Britain and America in the last years of the nineteenth century; the bicycle is popular because there is no choice. If the Chinese could afford cars, and cars were made available to them, then there would be more Chinese drivers than of any other nationality, a frightening thought.

Since the early 1970s bicycle sales in Britain and America have gone up and up. Nearly 1.75 million bicycles were sold in Britain in 1982 in contrast to just over 1.5 million cars, and although the recession may have artificially depressed car sales, so too it may also have depressed the sale of bicycles and therefore must be regarded as a healthy sign. The bicycle boom taking place now is different. The Western World does have a choice, and yet it goes on buying bicycles and cycling goes from strength to strength, perhaps surprisingly as road conditions are not ideal for cycling. It is true that many recent converts also own a car but cars are a necessary fact of life; the more cyclists there are the more chance there is of improving road conditions, not only because a car driver who also rides a bike will be more aware of cyclists and their problems but because the more of us there are the more our governments will listen to our point of view, if only to catch votes.

A measure of the popularity of a sport or pastime is the number of newspapers and magazines devoted to the subject and a glance through them will give one an interesting insight into the kind of people involved or interested in the activity that they cover. It used to virtually be a rule that the better off the readership the higher the quality of the contents of the magazines – excluding society magazines – that catered for them. *Yachting World* is a good example of an excellent publication aimed at a prosperous public.

Currently there are five periodicals for cyclists; *Cycling*, a weekly newspaper in magazine format primarily concerned with cycle racing, and *Cycling World* a monthly newspaper dealing with touring, tricycling, readers letters, stories and all sorts of fascinating oddments. The other three, *Bicycle*, *Cyclist* and *Bicycle Times* are all monthlies. All the magazines are well written and produced.

The predictions, for what predictions are worth, are that cycling as sport, exercise or merely transport will continue to expand worldwide. Experience and common sense suggests that these predictions, unlike so many others in the past, may well be right. Let us hope they are, for all our sakes.

Chapter 11

BICYCLE MAINTENANCE

My old Dad always used to say 'If you want anything done properly you must do it yourself'. He was, quite literally, always saying it, which did make it boring but nonetheless true and it is the best of all possible reasons for doing all your own maintenance and – as far as is possible – your own bike repairs. Not that all bicycle mechanics are uncaring louts whose knuckles are too near the ground – far from it – but however good they may be they are bound to be busy. Which brings us to the other good reasons why you should do it yourself – it's cheaper, quicker, and a lot more convenient. And if anything should go wrong when you are touring the Balkans, then you will probably be able to cope.

There is no need to make a religion of it. *Seventh Day Adventism and the Art of Bicycle Maintenance* is not required reading. It is not even necessary to enjoy doing it – although you almost certainly will. You don't need an extensive, expensive toolkit and you don't need a workshop, although workshops are nice. What you do need is a reasonably comprehensive toolkit, somewhere to work – like the kitchen – and a fund of patience and commonsense. I am very short of the last two but even I can do my own maintenance. The car goes to the garage, but I maintain my own bike.

Actually, patience is very important. Try not to do things in a hurry. What are known as inanimate objects are nothing of the kind. Beneath their bland exteriors beat hearts of steel or alloy. If they think that you are in a rush they will mess you about. Never show fear. If they think you can't cope they will clobber you. If you remember that all mechanical things are out to bruise, gouge

186

or draw blood, you won't go far wrong.

One of the aspects of maintenance that requires particular patience is to refrain from laying spanner to anything before you understand how it functions. In the interest of weight saving, bicycles, especially lightweight bicycles, are only as strong as they need to be and they will not stand up to brutality. Never apply excessive force to nuts, bolts or Allen screws unless absolutely necessary and there is no other way to undo them. Never, ever, apply excessive force when doing them up. It isn't necessary and you will strip the threads on the nut, bolt, or screw if you do. Don't use long handled spanners when working on bicycles. The long handle gives too much leverage which makes it all too easy to apply too much torque – the technical term for a twisting movement measured in pounds per foot. If a long handled spanner is all that you have, hold it near to the business end – reducing the leverage – tighten down firmly, and leave it at that. Do not give a final sharp tweak to make sure. It's the final tweak that can do the damage. In case you have led a sequestered life, most nuts, bolts and screws are tightened down clockwise and are untightened anti-clockwise. This means that they have a right-hand thread. There are left-hand threads but they are fairly uncommon.

Keeping a bicycle clean is part of its maintenance. Preventive medicine is better, and cheaper, than cure. As you clean it, look out for things that need to be done and put them right before they become a serious problem that will cost money in replacement parts. A clean bicycle is quiet, smooth, efficient, and a pleasure to ride, and it won't let you down. Clean the paint, alloy and chrome with warm soapy water, rinse off with clean water and dry with a leather or rags, finishing off with a polish with a clean duster. If you use a wax polish don't get it on the wheel rims where it will do the brake blocks no good at all. Paraffin is probably the best thing for cleaning such mucky things as gears, sprockets and chains – either on a rag or a brush, or both. When you clean these parts be sure to re-lubricate.

Before setting out to service your bicycle you will need tools, oils, grease and rags. Starting with spanners, you won't need very many, as bicycles carry very few sizes. Buy the best that you can afford. Capagnolo and Ofmega are nice but pricey. Here is a brief list of things you'll need:

A set of thin cone spanners 13, 14, 15 and 16mm sizes.

A French made Inox box spanner, cast in bronze, that fits eight different sizes of metric nuts and bolts (not to be confused with the cheap 'dumb-bell' multi aperture spanner which is not a good thing to use if you have any choice, but better than the flat multi size 'giveaway' spanners which are horrible). A set of three spanners. Open spanner one end, ring spanner the other. 8, 9 and 10mm sizes.

A good 6″ adjustable spanner. MUST be a good one. Cheap adjustables are destructive.

A set of metric Allen keys. 4, 5, 6 and 7mm sizes.

A C Spanner for the lock ring on the bottom bracket, or for fixed wheel lockrings.

A pedal spanner. This must be a long handled spanner giving sufficient leverage to unscrew pedal from crank. 15 and 16mm sizes.

A flat spanner to fit the big nut at the top of the headset.

A 'Third Hand' tool for holding brake blocks during brake adjustment.

A tool for removing cotterless cranks (if you have cotterless cranks), either for your make of crank, or a universal tool that fits everything except T. A. and Stronglight.

A pair of pliers. A pair of sharp nosed pliers can also be useful. Never use pliers on nuts.

A hammer. Not a coal hammer or a toffee hammer but something in between.

Two good screwdrivers. ¼″ and ⅛″ straight tips.

A pair of cable cutters.

A small file.

A spoke key.

A chain rivet remover.

A freewheel remover to suit your freewheel. There are six or seven types.

A puncture repair outfit.

Tyre levers.

Tyre pressure gauge.

A portable vice.

Alternatively you can buy some very nice tool kits, but you will still have to supply the hammer, pliers, files, etc.

Then there are lubricants. Oil is a must. SAE 30 or Sturmey-Archer cycle oil should be used for chains, gears, sprockets and brake levers and mechanisms. Also cables, although grease or tallow are better, oil is better than nothing. Alternatively there are aerosols of spray-on lubricants such as LPS Chain Lube. This is less messy as it doesn't throw off the chain (or so the label on the can says), and it doesn't collect a grinding paste of grit and road dirt to chew away at the chain. Some people consider that these spray-on lubricants evaporate fairly quickly and use oil instead. LPS 3 is also recommended for lubricating cables and for hub bearings, freewheels and headsets.

Rust and road dirt can seize nuts onto bolts and make them very difficult to shift. Always keep an aerosol of WD40 or LPS 1 in the workshop. Spray obdurate threads and then wait patiently while the fluid penetrates and lubricates. They should then come undone quite easily. Only use brute force when all else fails.

WD40 and LPS 1 can be used for cleaning bicycles.

Grease is the old fashioned and effective way, of keeping the lubrication in and water and rust out of bearings. It is probably the best thing for bearings, especially when reassembling them, as the ball bearings stick to the grease and do as they are told. The only snag is that you have to strip down the component to apply it. Modern bicycles don't have grease nipples. You can buy special waterproof greases in cycle shops, or big tins of grease by such makers as Castrol, in car accessory shops.

Also useful to have by you – especially if you tend to suffer from dermatitis or other skin diseases – is a barrier cream to stop dirt and grease getting into the pores of your hands, and a hand cleaner – Swarfega, Dirt Squad, Bars Handy Clean, Dirty Paws – for removing dirt and grease from your hands. Both will be water soluble, which destroys the effectiveness of the barrier cream.

Some method of holding the bicycle still whilst you work on it is essential. Leaning it against a wall doesn't work. Most of the time you will be wasting a much needed hand in restraining it from trying to escape or fall over. You will also be constantly turning it round to work on the opposite side. This is all very bad for the temper and bicycle/rider relationships. What you need is a well-behaved and immobilized bicycle and easy access to both sides. Whether you will be working in the garage, the kitchen, or the backyard, the best way to achieve this is a work stand. Such stands hold a bicycle rigidly – the right way up, which is a tremendous help – and do away with undignified and bad tempered struggles. A ready-made stand will cost you between £30 and £50 and will greatly enhance the pleasure of getting your hands dirty. If you are reluctant to spend that kind of money on a workstand it is possible to build one out of timber for a fiver. Mine took me a day to build, designing it as I went along. It is fairly crude, but it works very well. No special tools are needed and no skill whatsoever. See the list below for materials. See Fig. 1 for dimensions. Everything, with the exception of the top clamp and the two pieces of timber that keep the uprights and the top clamp apart, is 2" x 1". The actual size is 44mm x 20mm. I have painted the stand with black emulsion, partly because I happened to have some and partly because matt black paint doesn't show up rotten workmanship, or filthy finger marks.

See Figure 1.

MATERIAL LIST

21' 0" of 2" x 1" or 44mm x 20mm
2' 6" of 3 ¾ x ¾" or 95mm x 20mm
2' 0" of 1 ¾" x 1" or 40mm x 25mm
1 Hinge.
14 2½" No. 10 screws
22 1½" No. 10 screws
3 3" x ⁵⁄₁₆" coach bolts with washers and winged nuts.
One small container of Evo-Stik Resin W wood adhesive.
Something to stop the clamps from scratching the frame. I have used strips of draught excluder.

If you don't buy or build a workstand it means working with the bicycle upside down resting on saddle and handlebars. This is all very well with a roadster, or any bicycle with flat handlebars, but extremely bad for the brake cables of a drop handlebar bicycle. Placing the bars on a narrow box – preferably a wooden box with slots cut in it to take the cables – gets over that problem but it is a slightly shaky arrangement and a piece of board – say 18" long x 6" wide – lashed horizontally to the top of the saddle is a fairly effective if primitive steadying influence.

All you need now is a few bits of clean rag (not the kind that leaves fluff over everything), a tray to hold paraffin, a few containers to put nuts and bolts in and you are ready to start work. But before you do, may I suggest that you read up on any job first. Read the relevant text right through and study the illustrations, making sure that you understand just what is entailed. If you know what you are doing you will find the job quicker and easier and will avoid any unpleasant surprises.

FRAMES AND FORKS

Apart from the headset and the bottom bracket, which we will look at next, the frame and the forks need no maintenance, other than keeping them clean and free from rust. If the frame should be damaged, having been twisted or bent in an accident, do not try to straighten it yourself. Even if you succeeded, which is not very likely, it could have been dangerously weakened and may break at a most inconvenient moment – like when you are leading the Milk Race. Take it to a reputable frame specialist to be properly dealt with. The same applies for a dent in the frame. Don't fill it and paint over it and hope for the best, as it could have seriously weakened the tube.

In the case of bent forks, buy new ones. It is the cheapest and easiest course and the safest. Front fork failure can be a nasty experience.

THE HEADSET
See Figures 2, 3 and 4.

The front forks are attached to the frame by a tube known as the fork stem which is brazed in a vertical position to the centre of the fork crown. The purpose of the headset is to support the fork stem and allow the forks to pivot freely whilst at the same time preventing unwanted movement. A headset comprises two pairs of ball races (so called because ball bearings can race around within the confines of their concave profiles, although in practice they do no such thing), ball bearings, a large chromium plated washer and a chromium plated locknut.

A ball race is screwed, or force fitted, into the top and into the bottom of the head tube. These ball races are known as the top and bottom set races and their other halves are fitted to the top and bottom of the fork stem (see section below on dismantling the headset).

191

The bottom ball race on the fork stem is known as the fork crown race. It is a tight fit on the fork stem and sits, hollow side uppermost, hard against the fork crown.

Before the forks are fitted to the frame, the fork crown race and the top set race are packed with grease and the correct number of ball bearings (46-50 on average divided equally between top and bottom ball races) are packed into the grease. The fork stem is then inserted into the head tube and pushed upwards until the ball bearings in the fork crown race fit snugly up into the bottom set race and are no longer visible, and the threaded part of the fork stem protrudes above the top set race.

The remaining ball race, known as the top race, is fitted hollow side down onto the threaded fork stem and screwed down until it fits over the ball bearings in the top set race tightly enough to prevent any up and down or sideways movement; but not tightly enough to prevent the fork stem spinning freely in the headset. The large washer is then placed over the fork stem, followed by a front brake cable hanger bracket if the bicycle has a centre pull front brake, and the headset locknut is then screwed down the fork stem and tightened sufficiently to maintain correct adjustment of the bearings.

To dismantle the headset – which ideally you should do once a year to regrease the bearings – carry out the assembly operation in reverse, but be very careful or you will have ball bearings all over the place. It is best to work over a newspaper, or a sheet of white paper spread out on the floor. Remove the front brake caliper from the forks. If the brake is of the centre-pull type, remove the cable adjuster from the cable hanger bracket and remove the cable from the rear brake calipers, remove the handlebars with all controls *in situ*. Then remove the front mudguard and the front wheel (all these operations are easy enough but consult the relevant maintenance section if need be). Now, keeping the bicycle upright, hold the front forks up tight to the headtube in their normal position. It is best to lash them up to the frame with an aero elastic which leaves both hands free to deal with errant ball bearings. Take off the locknut, the brake cable hanger, or lamp bracket, remove the washer and unscrew the top race. As you undo it some ball bearings will come away with it, some will jump clear, and others will stay in the lower half of the ball race (the top set race). Before you do anything else, pick them all up, count them, making sure you have got them all and drop them into a container. Now, carefully unlash the forks and lower them gently away from the headtube, gather up the ball bearings – once more making sure that none have escaped – count them and put them into another container. A tin lid full of paraffin is a good idea for ball bearings, but put it where you won't tread in it.

Any problem that you can possibly have with a headset that cannot be cured by simple adjustment – i.e. loosening off the locknut and tightening down the top race – will manifest itself by grindings, roughness and juddering forks. If you do have such a problem, strip out, clean and examine all parts. If the ball bearings are pitted, cracked, or broken, replace them. Are the ball races damaged or distorted in any way? If so, replace them. Are the top set and bottom set races square in the frame? If not, remove and replace them as follows. If the races in the head tube are threaded (the problem may be that they have been put in cross threaded), unscrew and replace. This may be easier said than done if they are badly cross threaded, but strength through joy and penetrating oil will eventually triumph. If the races are force-fitted – this means a tight push fit – into the head tube, insert a length of piping or rod until it rests on the inside shoulder of the race and 'drift' it out with taps from a hammer, moving the 'drift' around the race as you go. To refit these races, use a block of hardwood to insulate them from the hammer. Do not belt the daylights out of them, but be firm if necessary, and make quite sure that the outside of the races are hard down on the head tube, all the way round, or you will be back in trouble again.

· The other possibilities are that the thread on the top of the fork stem may have stripped or that the thread on a ball race may have stripped and is loose in the head tube. If this is the case take them to a frame specialist to have the threads recut. It is a simple enough job and not worth going to the expense of buying your own taps or dies for. After all, it shouldn't happen that often.

Should it be necessary to remove the fork crown race from the forks, prise it up gently with the end of a screwdriver, a little bit at a time, working first on one side and then the other.

If there wasn't a problem with the headset and the strip-out is for routine re-greasing examine everything very carefully just the same before re-assembly, and replace anything that looks a bit suspect. Put it all back together methodically. When properly greased and adjusted a headset should be totally silent and absolutely smooth with no hint of freeplay.

There is a variation to the headset setup just examined that you are only likely to come across on a very cheap bike or, oddly enough, an expensive one. This is the clipped bearing arrangement. The cheapies prefer it as they can use less ball bearings – nine or so instead of the more usual eighteen, or similar number. The up market bicycle constructor will use it for ease of assembly. In the first case, throw it away and replace with individual ball bearings. The expensive type work very well. Clean, check over and if all is in order, re-grease and replace in the ball race.

HANDLEBAR STEM AND HANDLEBAR ADJUSTMENT AND REMOVAL

See Figure 5.

To adjust or remove stem, undo the centre bolt, either with a spanner or an Allen key, according to the bolt head. The method of holding the stem into the fork tube will either be by a conical nut or a wedge arrangement (see illustration). If by the former system, the bolt when undone will unwind to stand proud of the stem. Undo ½" or so and then tap down – using a block of wood and a hammer – to drive the expender nut out of the end of the stem. If by wedge arrangement, the bolt head will spin loosely and remain seated on top of the stem. If you wish to replace the stem in exactly the same position, wrap a short piece of masking tape around it to mark where it goes into the headset. Soft pen marks are no use, they wipe off too easily. Always leave some 2½" of stem inside the headset.

To adjust the handlebars, slacken off the clamp bolt. To remove the handlebars, remove cables, brake levers, etc. and then undo the clamp bolt.

SADDLE POST (OR SEAT PIN) ADJUSTMENT AND REMOVAL

See Figures 6 and 7.

There are two kinds of seat pins, those with micro adjusters and those without. See illustration. For replacement, mark the position with masking tape, as with the handlebar stem.

BOTTOM BRACKETS

See Figures 8 and 9

Not all of this section is applicable to BMX, or to some American bicycles. For these see next section.

The bottom bracket shell has a twofold purpose: to connect the bottom of the down tube and the seat tube with the inner ends of the chainstays, and to provide a housing for the bottom bracket set. This set is made up of a spindle to carry the crankset and chainwheel, and two steel, or dural, cups to carry the bearings which support the spindle. The cups are screwed into the threaded bottom bracket shell, one each side. In most cases the cup on the chainwheel side is not adjustable, but bottom bracket sets are now available that have adjustable cups on both sides to allow precise positioning of triple chainrings in order to get the best possible chain alignment. Once this aim is achieved they can be serviced in the same manner as a conventional bottom bracket set.

Bottom brackets have to put up with greater loadings than any other stress bearing component on a bicycle and accordingly need loving care. Old fashioned bicycles had access for oiling the overworked bottom bracket bearing; modern bicycles don't have this facility and the bottom bracket should be stripped out once a year for routine re-greasing. Maintenance-free bottom brackets with sealed bearings are now on the market – Phil Wood & Co. make a very nice unit – but even they may need occasional attention, (using an LPS aerosol rather than grease).

To strip down the bottom bracket, first remove the chain from the chainwheel. Then take off the chainwheel and cranks (see section on cranks). Lay the bicycle chainwheel side down on a large piece of paper, if you have no workstand. You are now face to face with the end of the adjustable cup that holds the bearings in place. This cup has a number of round, blind holes in it. Holding the cup in place is a locking ring. Undo and remove the locking ring by turning it anti-clockwise with a C spanner, or by drifting if off with a hammer and punch – you can use a screwdriver instead of a punch, but a punch with a flat tip is better. Now, undo the adjustable cup by placing the punch against the edge of one of the blind holes and lightly tapping it round, in the normal direction, with a hammer. Remove the cup carefully, holding the spindle in place against the bearings on the opposite side. The bearings may be loose, individual, ball bearings, in which case they will be all over the place when you lift out the cup. Or they may be clipped ball bearings. If loose ball bearings, make sure you have them all, count them – making a note of their number – and place them in a tin lid full of paraffin. If the ball bearings are clipped together, lift out and do the same thing, except there is no need to count them.

Now, carefully lift out the spindle and gather your bearings. If loose, count them. There should be the same number as you picked out of the other side. Dump them in the paraffin. This leaves you with a bottom bracket shell containing a fixed bearing cup and possibly a plastic sleeve. This sleeve is there to stop rubbish from raining down the inside of the seat tube and getting mixed up in the bearings. If there is a sleeve, remove it and clean out the shell. If the bottom bracket was working quietly and smoothly before you removed it, you will very probably find nothing wrong. Nevertheless, clean everything thoroughly and examine for cracks, pitting or roughness. If clipped ball bearings, or roller bearings, spin freely and quietly they are OK. Buy new spindle or bearings if necessary.

Now, replace the plastic sleeve, and pack the ball bearings in grease in the fixed cup. The clipped bearings should also be greased and replaced with the balls to the cups – that is, facing outwards. If the spindle has roller bearings attached, these must be re-greased. Replace the spindle. Pack the ball bearings in grease in the adjustable cup, place it carefully over the spindle and screw fully home, but not brutally. Reverse the cup roughly one eighth of a turn and replace the locking ring. When this is tightened, make sure that the spindle spins freely with no trace of sideplay. Replace cranks and chainwheel. The bottom bracket should now be fit for another twelve months hard labour.

ADJUSTMENT

Any sign of sideplay at the bottom bracket can be treated by removing the locking ring and adjusting the cup in the manner already explained. You may or may not have to take off the crank. Clicking noises seeming to come from the bottom bracket may be a loose spindle but more probably emanate from a pedal or a slightly loose crank.

BOTTOM BRACKETS FOR BMX BICYCLES

See Figure 10.

These are a somewhat agricultural arrangement in as much as the bottom bracket spindle and cranks are all in one piece. Some aspects of servicing are similar although the bearings are different so we will go through it briefly.

ADJUSTMENT

As is the case with the conventional spindle, all adjustments are made from one side, that is, the side opposite the chainwheel. If the bottom bracket is too stiff or too loose, take off the chain and undo the big locknut in a clockwise direction. Then, using a punch and a hammer (or a screwdriver and a hammer if you must), against a slot in the cone behind the locknut – the bit you can see is not shaped – tap it up anti-clockwise as far as it will go without force. Then tap it back again roughly one eighth of a turn until the spindle spins freely but there is no play at all. Re-tighten the locknut and replace the chain.

TO STRIP OUT TO RE-GREASE OR RECTIFY A PROBLEM

First, remove the pedal from the crank on the opposite side to the chainwheel. This is a left hand thread and will undo clockwise. Remove the chain. With the one piece crank there won't be a shower of ball bearings as they are held in a clip. Undo the locknut and slip it down the crank. Undo the cone and slip that down the crank. Take out the ball bearing clip and slip that down the crank. Push the crank through the bottom bracket shell. Reach round to the chainwheel side, tilt the whole thing and pull it through and clear of the shell. The chainwheel side bearing clip will come away with it. Remove this from the unit.

This leaves the bottom bracket shell containing two cups, which are a tight push fit in the ends of the shell. Clean and examine them. If they are pitted or badly worn, drift them out with a steel bar and a hammer from the opposite side. Push new cups into the ends of the shell and tap them right home, using a block of hardwood and a hammer. Clean and check the bearings. If they are pitted or cracked, replace with new bearings. If all is well, re-pack with grease. Reverse sequence to reassemble.

CRANKS AND CHAINWHEELS

The crank's mission in life is to provide a place to mount the pedals and to provide the leverage to turn the chainwheel. Cranks are attached to the bottom bracket spindle either by old fashioned cotter pins (a kind of slender wedge, now only used with steel, one piece single chainwheels on 'cooking' bicycles), or by the 'cotterless crank' system now used on sporting bicycles, which involves a square and tapered hole countersunk into the 'big end' of the crank that fits snugly on to the tapered end of the bottom bracket spindle.

COTTERED CRANKS

See Figure 11.

I have had a joyless time with cotter pins. When they work loose and the crank begins to flop about, tap the plain end with a hammer. Then tighten down the nut that's on the other end. Do not tighten down too hard or you will strip the thread. A firm hand is all that's needed (I suppose one has to strip a thread or two to get the feel of knowing when to stop). If, when tightened down, the crank is still loose on the spindle, take the nut and washer off the cotter pin, drive it out using a punch and hammer, and replace it with a new one.

If you are removing the cranks for some other purpose and the cotter pins have been behaving well, undo the nut until the top flat is flush with the end of the cotter pin, then tap out gently with a hammer. This method ensures that they survive for further service. IMPORTANT. Whilst all this hammering is going on, support the crank being hammered on a block of wood with a cutaway to take the cotter end. Don't let the bottom bracket take the strain. The shocks will damage cups and balls.

COTTERLESS CRANKS

See Figure 12

These are held firmly on the taper by a bolt screwed into the end of the bottom bracket spindle, with its shoulder up against the bottom of the round hole in the centre of the crank. The head of this bolt is covered by a slotted cap. If the crank is loose on the spindle, unscrew and remove the cap and tighten down the bolt head that you see. For this you will need a special spanner. Once more don't be violent. If you should shear the bolt head off the shank, or strip the thread inside the spindle, you may have to strip out the bottom bracket and replace the spindle with a new one.

If you wish to remove the cranks, first take off the chain. Remove the cap as before, then undo the holding bolt with special spanner. This special spanner comes with a crank extractor set for your make of crank. You now need the extractor. This is a fine threaded bolt that screws into, and right through, the top of a short, fat, hollow bolt that is threaded on the outside. Carefully insert the short, fat, hollow bolt of the extractor into the round hole in the crank and screw gently until fully home. Do not over tighten. Cotterless cranks are made of dural and threads cut into dural, or any kind of aluminium, are more vulnerable to stripping than threads cut in steel. Now, screw down the long centre bolt of the extractor until it bears against the spindle end and begins to push back on the hollow bolt. Then tighten down progressively and firmly until the crank comes off the taper and can be pulled away. If the crank plays hard to get and will not budge, tap the end of the extractor bolt with a hammer. And I mean just tap. Don't belt it, or the bottom bracket bearings will be damaged. To replace the cranks, make absolutely sure that they are seated well home on the tapers before the final tightening down.

The exception to the above rules is the Shimano 'One Key Locking System' which need no extractor, the cranks being held in place by Allen keys.

CHAINWHEELS AND CHAINRINGS

The purpose of a chainwheel is to tow the chain around, providing the bicycle with drive. The bigger the chainwheel, the higher the

199

gearing and vice versa. Chainwheels came in two types; in steel and in one piece with the offside crank, or in dural, in ones, twos or threes, and detachable from the cranks. These are known as chainrings.

There is not a lot that can go wrong with either type, except that teeth can get chipped or bent, or that the whole chainwheel can be bent or twisted in an accident. And, of course, they will eventually wear out.

By all means inspect the chainwheel when doing routine maintenance, but you will soon know when something's wrong. If the chain makes a jarring 'clunking' sort of sound at each revolution, you may find that a tooth is bent. Remove the chain and chainwheel, or, in the case of a sports or racing bicycle, remove the chainrings from the crank. This is easily accomplished by undoing the bolts or Allen screws that are holding it on. Then, holding the chainwheel down against a flat surface, clamp a large adjustable spanner on the tooth that hurts and heave it back into line – as gently as possible in the case of a dural chainring. This kind of home dentistry is rather less practical if the whole unit is running out of true, although with the one piece steel chainwheel, you may achieve something by working it over on a solid flat surface with a large hammer and a block of hardwood. A dural chainring will not respond favourably to such treatment and my advice is to take it to a specialist for more scientific attention.

PEDALS

See Figure 13.

The pedal is a very simple mechanism but it took bicycle builders a long time to think of it. Basically, it is a spindle between $3\frac{1}{2}''$ and $4\frac{1}{2}''$ long which is screwed into the small end of the crank. The pedal platform is pushed over this spindle and supported on ball, or sometimes roller, bearings at either end that allow it to remain flat, or spin freely, instead of slavishly following the circular motion of the spindle. All pedals work on this principle.

Pedals live a down-trodden life into which a lot of rain must fall, or bounce. Consequently, they are in need of care and attention at least every six months or more frequently if they bind, grind or grumble. The only exceptions to this are very expensive, maintenance free pedals, and even they ought to be looked at occasionally.

To service the pedals, remove them from the cranks with a long handled pedal spanner. CAUTION. The nearside – that is the left hand side – pedal has a left hand thread. This means that it is unscrewed the way that most things are done up, i.e. clockwise. Pedals are marked L and R respectively. L stands for left and R for right. Remember this when replacing the pedals or you will find it a longish job.

Pedals are nice things to work on as you can sit down at a table or workbench, unencumbered by the rest of the bicycle and do your maintenance in some comfort. As with any component containing ball bearings, work over a newspaper. First, remove the dust cap. On most lightweight pedals this is unscrewed with an Allen key or a spanner. On roadster rubber platform type pedals use a spanner, or if provision is not made for unscrewing, prize off with a screwdriver. Next, undo the locknut, which is the first nut you come to. Then, undo the adjusting cone. Whilst you are undoing the cone, hold the spindle into the back of the pedal or you will lose some ball bearings. Remove the cone from the spindle, tip out the ball bearings and place them in a tin lid full of paraffin. Next, with a hand cupped to catch leaping ball bearings, hold the crank end of the spindle and slide the pedal from it. Make sure that you have all the ball bearings. Clean out all grease and muck from the inside of the pedal and outside of the spindle. Inspect very carefully. Check that the cups that carry the ball bearings, and the cones that hold the balls in the cups for signs of wear. Check that the ball bearings are not pitted or cracked, as well as being all present and correct. Make sure that the spindle is straight. You would almost certainly have noticed if it was not, but spindles are easily bent and if it is only slightly out of true this will accelerate wear on the bearings. If it is bent, then buy another one, don't try to straighten it out. Renew anything suspect. Pack the cups with fresh grease. Put the balls into the cups on the crank side of the pedal. Drop the spindle carefully into the pedal, making sure that it is sitting down comfortably. Then, holding the spindle firmly in place and vertically, with outer end upwards, put the balls into the cup on that side. Screw on the cone. Tighten it fully home, but without using force, then back off again until the pedal spins freely but without any play. Then replace and tighten up the locknut whilst holding the cone with a spanner. Check that locking the cone has not mucked up the adjustment. If all is well, replace the pedals on the cranks, remembering that L is for left and R is for right.

ADJUSTMENT

If the pedals feel sloppy, make sure that they are not loose on the crank. This is not very likely, but possible. It is more likely to be cones in need of adjustment. If this seems to be the case do not remove the pedal from the bicycle. Remove the dustcap, loosen the locknut, and tighten the cone fully. Then adjust and retighten as already described.

CHAINS

See Figure 14.

Chains are nasty, dirty things that work very efficiently with only a modicum of attention and nobody has yet thought of anything better. There are three sizes of bicycle chains in common use. The most common are $\frac{1}{8}''$ and $\frac{3}{32}''$, and these measurements refer to the distances between the inside of the inner link plates – or the thickness of the chain rollers – plus a 'gnats'. On both sizes of chain, the chain rivets, or link plates, protrude slightly beyond the outer walls of the outer link plates, but in the third size of chain these rivets are made 'flush' and don't protrude beyond the outer wall. This makes for a narrower chain overall, although the inner measurement is still $\frac{3}{32}''$.

$\frac{1}{8}''$ chains are used for shopping bicycles, roadsters and similar machines fitted with single speed freewheels or hub gears. The $\frac{3}{32}''$ chains are used for sports or racing bicycles with derailleur gears and 5 or 6 speed freewheels. The narrower flush sided version is used for touring and racing lightweights with narrow 6 or 7 speed freewheel blocks.

Chains used with derailleur gears are not joined up with spring links; instead the ends are riveted together. However, the recently developed Super Link which sells for around £3.75 can be used and greatly simplifies the job of chain removal. It is NOT suitable for narrow chains.

To remove a rivet from a bicycle, use a chain rivet extractor (see illustration). Push the rivet until the end in contact with the extractor is clear of the inner link plate on the opposite side of chain. Remove the extractor and twist the chain to disengage the ends. Rivets are replaced by using the extractor as an 'inserter'.

Chains need lubricating once a week, whether with a spray-on LPS Chain Lube, Triflon, or good old fashioned messy oil. Oil lasts longer but attracts abrasive grit and dust. Whatever method used, the chain will still get filthy. For this reason they should be taken off the bicycle once every three months and thoroughly washed in paraffin. Total immersion is the best method. Complete this baptism by re-oiling or dipping the chain in molten paraffin wax. This is not such a production as it sounds. Place the wax in a shallow dish and warm over an electric cooker or a gas ring. Remove the dish from the flame with care. Put the chain into the dish, and leave it in long enough for the wax to penetrate the darkest recesses of its rollers. Take it out again and hang over the dish to drip. Organize this operation in advance. Wandering about the house with a chain dripping hot wax does not make one very popular. Alternatively, I'm told that spraying the chain with Teflon, having cleaned it thoroughly, is just as efficacious as all that waxwork stuff.

Due to the appalling conditions in which chains have to work, they don't last long, no matter how you cosset them. If you get the miles in, chains wear out – in two years at the very most. To check for imminent exhaustion, take the chain from the bicycle, grasp firmly with both hands 6″ or so apart and bend chain sideways. If it deflects much more than an inch it is pretty badly worn. The remedy is very simple. Buy a new chain. Before you buy a new chain count the links in the old one and buy a new one with exactly the same number.

FITTING NEW CHAINS

For a bicycle with a single fixed wheel, a single speed freewheel, or a hub gear, the chain tension is correct when there is ½″ up and down movement in the top run of the chain. Move the chain round by turning the pedals and check in several places. Variations in tension may mean a bent chainwheel, or a bent tooth or teeth on a chainwheel or a sprocket. If nothing is out of line, then you have been sold a rotten chain. Take it back to the shop and complain politely, at first, however irritated you may feel. Cycle dealers, like everybody else, have to rely on quality control at the factory that made the goods. He cannot possibly check up on all his stock.

On a bicycle with 10 or more speeds the derailleur takes care of the chain tension, but the same up and down play of $\frac{1}{2}''$ will give a good result. This test should of course involve no forward movement of the derailleur machine.

FREEWHEELS (OR 'BLOCKS')

The primary function of a freewheel is to give the rider a choice. To pedal, or not to pedal. Up to the mid-1880s riders had no choice; whilst they were moving they pedalled – furiously. The secondary function of multi-speed freewheels is to give the rider a choice of pedalling rates.

The freewheeling facility of both single and multi-speed freewheels is achieved by a complicated system of balls, springs and rachets. If a freewheel declines to freewheel there is not a lot you can do about it. Remove from the hub – we will come to that in a minute – and soak in penetrating oil. If it doesn't free up and run sweetly, treat yourself to a new one.

If the freewheel works well enough, revolves in a forward direction but doesn't provide any drive, there are only two possible causes. Either the freewheel is suffering a serious internal disorder and should be put out of its misery, or the thread has stripped either on the inside of the freewheel or the outside of the hub. Remove the freewheel from the hub to discover what's happened. In the case of a stripped thread this can be fun. Replace the defective freewheel or hub. Happily, such occurences are rare.

TO REMOVE FREEWHEEL

See Figure 15.
For this a special, but simple, tool called a freewheel remover is

required. Your freewheel may be internally splined, or have sockets for pegs to drop into. A quick glance at the freewheel *in situ* will tell you. Buy remover for the make and type of freewheel that you wish to remove. First, remove the wheel from the frame. Remove the nut and washer from the freewheel side of the spindle. Or, in the case of a quickly detachable wheel, remove the winged nut and spring from the spindle. You may find another nut holding a spacer. Remove both. Now, screw in, or drop in, remover tool. Freewheels are all right-hand-threaded on to the hub. Put the appropriate spanner on the end of the remover and turn anti-clockwise. It may be a bit of a struggle but leverage and a stout heart will eventually triumph.

A freewheel is easily screwed back on to a hub, provided you remember that it has a right-hand thread. Don't bother to heave it down hard; it will wind on tight as you pedal. Don't use a well-worn chain on a brand new freewheel, as it would be bad for the teeth on the sprockets; it is best to buy a new chain to go with it.

New or old, chain alignment is very important both for chain life and for smooth running. Single sprockets should be exactly in line with the chainwheel. In the case of both 5 and 7 speed freewheels, the middle sprocket should line up exactly with a single chainring, or with middle ring with triple chainrings. With a double chainring it should line up with a point midway between the two rings. The middle two sprockets of a 6 speed freewheel should line up with a double chainring, or with points either side of a single chainring and either side of the centre ring in a triple chainring setup.

The sprockets may well not line up if you fit a new block with more – or less – sprockets. If they are too far to the right, or the offside of the bicycle, either the wheel must be dished (see section on wheels) or the chainwheel or rings adjusted to compensate. If the bottom bracket spindle isn't adjustable – not many are – buy a spindle that is suitably longer, if possible. Wheel dishing may be the only solution. Discuss the alternatives with a specialist cycle shop. If the block is too far over in the direction of the wheel, remove it from the hub and pack out with a suitable shim obtainable from specialist cycle shops. This may bring the block too close to the frame. Fit a spacer on the spindle or shim the existing one. Remember that if you have fitted a wide ratio block with much bigger sprockets – or a close ratio block with much smaller sprockets – than you were previously using then you may

205

have to lengthen, or shorten the chain.

A notice with the words 'Patience is a virtue' printed upon it is essential to any good workshop, even if only to rip off the wall and jump on in moments of stress.

MAINTENANCE

This is exceedingly simple and can be briefly summed up as 'leave well alone'. Do not attempt to oil the internals. Freewheels are packed with grease at birth. There is no way it can escape and dribbling oil into it will do more harm than good. Give sprockets a spray with LPS Chainlube, or similar substance, once a week. Do not attempt to straighten bent sprockets unless as a necessary, and very temporary 'bodge-up'. New sprockets are quite cheap and easily fitted and even an entire new freewheel block doesn't cost the earth.

WHEEL REMOVAL. FRONT WHEELS

First, use the quick release mechanism if fitted on the front brake. This will open the brake callipers just enough to allow the tyre to pass between them. Then, undo the nuts, or pull back the quick release lever on the spindle. With nuts, unwind sufficiently to clear the fork ends, or 'drop outs'. Pull the wheel clear.

WHEEL REPLACEMENT. FRONT WHEELS

Wheel with nuts and washers: The washers go on the OUTSIDE of the fork ends. Nip the nuts up lightly. Check that the wheel is fully home and central in the forks. Tighten the nuts and release the quick release brake mechanism, or re-adjust front brake.

Wheel with quick release spindle: The wheel goes back in with the lever on the nearside (left hand side) of the fork. Make sure that the spindle is hard up against the 'drop-outs' and that the wheel is central before palming the lever fully home. In the fully tightened position the lever should point upwards, close to, but not touching, the front fork. Release the quick release brake mechanism, or re-adjust brake cable.

WHEEL REMOVAL. REAR WHEELS. BICYCLES WITH DERAILLEUR GEARS

Due to the current fashion of very short chain stays, you will very probably have to deflate the rear tyre in the interest of frame stiffness before the wheel can be removed. Turn the pedals and set the derailleur mechanism in top gear, that is, with the chain on the smallest rear sprocket. Most sporting bicycles have a small peg welded on the inside of the offside seat stay, about three inches above the drop out. Hook the chain over this. Operate the quick release rear brake mechanism. Undo the spindle nuts or quick release lever, and holding the derailleur from swinging forward and fouling the freewheel block, slide the wheel spindle down the drop outs and pull the wheel clear of bicycle.

Bicycles with hub gears: Put the lever into top gear. Disconnect the control cable at the hub end of holding the metal sleeve on the upper part of cable and undoing the knurled locknut from it. Undo the wheel nuts and remove the chain from the sprocket as the wheel is pulled clear.

WHEEL REPLACEMENT. REAR WHEELS

Bicycles with derailleur gears: Slip the wheel spindle back into the drop outs. Unhook the chain and drop it on to the smallest sprocket. Pull the wheel right back, either into drop out ends, or up against the wheel adjuster screws. Make sure that the wheel is central between chainstays. Palm the quick release spindle lever tight shut. The lever should be horizontal and facing forward. Release quick release brake mechanism.

Bicycles with hub gears: Slip the wheel spindle back into the drop outs and replace the chain. Make sure the wheel is central between the chainstays and that the chain has ½″ up and down freeplay. Tighten the wheel nuts with washers outside the frame. Re-connect the gear cable and adjust.

WHEELS

Wheels are made up of a rim, a hub and a variable number of spokes. As a general rule there are twenty-eight, thirty-two or thirty-six spokes to a racing wheel and thirty-six or forty to a touring wheel. By being kept in tension, the spokes not only keep the wheel and its hub equidistant from each other and running 'true', but impart surprising strength and great resilience to a light alloy or steel lightweight wheel. However, there are limits to what a wheel will stand without going out of true.

SPOKES AND RIMS

The only maintenance required for rims and spokes is keeping the spokes in proper tension and the rims in true. This is easier said than done. All my own efforts to 'true' a wheel have been a failure. Nevertheless, it should be simple, so, in case a wheel should buckle when you are miles from anywhere, we will go into the theory and the practice. But, if a wheel is really badly buckled – say, more than ½″ out of 'true' – then you may have 'had it' anyway. The only remedy will be a new rim.

For lesser bucklings, remove the wheel from the bicycle and the tyre and tube from the wheel. A tightened spoke might just protrude through the rim into the inner tube. Then put the tyreless, tubeless wheel back into the bicycle where the frame or forks will make a handy wheel jig. Wheels can buckle vertically or sideways. To treat an oval rim, spin the wheel whilst holding a piece of coloured chalk, a lipstick, or a sticky bar of chocolate – anything to make a harmless mark – high up on a seat stay or the forks, and then sliding it down until it marks the high spots on the top edge of the spinning rim. Then, taking a spoke key, tighten the nipples of the spokes around the marks by turning them anti-clockwise half a turn at a time. Loosen off the nipples of the same number of spokes on the rim opposite the marks, and by the same amount. Keep up the treatment until the rim is once more in the round – or round enough to ride down to the cycle shop for skilled attention.

For sideways bucklings, hold your marker to the side, or braking surface, of the rim so that only the buckle comes into contact with it. Then loosen half a dozen spokes around the marks, but only the spokes that tension the rim in the direction of the bulge. Then tighten up the nipples of the spokes that are in between the spokes that you have loosened. These are the spokes that run down to the hub on the side opposite the bulge. In theory, this will straighten up the rim. Be sure to file down any spoke ends that might poke into the inner tube.

Check your wheels occasionally for loose spokes. Spokes should 'ring' when flicked with a fingernail. Those that don't are loose or broken. Loose spokes should be tightened carefully until they 'ring' more or less on the same note as the other spokes. Broken spokes should be replaced. To achieve this, remove the tyre and tube. If working on the back wheel with the broken spoke on the freewheel side of the hub, remove the freewheel. Take the ends of the broken spoke from the rim and hub, noting whether the head (the bent end of the spoke) was against the inside or the outside of the hub flange. Place new spoke in the same direction and make sure that it passes over and under the other spokes – this is called 'lacing' – in exactly the same manner as the corresponding spokes. If a lot of spokes are broken take the wheel to a cycle shop, unless circumstances leave you little choice but to soldier on – or you have masochistic tendencies.

HUBS

Hubs work on the same principle as bottom brackets, except that in the hub it is the spindle that stands still – held by the frame or forks – and the outer casing that whizzes round it, supported on the spindle by ball bearings.

MAINTENANCE

If your hubs have oiling caps, or holes covered by sprung metal clips, they should be lubricated once a month with generous squirts of cycle oil. Modern bicycles rarely have such convenient facilities for lubrication and have to be dismantled and regreased. This is a simple matter and – ideally – should be done every six months and certainly once every year, even if you are only a fair weather cyclist.

TO DISMANTLE

See Figure 16.

Remove the wheel from the bicycle. Remove the nuts and washers, or quick release conical, or winged nut and inner spindle, being careful not to lose the conical springs. If working on the rear wheel of a bicycle that is fitted with a derailleur gear, remove the freewheel block (see relevant section under Freewheel heading). Working on a bench or table over a sheet of newspaper, lay the wheel on its side and undo the locknut and the cone. Remove them from the spindle whilst holding the spindle into the hub. Still holding the spindle into the hub, remove the dust cover – that is the next thing that you come to. Dust covers are only pushed in. Prise it out gently with a screwdriver, taking care not to bend it. Now, tip out, or carefully remove the ball bearings, and place them in a tin lid full of paraffin, making sure that you have got them all. Then, cupping your hand over the empty end of the hub to catch the next lot of ball bearings, turn the wheel over and lift out the spindle. Collect up the ball bearings (there should be the same number as there were on the other side), and drop them into the paraffin. Leave the locknut and cone *in situ* on the spindle, if in a fit condition to be put back into the hub. Clean out the hub and inspect the fixed cups left inside it. If they and all the other parts are as they should be – not cracked or pitted or noticeably worn – re-pack the fixed cups with grease. Place the clean and dry ball bearings in the grease and re-assemble. Fully tighten the cone and then back off until the wheel spins sweetly with no trace of side play. Tighten the locknut up to the cone and recheck adjustment.

WHEEL BEARING ADJUSTMENT

If a wheel turns stiffly, or side play can be felt when the rim is pushed and pulled from side to side, the bearings need adjustment, if not more serious attention. Remove the wheel from the frame. There is no need to remove the nuts, the quick release spindle and winged nut, or the freewheel. Undo the locknut, run the cone fully home and back it off again until the wheel runs smoothly. Re-tighten the locknut and re-check adjustment. If the bearings are still too stiff, or sloppy, dismantle and investigate.

LUBRICATION AND ADJUSTMENT OF BEARINGS in 3, 4 and 5 SPEED HUB GEARS

A generous squirt of oil should be applied every month. Bearing adjustment is carried out in the same manner as with a normal hub, but on the side opposite the sprocket. If adjustment does not cure the trouble, my advice is DO NOT STRIP IT DOWN, as these hubs have terrible internal complications. Take it to a cycle shop.

FRONT DERAILLEURS

See Figure 17.

A front derailleur or changer is a simple metal cage pivoted on two parallel arms from a mounting low on the seat tube. The chain passes through the cage, which can be moved from side to side, altering the overall gearing by switching the chain from one chainwheel to another. The bottom of the offside (right hand side) sideplate of the cage should be set to sit about $\frac{1}{2}''$ or slightly less above the larger chainwheel, and with the curvature of the cage matching the curvature of the chainwheel and parallel with teeth. The height of the cage is determined by the position of the mounting bracket on the seat tube. The Sun Tour changer illustrated is spring loaded towards the larger chainwheel. Most front changers are spring loaded towards the smaller chainwheel.

The sideways travel of the changer cage is governed by two adjusting screws, the screw ends limiting the upward movement of the pivot arm. The chain should just clear the side plates of the cage.

ADJUSTMENT

Make sure that there is no slack in the control cable. Holding the rear wheel clear of the ground, spin the pedals and change gear, with the chain on the largest rear sprocket and smallest chainwheel. If the inside of the cage touches the chain, adjust screw L until the cage just clears. Now change into top gear with the chain on the smallest rear sprocket and the largest chainwheel. The chain should now clear the opposite side of cage. If it doesn't, adjust screw H.

If, in spite of all adjustment, the cage persists in rubbing on the chain, this can mostly be compensated for by a slight adjustment of the gear lever after changing. If the cage – once more, in spite of all adjustment – throws the chain too far so that it rides off either chainwheel, check the chain for excessive wear, for bent teeth on the chainwheel, or for misalignment of the freewheel and chainwheel.

MAINTENANCE AND LUBRICATION

Keep clean, and in correct adjustment. Also keep an eye on exposed cables for fraying and make sure that the tension screw in the middle of the control lever is tight enough to stop the cage drifting in the direction of its loading spring. Spray with LPS aerosol or a similar lubricant once or twice a month. To remove the changer for a thorough cleaning the chain must be disconnected.

REAR DERAILLEURS

See Figures 18 and 19.

All rear derailleurs work on the same principle. The lower run of the chain passes over and between two small sprockets – known as rollers – that revolve in a metal cage which is spring loaded to the rear, keeping the chain in tension, no matter what size of freewheel sprocket the chain happens to be on. The chain passes behind and over the lower tension roller and then upwards and over the front of the upper jockey roller and thence to the sprockets on the freewheel. The cage that holds these rollers is pivoted off the main body of the changer mechanism.

The changer mechanism can move laterally to and fro controlled by the gear lever via the gear cable. As it moves sideways it derails the chain, which is held captive by the roller cage, from one sprocket to another. The changer body may also be spring loaded, but in the direction of the smallest sprocket. As the gear change lever is operated and the changer body moves sideways, so the roller cage moves back and forth compensating for the differing chain tension.

ADJUSTMENT

See Figure 20.

Some derailleurs provide for adjustment of the spring tensioning the chain via the roller cage. All derailleurs provide for adjustment to limit the sideways travel of the changer body. There are so many different makes and models of derailleurs that it is not practical to give a run down on the adjustment of them all. The derailleur illustrated is the Sun Tour VGT which is fairly typical. Adjustment for chain tension is provided by the top screw marked T. The limits of lateral movement are controlled by the screws marked L and H. These must be set so that the changer doesn't carry the chain too far and completely off the sprockets in either direction. If the changer body is throwing the chain off the smallest sprocket so that it drops on to the spindle, put the chain on the smallest sprocket and the biggest chainwheel, and adjust the screw marked H, turning it slightly in a clockwise direction until the body of the changer has moved inwards sufficiently to cure the tendency to throw the chain too far. If the changer is throwing the chain into the wheel, put the chain on the largest sprocket and the smallest chainwheel, and adjust the screw marked L, turning it clockwise bit by bit until the changer moves outwards enough to cure the trouble.

Before touching the adjusters, make sure that there is virtually no slack in the gear change cable – the cable adjuster is mounted on the changer body in this case – and that the roller cage is in line with the chain. If, somehow, it has become bent, take it to a specialist for treatment.

Keep cables in adjustment and check exposed cables for fraying. At the first sign of deterioration, replace them immediately. Keep the tension screw in the middle of the gear change lever tight enough to stop the lever drifting forward, but not so tight that the lever is hard to move. If the control cable is slightly

213

slack, it may prevent the changer moving sufficiently to get into bottom gear.

LUBRICATION

Spray LPS or similar lubricator on to all pivot points, cables and jockey and tension rollers. Do this once or twice every month, depending on mileage and the weather. Keep the mechanism clean.

HUB GEARS – 3 AND 5 SPEED

We have covered lubrication and maintenance in the section on hubs. These gears are very reliable and rarely give trouble. Slipping out of gear is mostly a matter of cable adjustment.

CABLE ADJUSTMENT – 3 AND 5 SPEED HUB GEARS

See Figure 21.

If the gears are slipping, first make sure that the control levers are functioning correctly and smoothly. If so, try adjusting the cable. At the hub end you will find a knurled barrel adjuster with a locknut beneath it. Undo the locknut and turn the adjuster to take up all but the slightest amount of slack in the cable. That should do the trick. If it doesn't, have a look at the position of the indicator rod. You will find it poking out of the inside of the hub spindle on the end of the short length of chain below the locknut. With the gear lever in N (neutral), the end of this rod should be level with the end of the spindle, viewed through the hole in the side of the wheel nut. If it is not level, disconnect the cable at the adjuster. Check that the indicator rod is properly screwed into the hub, then re-adjust the cable. If the gears are still slipping, fill the hub with penetrating oil or paraffin. Never use petrol. Then churn it around and leave it to soak for a while. Drain out and refill with cycle oil. If you are still in trouble, resist the temptation to pull the hub to pieces. You will be sorry if you do as hub gears are full of tiny springs and need expert attention.

TYRES

Basically, there are two types of tyre. The wire-on type which has a separate inner tube, and the tubular type in which the tubular casing held on by the rim by glue, contains the inner tube.

Tyres of roadster and shopping bicycles vary in diameter – 20 and 26 inch wheels are the most common sizes – and in width, from 1 ¼″ up to 1 ¾″. The fatter the tyre, the lower the tyre pressure (up to 60lbs psi (per square inch) for the narrower tyres, and down to around 45 for the bigger section 'squidgies'), and the harder the work to pedal the bicycle along. Most of these tyres have inner tubes fitted with car type Schraeder valves which means that they can be inflated – or blown right off the rims – with a garage air line. So watch the pressure gauge.

Lightweight bicycles have 27 x 1¼″ tyres, or 700C. These are called high pressure tyres and need pumping up to around 85/90lbs. This must be done with a hand, or preferably a foot pump, as wheel rims for this type of tyre are too narrow to take the Schraeder valves and are fitted with slender Presta valves instead. You will need a pressure gauge to ensure correct tyre pressures. Do not over inflate. I recently over inflated my rear tyre by 10lbs in the hope it might make life a little easier and it exploded miles from home, blowing the tyre right off the rim and ruining the tube.

MAINTENANCE

Other than regular weekly checks on tyre pressures and more regular checks for sharp flints, glass or other foreign bodies embedded in the treads, there is nothing to be done except mend the inevitable punctures.

Always carry a spare inner tube, or 'tub' if riding tubulars. If you experience a 'blow out', the tube will be irreparably damaged, and messing about with patches and synthetic rubber solution at the roadside (or needle and thread, as is the case with 'tubs'), is something one can do without. But carry a puncture outfit as well as a spare tube. It is always possible to get two punctures.

MENDING PUNCTURES

Punctures are more easily dealt with when the affected wheel is unencumbered by the bicycle. Before removing the wheel, just check that it is not a loose valve core that is causing the trouble. The core of a Schraeder valve can sometimes work loose. Invert the valve cap, insert in the top of the valve and tighten the core. If the valve is of the Presta type there is nothing to be done with it.

To mend a puncture in a wired-on tyre with separate inner tube, find the cause, if possible, and mark the spot. Remove the wheel, the valve cap and the valve holding nut. Then, starting opposite the valve, prise one side of the tyre off the rim with tyre levers. Insert the lever under the wire edge and lever it over the rim. Clip the other end of the lever on to the spoke and insert and pull down on the second lever. Be very careful when using levers on a tyre. It is very easy to pinch and damage the inner tube. Now try and pull the tyre off the rim with your fingers. If you cannot manage it, use one more lever. Then, working with your fingers, and in both directions, pull that side of the tyre off the rim until you come to the valve. Push the valve up into the inner tube and pull the one side of the tyre completely off the rim. Remove the tube, and remove whatever caused the puncture. Check for sharp ends of spokes that might be sticking through the rim tape and file them down if need be. Run your finger round the inside of the tyre, checking for intruders. Inspect the inside of the tyre. If there are any splits or cracks, the tyre should be discarded. At once, if convenient, but if not, as soon as possible.

If you cannot find the puncture, inflate the tube. Look and listen. If you find it mark the spot. If you don't, inflate it again and immerse it in water, watching out for bubbles. When the puncture is found, dry the tube and mark the spot. Then open your puncture outfit. Roughen the tube around the hole with emery cloth, or whatever is provided in the outfit for that purpose. Spread the rubber solution or cement provided on the roughened area. Let it go tacky. Remove backing from a patch and press firmly on to cement. Let it dry for a while.

Then, slightly inflate the tube. Shove the tube back into the tyre with the valve through the valve hole, and holding the nut loose on the thread. Keeping the valve stem upright, push it up into the inner tube and replace tyre on round on either side of it. Now work the tyre back on to the rim in both directions, without pinching the tube between the tyre and rim. You should end up opposite the valve. Pull the last bit of tyre back on to the rim with bare hands. Check all the way round for nipped up inner tube. Inflate to recommended pressure. Do up the valve holding nut and replace the valve cap.

MENDING A PUNCTURED TUBULAR TYRE

Mend the tube in exactly the same manner as above. It is only the method of getting at it and replacing it that differs. Remove wheel and let out any remaining air. Pull the tube from the rim with your hands, and find the puncture, as above. Prise 6″ of tape from under the side of the tyre in affected area. Cut stitching at points two inches or so each side of the puncture, being careful not to cut the tyre. Pull out the section of tube in need of repair. Repair it. Dust the tube with talc before replacing it in the outer casing. Pinching the casing up clear of the tube, re-stitch with needle and thread through existing holes. Overlap the new stitches into the existing stitches at either end of the mend. Cement the underside of the casing, beneath the tape that you removed. Wait for it to go tacky, and press down tape. Inflate to check repair.

Before replacing the 'tub' on the rim, clean off all traces of old adhesive with a suitable solvent. Then re-coat the rim with tub cement (Dunlop make a good one, complete with a brush in the container) but leaving a space 2″ or so on either side of the valve hole uncoated. If the entire rim were to be coated with cement it will be difficult to remove the tub. Deflate the tyre and then replace the valve in the hole and put the tub back on to the cemented rim. No levers are required, just a good strong pull. Make sure the tyre is evenly on the rim before the cement dries. Double sided tape can be used as a less messy alternative to cement.

BRAKES

There are four types of brakes for bicycles, the old-fashioned rod operated stirrup brake fitted to heavy roadsters, the equally old-fashioned and rather uncouth back pedal brake recently come back into fashion on BMX bicycles, the disc brake, and the universally popular calliper brake fitted to almost everything with pedals on two or three wheels.

We can dismiss the first three types fairly briskly. Back pedal brakes either work, or they don't. They are complex and unrewarding to work on, so in the event of trouble take it to a cycle shop and pay them to struggle with it. Disc brakes are excellent things, especially for tandems, or for touring in mountains with heavy loads. However, they are as yet fairly uncommon, and as anybody who has one will almost certainly also have instructions on how to maintain it, there seems little point in devoting limited space to such rarities. Stirrup brakes (so called because they look much like stirrups), come into the same category, although they are shuffling off this mortal coil rather than on to it.

CALLIPER BRAKES

See Figures 22, 23 and 24.

Basically, there are two kinds of calliper brakes, side-pull and centre pull. The names are derived from the position of the operating cables on the callipers. Side-pull brakes have only one, central, pivot point, whereas centre-pull brakes have two pivot points.

MAINTENANCE

This is simple enough and boils down to lubrication and adjustment. It is best not to use oil on the callipers, as it tends to get on to the wheel rims and cuts down on friction in the only area where you are actually in need of it. Oil at the lever end of the brakes is messy and gets on your hands. Use an LPS or similar spray or dry lubricant at least once a month on the brake lever pivots, on the calliper pivots, on the exposed ends of cables, on the inside of the cable housings, on the yoke cable anchor points and inside the cables. Alternatively, strip out the inner wires from the outer cables occasionally and grease them thoroughly. Keep all lubricants away from the rims.

There are only two adjustments to be made to side-pull, or

centre-pull brakes. They are cable adjustment and brake shoe adjustment. The less movement at the brake callipers, the better the brakes will work. Adjust the cables so that the brake shoes are only just clear of the rims. This is done at the cable adjuster. On a front centre-pull brake this is located on a hanger mounted on top of the headset. On a centre-pull rear brake the adjuster will be mounted on a hanger suspended from the seat pin bolt. On a side-pull brake the adjuster is on the yoke that carries the cable housing. Undo locknut on adjuster. Wind anticlockwise for less brake shoe clearance, or clockwise for more clearance. Tighten the locknut after adjustment.

Quick release mechanisms are operated either by a small section at the top of each brake lever that can be pivoted inwards, allowing the lever to move further up in its housing or 'hood', or by mounting the cable housing on a cam on the cable hanger which can be moved downwards by depressing a lever. Both systems have the effect of lengthening the brake cable, thus letting the callipers spring further open.

Brake shoes are correctly adjusted when, with the brake applied, the shoes sit squarely against, and in line with, the rim, protruding neither above or below it. This is easily achieved by slackening off the nut that holds the brake shoe on to the calliper. Slacken just enough so that the brake shoe can be moved. Adjust and retighten.

Bicycle brakes are simple mechanisms and give little trouble. If a brake judders when applied, it means that something is loose. Stop. Apply the brake and rock the bicycle backwards and forwards. You will then see if the pivot bolts need to be tightened. If all is well with the brake mechanism, the rim may possibly be buckled.

If the brakes don't work very well, there may be oil on the rim and the brake shoes, or the brake shoes may not be in proper contact with the rims. Alternatively, the shoes could be worn out. When buying new brake shoes remember that a soft compound will give you better braking but won't last as long as a harder shoe. PLEASE fit new shoes on to brake callipers with the closed end of the metal holder facing forwards. Otherwise, at the first serious brake application the shoes will pop out and desert you just when you need them most.

219

CABLES

Brake cables can be another source of trouble. Keep an eye on them and replace them if the outer cables become kinked and stiff to operate, or the inners become frayed. Teflon coated cables are a good idea – Aztec make an excellent range. Whilst much more expensive than conventional cables, they do provide ultra-smooth and sensitive brake operation and require no lubrication.

USEFUL ADDRESSES

Cycling organizations

The British Cycling Federation
16 Upper Woburn Place
London WC1H 0QE

The Cyclists' Touring Club
Cotterell House
69 Meadrow
Godalming
Surrey GU7 3HS

Tricycle Association
c/o Stan Bray
307 Moor Green Lane
Birmingham B13 8QR

Some knowledgeable and helpful cycle dealers

Beta Bikes
275 West End Lane
London NW6 1QS

Condor Cycles
144-148 Gray's Inn Road
London WC1X 8AA

F. W. Evans Ltd
77-79 The Cut
London SE1

Border Cycles
133 Lowther Street
Carlisle

Tower Cycles
170-178 Gravelly Lane
Erdington
Birmingham

W. F. Holdsworth Ltd
132 Lower Richmond Road
Putney
London SW15 1LN

Also branches at . . .

55 High Street, Penge, London SE20
69 Belle Grove Road, Welling, Kent
362 Staines Road, Hounslow, Middlesex

Bob Jackson
148 Harehills Lane
Leeds LS8 5RD

John's Bikes
1 Cleveland Place East
London Road
Bath
Avon

Ron Kitching
Hookstone Park
Harrogate
Yorkshire

Mercian Cycles Ltd
28 Stenson Road
Cavendish
Derby DE3 7JB

Harry Hall Cycles
30-32 Cathedral Street
Manchester 4

Colin Lewis Cycles
5-7 Manor Corner
Paignton
Devon

Madison Cycles Ltd
275 West End Lane
London NW6 1QS

Geoff Wiles
47 Cuxton Road
Strood
Kent

Cliff Pratt Ltd
84-86 Spring Bank
Hull HU3 1AA

Robin Williamson Cycles
26 Hamilton Place
Edinburgh EH3 5AU

Dave Kane Cycles
309 Upper Newtonards Road
Ballyhackamore
Belfast

Hetchins Bike Shop
117-119 Hamstel Road
Southend
Essex

Harry Quinn Ltd
7-9 Walton Road
Liverpool 4

Solec Cycles
51 Ermine Street
Huntingdon
Cambs.

Tricycle makers

Ken Rogers
71 Berkeley Avenue
Cranford
Hounslow
Middlesex TW4 6LF
(also for tricycle conversion kits)

Broadway Bikes
65 Windmill Hill
Enfield
Middlesex
(shopping and touring tricycles)

TGA Cycles
North Street
Sudbury
Suffolk
(shopping tricycles)

Tandem manufacturers.

Cycles Peugeot
Edison Road
Bedford MK41 0HU

Richmond Cycles
36 Hill Street
Richmond
Surrey

Mercian Cycles Ltd
28 Stenson Road
Cavendish
Derby

Madison Cycles Ltd
75 West End Lane
London NW6 1QS

Tom Avon Cycle
7 Chessel Street
Bedminster
Bristol

Frank Herety
180 Higher Hillgate
Stockport
Cheshire SK1 3QY

Tandem and tricycle makers.

W. R. Pashley Ltd
Mason's Road
Stratford-upon-Avon
Warwickshire CD37 9NL

Bob Jackson Cycles
148 Harehills Road
Leeds 8

Swallow Frames
30 Sunray Avenue
Hutton
Brentwood
Essex CM13 1PR

Jack Taylor
Church Road
Stockton-on-Tees

T. J. Cycles Ltd
114 Blackpool Street
Burton-on-Trent
DE14 3NT
(also for tricycle conversion kits)

Mail Order Catalogues

Freewheel Annual Equipment Guide
275 West End Lane
London NW6 1QS
(£1.15)

Richmond Cycles
36 Hill Street
Richmond
Surrey
(£1.00)

Some lightweight frame makers

Paris Lightweight Cycle Co
144-148 Gray's Inn Road
London WC1X 8AA

Holdsworth
55 High Street
Penge
London SE20

Woodrup Cycles
345-347 Kirkstall Road
Leeds 4

Mercian Cycles Ltd
28 Stenson Road
Cavendish
Derby

Claud Butler
The Holdsworth Co Ltd
1 Oakfield Road
London SE20 8DE

Shorter/Rochford Cycles
65 Woodhouse Road
Finchley
London N12

Hetchins
117-119 Hamstel Road
Southend
Essex

English Cycles
Freepost
Albert Street
Telford TF2 9BR

Condor
Condor Cycles
144-148 Gray's Inn Road
London WC1X 8AA

Bob Jackson
148 Harehills Road
Leeds LS8 5RD

Dave Lloyd
Dave Lloyd's Bike Shop
18A The Village
Bebington
Wirral
Merseyside

Harry Hall
Harry Hall Cycles
30-32 Cathedral Street
Manchester M4 3EX

Index

229

THE CASTROL MOTORCYCLE TEST MANUAL
How to Pass Parts 1 and 2
Gordon Cole

As soon as a motorcyclist gets on his machine he joins a million or so others who are using the roads at any one moment. For your own safety and that of other people it is very important that you should learn the correct way to ride your motorcycle by taking a training course, and that you should be able to demonstrate your competence by passing a test.

Over the years various books have been written to help the learner motorcyclist to pass his proficiency test, but until now none of them has explained the marking procedure in detail. THE CASTROL MOTORCYCLE TEST MANUAL explains very clearly just what the test candidate is expected to do, how many faults he is allowed to make, and, more important, how he can avoid making any faults at all while he carries out Part 1 and Part 2 of the motorcycle test.

THE CASTROL MOTORCYCLE TEST MANUAL has been written with the aim of getting you through both parts of the test at your first attempt. It will also help you afterwards to enjoy the freedom and independence that motorcycling has to offer.

0 552 99100 7   £3.95

RULES OF THE GAME
The Diagram Group

The complete Illustrated Encyclopedia of all the sports of the world.

More than one hundred and fifty sports and four hundred sporting activities are fully covered. Sports of a similar nature are grouped together; each group of sports are first presented in the contents page and later each particular sporting activity appears in its alphabetical sequence so that answers to sport questions are fast and easy to find.

The method of presentation is predominately visual, with the complex features of each and every sporting event clearly and graphically explained.

The guidelines of the books are the official international rules and laws and RULES OF THE GAME has been compiled with the cooperation and personal involvement of three hundred official governing bodies and individuals in twenty-one countries.

The information is presented in concise, clearly identified sections with two thousand five hundred illustrations in full colour to provide the reader with an easy to find reference work.

Different features of each sport are described, including major objectives, playing area and equipment, timing and scoring, rules and regulations, participants and officials, playing procedure . . . and misconduct and its consequences.

RULES OF THE GAME is designed to help all people interested in sport to enjoy and appreciate every type of sporting event.

'A spectacular volume that assembles a multitude of facts with remarkable clarity' *The Financial Times*

'The best attempt I have seen at an encyclopedia which clears out the brushwood from the rules jungle and leaves the trees clearly visible' *The Guardian*

'The best guide ever produced and certainly the most colourful and beautifully presented' *The Times*

0 553 01397 1   £5.95

A SELECTION OF NON-FICTION TITLES
AVAILABLE FROM CORGI BOOKS

WHILE EVERY EFFORT IS MADE TO KEEP PRICES LOW, IT IS SOME-
TIMES NECESSARY TO INCREASE PRICES AT SHORT NOTICE. CORGI
BOOKS RESERVE THE RIGHT TO SHOW AND CHARGE NEW RETAIL
PRICES ON COVERS WHICH MAY DIFFER FROM THOSE ADVERTISED
IN THE TEXT OR ELSEWHERE.

THE PRICES SHOWN BELOW WERE CORRECT AT THE TIME OF
GOING TO PRESS (MARCH '85).

☐ 07200 1	**Test Yourself (I.Q.)**	*William Bernard &*	
		Jules Leopold	£1.50
☐ 99100 7	**Castrol Motorcycle Test Manual**	*Gordon Cole*	£3.95
☐ 99105 8	**The U.S. Armed Forces Survival**		
	Manual	*John Boswell*	£2.95
☐ 01397 1	**Rules of the Game**	*Diagram Group*	£5.95
☐ 10435 3	**The Fast Men**	*David Frith*	£2.95
☐ 12493 1	**The Slow Men**	*David Frith*	£2.95
☐ 12019 7	**Beginning Windsurfing**	*Dan Morgan*	£1.50
☐ 98051 X	**The Complete Book of Self-**		
	Sufficiency	*John Seymour*	£8.95
☐ 99059 0	**The Lore of the Land**	*John Seymour*	£4.95
☐ 99067 1	**The Book of Clues**	*John Sladek*	£4.95
☐ 08456 5	**Bruce Tegner's Complete Book of**		
	Jukado Self Defence	*Bruce Tegner*	£1.00
☐ 23309 2	**Karate: From Beginner to Black Belt**	*Bruce Tegner*	£1.95
☐ 10747 6	**The Book of Lists**	*David Wallechinsky,*	
		Irving Wallace &	
		Amy Wallace	£2.25
☐ 11681 5	**The Book of Lists 2**	*David Wallechinsky,*	
		Irving Wallace &	
		Amy Wallace	£2.25
☐ 98058 7	**Yoga and Nutrition**	*Kareen Zebroff*	£1.25
☐ 11934 2	**The Concise Medical Dictionary**		£4.95

*All these books are available at your bookshop or newsagent, or can be ordered direct from
the publisher. Just tick the titles you want and fill in the form below.*

CORGI BOOKS, Cash Sales Department, P.O Box 11, Falmouth, Cornwall.

Please send cheque or postal order, no currency.

Please allow cost of book(s) plus the following for postage and packing:

U.K. CUSTOMERS – Allow 55p for the first book, 22p for the second book and
14p for each additional book ordered, to a maximum charge of £1.75.

B.F.P.O. & EIRE – Allow 55p for the first book, 22p for the second book plus 14p
per copy for the next seven books, thereafter 8p per book.

OVERSEAS CUSTOMERS – Allow £1.00 for the first book and 25p per copy for
each additional book.

NAME (Block letters) ....

ADDRESS ....

....